Expatriate

Compensation

Expatriate Compensation

A practical and informative textbook for
managing expatriate compensation, mobility, and
international assignments in the world of work

Dr Mark Bussin

KNOWRES
PUBLISHING

2015

First published in 2015

ISBN: 978-1-86922-523-0
eISBN: 978-1-86922-524-7 (PDF ebook)

Published by Knowres Publishing (Pty) Ltd
P O Box 3954
Randburg
2125
Republic of South Africa

Tel: (011) 706-6009
Fax: (011) 706 1127
E-mail: orders@knowres.co.za
Website: www.kr.co.za

Printed and bound: Mega Digital (Pty) Ltd. Parow Industria, Cape Town
Typesetting, layout and design: Stephani Krugel, steph.krugel@gmail.com
Cover design: Cia Joubert, cia@knowres.co.za
Editing and proofreading: Adrienne Pretorius, pretorii@mweb.co.za
Project management: Cia Joubert, cia@knowres.co.za
Index created with: TExtract, www.Texyz.com

ACKNOWLEDGEMENTS

This book would not have been published without the contributions from many very dedicated people – thank you for sharing your expertise.

Thank you to the authors of, and contributors to, the relevant chapters.

Thanks to John Rubino, a son of the soil and a legend in this field internationally, for the Foreword.

Knowledge Resources, thank you for co-ordinating the production and marketing of this book.

A special thank you to Chris Blair for your insight.

A giant thank you to Marina, Daniel, Kate, Genna and James for your inspiration and patience.

To you, the reader, I look forward to receiving your inputs and to building in the experiences that you have had with expatriate management and to how we can improve our knowledge and practice in this relatively poorly practised field of management.

Professor Mark Bussin
Johannesburg
February 2015

Please feel free to contact me with suggestions that can build on this version.

drbussin@mweb.co.za
www.drbussin.com
Mobile: +27 82 901 0055

FOREWORD

Working in the field of expatriate compensation is extremely complex. Designing and administering appropriate pay levels and other rewards for a globally mobile work force present multi-faceted difficulties and challenges for all organisations and international consultants. Not only must we deal with the technical exercise of calculating and equating quality-of-life standards for mobile employees, but we must also address the psychological issues of transferring employees from one culture to another, sometimes vastly different, one. There is a lot at stake here: from an organisational productivity and cost perspective all the way through to employee performance and motivation. Without question, successfully addressing and resolving all of the quantitative and qualitative issues and concerns with mobility are what separates premier global human resources consultants from just the average players.

Dr Mark Bussin has earned his place at the premier level. Through his many years of consulting activities and a plethora of published works, Dr Bussin has distinguished himself as a "go to" consultant who understands intimately what it takes to design and administer human resources and employee mobility programmes comprehensively and successfully.

Dr Bussin's latest book, *Expatriate Compensation*, is an aggregation of his extensive experiences working in the field. He and his cadre of expert authors comprehensively cover every aspect of dealing successfully with international assignments and the mobile employee: from the reasons to go global all the way through to setting appropriate market-based pay rates, tax implications, recognising and rewarding performance, and employee motivational issues. Moreover, Dr Bussin has the gift of taking this very complex subject matter and distilling it so that it can be easily understood and absorbed. Indeed, all of the information in the book is presented in a practical, straightforward, and real-world manner.

As the globe continues to shrink and the interconnectivity of business operations across multiple countries increasingly becomes the standard, this excellent book is critically important and very timely. The stakes for employee mobility are too high and the organisational and human costs are too great not to be able to get it right. Dr Mark Bussin's book offers everyone working in the field of expatriate compensation much-needed guidance to help ensure successful results. Enjoy!

John A. Rubino
President: Rubino Consulting Services – a global human resources consulting company
Pound Ridge, New York, USA
December 2015

TABLE OF CONTENTS

SOURCING OF FIGURES AND DIAGRAMS

Many of the figures and diagrams used in this publication have been accumulated over a 35-year consulting and development history by several people – executive and developmental practitioners. The following is a guide to key sources:

21st Century: from the files and archives of 21st Century Pay Solutions Group (Pty) Ltd.

Other sources are individually acknowledged.

ABOUT THE AUTHOR

Prof Mark Bussin

Mark is the Chairperson of 21st Century Pay Solutions Group, a specialist reward and human resource consultancy. He has remuneration and performance management experience across all industry sectors, and is viewed as a thought leader in the remuneration arena. He serves on and advises numerous boards and Remuneration Committees on Executive Remuneration and has held Global Reward positions for several multinational companies. Mark holds a Doctorate in Commerce. He has published or presented over 300 popular articles and papers and 25 peer reviewed academic articles. He has appeared on television and radio, and in the press, giving expert views on remuneration.

Mark is an associate Professor at the University of Johannesburg, Professor Extraordinaire at North West University, and guest lecturer at several universities. He supervises Masters and Doctoral theses in the HR, Reward and Performance area. He is an EXCO member of SARA (South African Reward Association), Fellow of the Institute of Directors, tutor for WorldatWork GRP courses, and a past Commissioner for the remuneration of Public Office Bearers in the Presidency. In his spare time, Mark likes flying Cessnas and spending time with his family.

Books written by Prof Bussin:

Bussin, M., (2011). *The Remuneration Handbook for Africa.* First edition. Randburg: Knowres Publishing.

Bussin, M., (2012). *The Performance Management for Emerging Markets.* Randburg: Knowres Publishing.

Bussin, M. (2013). *Performance Management for Government, Universities, Schools and NGO's.* Randburg: Knowres Publishing.

Bussin, M. (2014). Remuneration and Talent Management. Randburg: Knowres Publishing.

LIST OF CONTRIBUTORS

A giant thank you to all of you!

Advocate Nasreen Dawood, Executive Director, 21st Century Pay Solutions Group
ndawood@21century.co.za

Adrenè van der Merwe, Programme Manager, Carlson Wagonlit Travel, South Africa
AVanDerMerwe@carlsonwagonlit.co.za

Barbara Parry, Barbara Parry and Associates, Mobility Consulting
barbara@bpec.co.za

Cinzia de Risi, Personal capacity

Chris Blair, Chief Executive Officer, 21st Century Pay Solutions Group
cblair@21century.co.za

Craig France CA (SA), Executive Consultant, 21st Century Pay Solutions Group
craigfrance@21century.co.za

Craig Raath, Executive Director, 21st Century Pay Solutions Group
craath@21century.co.za

Dianne Trompetter, Head of Mobility, Sasol
Diane.Trompetter@sasol.com

Elmien Smit, Junior Consultant, 21st Century Pay Solutions Group
esmit@21century.co.za

Fermin Diez, Director, Fermin Diez & Associates, South East Asia
fermin@fermindiez.com; fermin.a.diez@gmail.com

Ian McGorian, Executive Director, 21st Century Pay Solutions Group
imcgorian@21century.co.za

JC Nel, Executive Consultant, 21st Century Pay Solutions Group
jcnel@21century.co.za

John A. Rubino, president, Rubino Consulting Services, a global human resources consulting company
rubinoconsulting@aol.com

Laurika Fourie, Product Manager, 21st Century Pay Solutions Group
lfourie@21century.co.za

Mack Moey, Director, SNEF (Singapore National Employers Federation)
mack_moey@snef.org.sg

Dr Marius van Aswegen, CEO, XpatWeb
marius@xpatweb.co.za

Mertz Aucamp, Chief Human Resources Business Partner, African Development Bank, Tunisia
mertza35@gmail.com

Morag Phillips, Executive Director, 21st Century Pay Solutions Group
mphillips@21century.co.za

Nazlie Samodien, Executive Manager – Remuneration, Benefits & Wellness, Edcon
NSamodien@edcon.co.za

Peter Karlak, GM Western Cape, Namibia & South East Asia, 21st Century Pay Solutions Group
pkarlak@21century.co.za

Ray Harraway, Personal capacity

Dr Ronel Nienaber, VP: Global Rewards and Benefits, Sasol
ronel.nienaber@sasol.com

Simon Davies, Sales Director, K2Corporatemobility
simon.davies@k2corporatemobility.com

Steven McManus, Executive Consultant, 21st Century Pay Solutions Group
smcmanus@21century.co.za

Vishal Nundlall, Manager, Global Employer Services, Deloitte
vnundlall@deloitte.co.za

PROLOGUE AND PREAMBLE

I have been talking at conferences and lecturing to thousands of people for several years. Whenever the opportunity presents itself, I can't resist asking the audience just one question:

> "Who here can say that they have a seamless methodology for managing mobility in their organisation, that all International Assignees are happy, and that the process works well?"

This book is inspired by the 99% of people who did **not** put their hands up. I had the opportunity of managing a mobility section for a large financial institution and I can honestly say that it was one of the toughest jobs I have ever done. There are thousands of books and gurus on the subject. Yet there are so few examples of where it is practised well. Why, I ask myself? What is missing? Everyone knows what needs to be done, has read the books, has heard the gurus, yet there are so few outstanding success stories.

This book is different for the following reasons:

1   It is based on years of personal experience.

2   Contributors to the book have actually done and experienced what they are writing about.

3   It is underpinned by empirical research.

4   It is practical and, for once, tells you how to do it, with no missing steps or information. There are tool kits, forms and checklists that can be used instantly.

5   It is written in plain English, with no bamboozling jargon.

6   If you feel that clarification is required, our contact details are supplied. We are not some sort of black hole that no one knows how to approach.

Getting nomenclature out of the way

In this book:

1   The terms *compensation* and *remuneration* are used interchangeably. It is a matter of country and company preference as to which term is used. Therefore, Compensation Committee is the same as Remuneration Committee.

2   The terms mobility function, expatriate and international assignments are used interchangeably. They refer to the movement of people around the world.

Finally, the tax, legal, cost-of-living (COL) and other professional advice in this book serves as a useful guideline. Given the fast-moving field, it should always be checked with a reputable service provider.

CHAPTER 1
INTRODUCTION AND CONTEXT
Fermin Diez

1.1   INTRODUCTION

International assignments are a part of life and doing business for most multinational organisations. It is a great way to give leaders international experience and grow the talent pipeline of CEOs. It often makes good business sense too, yet the costs of getting it wrong are enormous, and potential brand damage is considerable.

Selecting the right candidate for the right assignment at the right cost is an international challenge and is often done by negotiation. We need to get better at this, and using more robust systems and methodologies goes a long way in doing so. This is one of the main objectives of this book – to make the process more robust to increase the chances of success, thereby saving time and money.

1.2   BACKGROUND

Globalisation is a predominant theme affecting most business organisations today. Whether because of domestic competition from foreign companies or because of new business opportunities abroad, virtually every company is learning to operate in a global marketplace.

Organisations define themselves differently according to their operations. The following terms define organisations according to how they operate with regard to other countries:

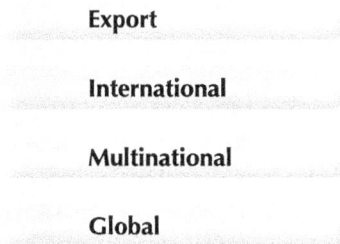

Export

International

Multinational

Global

Figure 1.1: Terms used to define organisational operations (WorldatWork, 2014)

The definitions of each of these from a compensation and mobility point of view are important. For example, if you want to conduct market pricing benchmarking, you should draw comparators from a pool similar to yours.

Export organisation: First overseas processes in place, but the bulk of all business is done in the home country.

International division: These organisations concentrate on the home market, with some international business activity managed by the headquarters country. Commonly less than half the revenue comes from international activities.

Multinational organisation: These organisations administer business in multiple countries, with each operation typically managed by local employees following a centrally co-ordinated strategy. Typically, more than half the revenue comes from international activities.

Global organisation: This refers to organisations with worldwide operations, whose policies and resources are used globally regardless of national or geographic boundaries. There is often a fairly even spread of revenue across each region.

1.3   WHY GLOBALISE?

Figure 1.2, below, highlights the main reasons it is important to globalise.

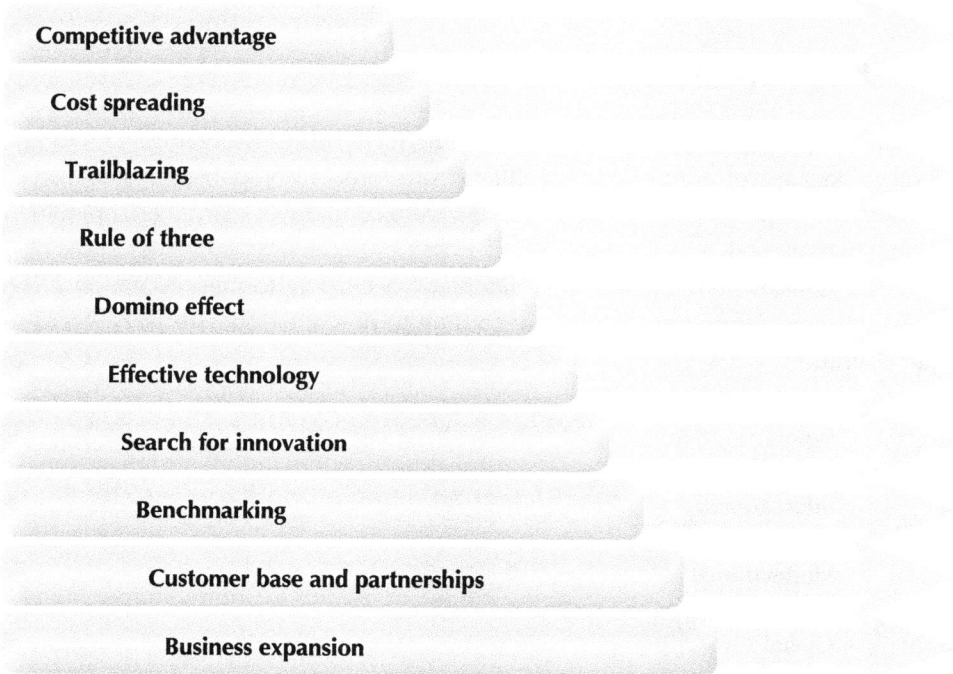

Competitive advantage

Cost spreading

Trailblazing

Rule of three

Domino effect

Effective technology

Search for innovation

Benchmarking

Customer base and partnerships

Business expansion

Figure 1.2: Reasons it is important to globalise (WorldatWork, 2014)

WorldatWork (2014) describes each of these reasons as follows:

Competitive advantage: This could be seen as the top reason for organisations to globalise. Reduction of costs and increase in profits often provide the motivation.

Cost spreading: This is normally recognised through mergers, alliances and joint ventures in an effort to spread or share costs for various capital-intensive investments

Trailblazing: This is subject to vision. Currently, many organisations are attempting to expand into the emerging markets.

Rule of three: This refers to the statement: "Three organisations will always garner the lion's share of the market, while those that arrive late receive only crumbs." For organisations to recuperate from start-up expenses, they must understand the importance of establishing a major presence in emerging markets

Domino effect: This signifies that success in a new territory makes it easier to enter another. This is true when interring country cultures and customs are similar.

Effective technology: This is easily accessible to most organisations and it levels the global playing field.

Search for innovation: Organisations that are aware of worldwide trends may lead to creative and innovative ideas for new products and services.

Benchmarking against other organisations drives organisations towards globalisation by:

- Teaching organisations how other organisations break through global boundaries.
- Generating richer data when the organisations practising benchmarking already have global operations.

Customer base and partnership: This leads to speedy delivery to customers, improves relationships with strategic partners abroad, supports local customers' international operations, and meets cultural needs of customers.

Business expansion: This avoids isolation, finds lower taxes and government incentives, accesses global technical and management talent, avoids local regulatory constraints, and accesses lower production and service costs.

1.4   KEY CONCEPTS

1.4.1   Expatriate

Expatriates are often defined as anyone not working in their home country. However, this definition is not 100% "pure". Sometimes we have foreigners working on local terms and we even occasionally find home-country employees working on expatriate terms. So to address these, we will define an expatriate as anyone working on terms which are different from the normal local terms in the country. As we will see later, this definition will allow us to define a variety of compensation approaches for these expatriates.

1.4.2   Compensation

When we talk about compensation, we mean all cash and cash-related modes of payment such as base salary, annual incentives, and long-term incentive plans. Sometimes we refer to this as "pay" or "remuneration". Expatriate allowances are typically considered part of compensation.

1.4.3   Total rewards

In contrast, "total rewards" means all elements of the employment relationship which the employee perceives to be of value. Besides compensation, total rewards include development opportunities, benefits, work–life balance, and even the culture of the company.

1.5   THE EVOLUTION OF INTERNATIONAL ASSIGNMENTS

An organisation's approach to international assignment policies is often linked to the level at which it is conducting business outside of the home country. Table 1.1 below illustrates the potential evolution of international assignment policies as an organisation matures from the export stage to the global stage.

Table 1.1: Potential evolution of international assignment policies

Issue	Export	International division	Emerging multinational	Mature multinational	Global
Business status	First overseas operation(s)	Few overseas operations (not inte-grated)	Growing International maturity	Heightened global cost conscious-ness; down-sizing	Worldwide integration and planning
Types of international assignment	All headquar-ters-based	• Most headquar-ters-based expatriates • Few TNs • Uses inter-national careerist	Headquar-ters-based increasingly replaced by: • TCNs • Local nationals	Increasing use of "cost-effective international assignees"	Global sourcing of talent with diminishing emphasis on nationality; well-devel-oped career planning and repatriation polices
International assignment philosophy	Get the job done	Improvisation	Developing awareness of need to plan: • Career paths • compensa-tion	Increased career risk, both at home and abroad	

Example:

1. A large cement company from Latin America started its global expansion in Europe. Each of the first home-country executives who arrived in the host European country had negotiated his or her "expatriate package" with the division head. As a result, each new assignee negotiated his or package by stating, "I want everything the prior person received, plus this other item." Each successive package became more generous, to the point where the first assignees started to complain that the "new people" had much better terms! After the second venture abroad, the company realised that this approach was much too expensive and implemented a global expatriate policy to standardise terms.

2. Mature multinationals are often faced with developing talent in smaller operations. A well-known fast-moving-consumer-goods (FMCG) company recently was facing the following problem in Asia: Some of their operations in

countries such as Malaysia were small, so their professional staff had very little room to progress in the country and often ended up leaving the company and migrating to larger firms in the same sector, even if not direct competitors. At the same time, the company was experiencing severe labour shortages in other countries such as India and China. The problem was that the expatriate policy in place was aimed at moving people from their US global headquarters to Asia, but was not useful for moving people from one country to another within the region. As a result, the company designed and implemented a regional expatriate policy with very different terms and conditions which allowed it to move people from their smaller to their larger operations more easily.

3. Global firms tend also to think of talent as global and have developed pay programmes that easily allow them to move people from one place to the next, regardless of the passport carried by the person or the location to which they are sent. Another consumer goods company implemented just such a programme by defining their "global talent" (key people in key jobs) and placing these few individuals on a global compensation package that did not change with assignment location.

Table 1.2 depicts reasons and subdivisions relating to acceptance of an international assignment.

Table 1.2: Why accept an international assignment?

Reasons	Subdivisions
1. Development	• Career development of expatriate • Pre-planned next assignment
2. Transfer of skills and knowledge	• Transfer expatriate's skills and knowledge to host location • Train local nationals
3. Project	• Project of defined duration • Common in construction and petroleum industries
4. Interested and willing	• Employee often young, highly mobile and inexperienced • Assignment often at request of individual
5. Senior Management	• Managing a major business • Frequently to give executive international experience before major promotion

Reasons	Subdivisions
6. Career expatriate/international cadre	• International mobile • On series of international assignments
7. Regional	• Mobile within geographic region but not globally

1.6   CONCLUSION

A deeper grasp of reasons why organisations go abroad and the various stages of becoming global will assist in making better decisions regarding the type assignment and compensation approach. There is a growing trend that "professional expatriates" spend their entire work career moving from country to country, and they just want to know a few things:

1.   That they will not be worse off than their colleagues who stayed.

2.   That their pay is fair.

3.   That they will not be worse off when they retire.

The next chapter covers the various approaches to assignments and the conditions associated with each.

1.7   REFERENCES

WorldatWork. 2007. *The world at work handbook of compensation, benefits & total rewards*. Hoboken, NJ: John Wiley & Sons, Inc.

CHAPTER 2
EXPATRIATE ASSIGNMENT APPROACHES
Mertz Aucamp

2.1 INTRODUCTION

International assignments play a pivotal role in the development of leaders of multinational organisations and should play a pivotal role in the attraction and selection of employees for expatriate assignments. Debatably, multinational organisations accomplish and sustain significant competitive positions through developing their leaders to have an in-depth understanding of their diverse employees, customers and business partners across their geographic spread (Marsh & McLennan Companies, 2013).

International assignments are just a great vehicle that provide leaders with the opportunity to obtain the necessary insight which is not achieved through a normal leadership development programme. The success of an effective programme for international assignees will depend at least in part on the extent to which employers (a) display their appreciation to valued employees by preparing them before they embark on the assignment and welcome them back when repatriated; and (b) emphasise international assignments as critical prerequisites for appointment to their most significant senior positions (Marsh & McLennan Companies, 2013).

2.2 MOBILITY AS AN IMPORTANT PART OF A GLOBAL LEADERSHIP DEVELOPMENT STRATEGY

Mobility is at the heart of a leadership development strategy in the most successful international organisations. Mobility is not only about enhancing their business by transferring key players to critical positions in very important parts of their operations, but among the objectives is to nurture leaders for broader and more significant roles with a larger accountability. Multinational organisations recognise their need for leaders who understand their markets, customers' preferences in those markets, and the buying habits of those inhabitants at large. In addition, organisations also require leaders who understand the culture and values of local employees, and who are able to motivate and inspire others to excel in their performance, as well as attracting and retaining the best. Internationally, assignees are provided with an opportunity to experience life personally and viscerally in different global areas within which organisations operate. Multinational employers equip their leaders to engage genuinely with people from different global alliances (Marsh & McLennan Companies, 2013).

2.3 LEADERSHIP DEVELOPMENT INTERVENTIONS

Figure 2.1 below identifies eight recognised leadership development interventions, of which two are directly associated with mobility, namely international assignment, which assists leaders to develop a global mind-set; and rotational assignments, which provide leaders with a foundation of a broad understanding of an organisation's inner workings and of its operational and geographical activities. Action learning, a third intervention, focuses on bringing together people from different backgrounds, nationalities, and functions in order to collaborate, and in the process, to learn what makes other people what they are and why they react as they do (Marsh & McLennan Companies, 2013).

Global Mind-set and Resilience	Diversity, Inclusion, Engagement	Organisational Breadth	Strategic Mind-set
International Assignments/ Mobility	**Multicultural Teaming**	**Rotational Assignments/ Mobility**	**Special Projects/ Action Learning**
Frequent Purposeful Travel	**Leadership & Management Development**	**MBA, MSc, Open Programmes**	**Coaching, Mentoring & Sponsorship**
Helicopter View	Skills, Culture, Behaviour	Broadening Knowledge	Application, Career, Practice

Figure 2.1: Leadership development interventions (Mercer, 2013)

2.4 THE PURPOSE OF INTERNATIONAL ASSIGNMENTS

In order to give context to expatriation in an organisation, it is important to outline why organisations need to assign their employees to an international assignment and why employees accept such an opportunity. The reasons organisations are assigning their employees to international assignment are:

- Filling a skills gap/providing technical expertise

- Launching new endeavours

- Development purposes for career planning

- Leadership or management required in a specific location

- Globalisation, such as building global networks

- Knowledge transfer that could focus on building technical and management expertise

- Transfer of corporate culture

- Transfer of technological knowledge and expertise

- Retention – preventing key talent from leaving and joining a competitor

- Political reasons – to move an employee into or out of a sensitive situation

- Self-initiated request (McNulty, 2009).

On the other hand, employees accept international assignments for the following major reasons:

- *Capability development* in areas such as building larger networks through enhanced communication, evolving of a global perspective, cultivating cultural understanding, knowledge transfer and developing new/fresh ideas

- *Staffing development and expertise* in areas such as enhancing local morale, retention of talented employees and maintaining strong leadership to ensure stability

- *Career development* as a source of personal competitive advantage, in areas such as building a Curriculum vitae, developing management, leadership and people management capabilities, constructing professional networks, attaining more visibility and exposure and gaining a global perspective

- *Personal or family gains* in terms of improved lifestyle, personal growth and travel opportunities

- *Financial gain* for the assignee through the different allowances that are being paid

- *Job security* (McNulty, 2009).

2.5 OVERVIEW: INTERNATIONAL ASSIGNMENT COMPENSATION APPROACHES

It is known that international assignments have progressed considerably over time, especially in the ways in which organisations compensate their expatriates. As the evolution of international assignments is accelerating, it is of the utmost importance for multinational employers to comprehend the breadth of the present approaches to compensation for different international assignments. Expatriation, as it is known, emerged in the late 1970s and early 1980s. It was during this period that multinational orgnaisations were investing around the world, and much of the project-based work required the presence of managers and senior executives from the head office country for overseeing the operations. During this period, in general, the early remuneration packages were excessively generous, as organisations supposed that pay remuneration packages needed to be lavish in order to persuade employees to work overseas. This period displayed that there was a lack of planning for period and purpose of the international assignment. Many policies were headquarters-centric, but a few multinational employers had a well-defined pay approach for their expatriates (Marsh & McLennan Companies, 2013).

During the 1980s and 1990s, organisations displayed some movement toward consistency. They adopted an approach where they examined assignments country by country and began to consider repatriation more carefully. Organisations were increasingly likely to get two- to five-year assignments motivated by a compensation strategy of "no gain, no loss". This approach did not function well when moving, for example, an automotive executive from a 3 000-square-foot, four-bedroomed home in the Detroit suburbs to a small inner city Tokyo apartment. Therefore, particularly in the United States, they have settled on the balance-sheet approach as a means of rationalising pay for globally mobile employees (Marsh & McLennan Companies, 2013). The latest approach to segmentation will be discussed further on in this book.

2.6 THE COMPLEXITIES OF EXPATRIATE COST-OF-LIVING ISSUES

At the core of protecting international assignees' purchasing power, employees should neither profit nor suffer financially from a temporary relocation overseas. Two main approaches exist to protect the purchasing power of employees during international assignments: multinational and home-host philosophy. When employees are being posted for their international assignments, organisations use a "cost-of-living basket" including key items in order to calculate differences in the cost of living between host and home locations (Marsh & McLennan Companies, 2013).

The multinational philosophy uses the principle that the assignees' expenditure will be similar on their "basket items", irrespective of their home location. When this approach is taken by an organisation, one basket is used for all transfers. On the other hand, the home-host approach is built on the principle that people spend differently subject to their country of origin. In order to attend to these differences, a dissimilar basket is used per nationality.

To answer the question on which philosophy is preferred, the right choice for an organisation will depend very much on the make-up of the expatriate workforce. If the expat group is drawn from a range of locations, the multinational approach is most likely to be the best option. In order to provide context, we have used Mercer as an example. The indices used in their multinational and home-host approaches are described below (Marsh & McLennan Companies, 2013).

2.6.1   Multinational philosophy

- **Mean-to-mean:** This is a comparison of the average prices in an employee's home location to the average in their host location for similar items at similar retail outlets. This index proposes the best indicator of entire price differences between locations without contemplation of assignee efficiency or obtainability of goods in the location.

- **Efficient:** This dimension supposes the assignee has an extensive variety of outlets and retail prices in the assignment location from which to choose, but based on the short-term nature of the assignment, it may not have the identical efficiency in purchasing compared to home.

- **Convenience:** In this dimension, it is on the basis that more stores are available in the host location. This is particularly applicable for locations where shopping convenience is crucial, or locations that do not have a wide variety of alternative retail shops. High prices are evident in the host country, and this results in a bigger allowance being granted (Marsh & McLennan Companies, 2013).

2.6.2   Home-host philosophy

- **Efficient purchaser:** This is based on the assumption that the assignee is acquainted with the local market and is more accustomed by buying a combination of international and local/regional brands at different outlets.

- **High-income purchaser:** This factor is designed for high-income employees from low-wage or lesser-developed countries who, as a result of their increased earning power, have developed spending practices that are more typical of the expatriate or international community than those of typical locals from their home country.

- **Expatriate:** This approach considers comparing prices in retail outlets frequented by local nationals in the home location to prices from retail outlets frequented by expatriates in the assignment location. This is appropriate for newly arrived expatriates or lesser-developed locations where local brands/outlets are inappropriate (Marsh & McLennan Companies, 2013).

2.6.3   Cost-of-living-trends

When faced with the cost-of-living (COL) dimension unfolding, one cannot ignore the 2012 Mercer *Worldwide Survey of International Assignment Policies and Practices*, which revealed that home leave, housing and COL were among the top three issues about which expatriate employees were complaining. Cost of living remains the item that is most complained about as it does not remain constant, and expatriate employees are worried about it as it impacts on their daily life with regard to weekly shopping and refuelling their cars. The survey further found that organisations limit COL expenses where the employee's salary determines the COL amount they will be receiving, and in some cases, a ceiling exists where employees earning more than a threshold amount are not entitled to COL expenses. According to the Mercer Survey of 2012, the three most popular pay delivery models identified are the split pay method, the home country currency method, and the host currency method (Marsh & McLennan Companies, 2013).

2.6.3.1   Split pay method

In this method, the organisation pays what is needed in the countries where income taxes in the home location are being paid, which means that the organisation pays for housing and goods in local currency in the assignment country. Under this system, currency fluctuations between host and home country have no influence on the employee, but organisations are required to pay close attention to price fluctuations. This method could create implications on the payroll as the terms are not standard, especially with regard to definitions or meanings that differ between home and the host country (Marsh & McLennan Companies, 2013).

2.6.3.2   Home country currency method

This is a well-liked option for short-range assignments and commuters. It does not require any extra administrative burden on the payroll as employees are being remunerated in their home country currency directly into their bank accounts in the home country. Then a portion of the salary will be channelled to the host country to pay for housing, spendable income, and potentially for school fees. A distinct advantage of this method is that employees from countries paying a high salary acknowledge that their "money is in the right place at the right time", which allows employees to maintain their home financial obligations such as their mortgage, and saving is easier for them (Marsh & McLennan Companies, 2013).

This method has some disadvantages with regard to issues such as tax and transfer pricing. Employees will be taxed in their host country, and in some countries such as Poland and Bulgaria, tax returns need to be completed monthly. In other situations, tax payments cannot be bound to the relevant authorities by the home company, but need to be paid in person or through a host country account owned by the assignee. Both these scenarios place a considerable extra administrative burden on assignees and organisations alike. Lastly, another disadvantage is the necessity to monitor exchange rate variations (Marsh & McLennan Companies, 2013).

2.6.3.3 Host currency method

With this system, the employee's full salary is paid in the local currency into a local bank account, which entails that the money is where assignees require it as they purchase their daily consumables. This method does, however, make it more difficult for employees to save in their home country. The distinct disadvantage is that if employees are not based in a "safe harbour", the systems to transfer funds home may not be secure, which causes anxiety among employees. At the same time, there may also be limitations on the amounts of money that can be sent abroad or to their home country. With this method, currency fluctuation also plays a role (Marsh & McLennan Companies, 2013).

2.7 MANAGING THE COST OF LIVING IN HIGH-INFLATION LOCATIONS

Inflation is another key cause of concern for assignees, but in fact only 11 of the 300 locations researched by Mercer experienced high price movement of more than 10 percent for the 12 months leading up to September 2012. As an HR practitioner, it is always interesting to see that employees are swift to spot that the inflation rates displayed in internal index tables do not add up to the official rate, and they will enquire about that. In order to manage this challenge, it is important to explain the organisation's policy and reassure employees that if inflation escalates in their host location, the index will change to reflect those higher prices and that employees' purchasing power will not be negatively affected (Marsh & McLennan Companies, 2013). (It is important to note that reference is made to "basket" inflation, not the official inflation rate, and that housing and school fees have been excluded from the basket.)

In conclusion, it remains a challenge in managing cost of living for expatriate workers, specifically as it is influenced by a multitude of issues such as base salary, currency fluctuations, choice of index, and price changes in both home and host cities. Success in managing the situation lies in good and thorough communication. Encourage assignees to consider overall policies rather than being focused on just one element, and as an employer, be prepared to test their perceptions if employees perceive that their purchasing power is being impaired in some or other way, and share with them the figures that will reveal the true picture. In order to do so successfully, ensure that COL indexes are updated regularly, especially for those countries or regions with high price movements (Marsh & McLennan Companies, 2013).

2.8   THE CURRENT ENVIRONMENT – MOVING TOWARDS SEGMENTATION

As organisations recover from the global recession, employers discover the need to move employees earlier in their careers, and are looking at mobility with regard to length and type of assignments. In reality, many more nationalities are involved, including employee movements that would have been unusual 10 years ago, such as those employees who are assigned from Angola to Central London (instead of the other way around). This emphasises the need for different pay models. In order to manage an increasingly diverse, fragmented population of globally mobile employees effectively, organisations need to look at segmentation, structured compensation, and structured mobility at different levels of the organisation (Marsh & McLennan Companies, 2013).

The segmentation of an organisation's expatriate workforce may require some change management on the "employer" side. For any HR practitioner involved in setting policies and administering them, the challenge is to ensure that business leaders are ready to endure *pay differences* or "defensible differentiation". It is important that attention is paid to cost awareness, cost modelling, strategic planning, and workforce planning. Particularly after an acquisition or a spinoff, it is helpful to examine the diversity of the expat population (Marsh & McLennan Companies, 2013).

The administration of global mobility programmes is complicated, as there are continues pressures to do more with less, and organisations measure the return on investment (ROI). It is important for global mobility managers to engage more with the talent management experts within HR to elevate the use of assignments. And emerging on the front burner are family and work–life balance pressures (Marsh & McLennan Companies, 2013).

2.9   TRENDS IN ALTERNATIVE APPROACHES

The use of a single international assignment policy approach is no longer workable for many employers. Organisations adopting more than one programme further complicate administration. Multi-tier policies, Expat-Lite and Local-plus packages, and flexible pay options are the three trends being adopted by organisations (Marsh & McLennan Companies, 2013).

2.9.1   Multi-tier policies

Multi-tier policies are defined by assignment type, location, region, position, or level in the organisation or assignment purpose, and outline what package will be chosen for particular assignment. Assignees need to understand that the choice of package is fair and not subjective. Table 2.1 represents a typical policy matrix indicating the remuneration elements that an employer could adopt in order to differentiate among four types of international assignments. The 2012 survey conducted by Mercer found that companies limit the payment of cost-of-living allowances (COLAs). In Europe only 15 percent of organisations select this approach, but at the same time organisations are placing a "ceiling" or "floor" on the allowance, where COLA could be paid for employees earning up to US$200 000, as an example (Marsh & McLennan Companies, 2013).

Table 2.1: Policy matrix (Mercer, 2013)

		Executive level	Long-term inter-national assignment (LTIA) policy	Intra-re-gional	Local plus
Pre-move	Relocation allowance	O	O	X	X
	Home sale closing costs	O	O	X	X
	Pre-move house-hunting trip	O	O	X	O
	Economy class airfare	X	O	O	O
	Business class airfare	O	X	X	X
On assignment	Housing deduction	O	O	O	X
	COLA	O	O	O	X
	Dependent education	O	O	O	O
	Tax prep	O	O	O	X
	Transportation	O	O	O	X

O	*Core benefit*
O	*Discretionary benefit*
X	*Not applicable*

2.9.2 Expat-Lite policies

In terms of expat "lite" best practices, these establish both the criteria and the benefits that will be excluded or reduced, with a clear value proposal to the employee. This practice has been in implementation for the past 10 to 15 years. It starts with a core policy and contemplates ways of decreasing benefits for certain parts of the population, which will contribute to a saving of money. This approach is used most often in the Middle East, especially the United Arab Emirates. In order to provide further context as to how organisations could adjust their expat lite programmes, some of the factors below are being considered:

- *COLA* – The organisation needs to decide whether to apply it, and if so, which one.
- *Pre-departure trips or exploratory trips* – The organisation needs to define whether to allow these, and if so, how many, and the extent of assistance necessary.
- *Cultural/language training* – Online training, in person, or none at all.
- *Housing* – Modified allowance or no allowance.
- *Travel* – Limited to economy class.
- *Taxes* – Employee responsible, instead of tax equalisation. In certain organisations, the remuneration could be tax free, purely because of the type of organisation and the nature of its separation
- *Home sale and storage of belongings* – Assistance provided to employees while they are internationally assigned.
- *Home leave* – The organisation needs to outline whether to allow leave, and if so, how much and to what extent the organisation funds the home leave regarding travel expenses.
- *Relocation* – Will it be allowed, and if so, how much?
- *Spousal allowance* – Normally this is expressed as a fixed amount for the spouse. (The purpose of a spousal allowance is to act not as an income substitute, but as recognition by the company of the disruption in the spouse's lifestyle. Organisations must not lose sight of the fact that the spouse income is lost when an employee is internationally assigned (Corporate Leadership Council, 2002).)
- *Pet shipment* – Surprisingly, this can be a contentious matter (Marsh & McLennan Companies, 2013).

2.9.3   Flexible pay options

This option entails employee choice or management discretion or a combination of both. Employees are assigned a certain number of credits that they can select to apply to benefits that appeal most to them. Evidently, some selections need to be made as to which elements are obligatory and which can be made elective, and whether this could be administered effectively (Marsh & McLennan Companies, 2013). Table 2.2 below is only an example to provide context to this option and a cafeteria "menu" that one employer has devised:

Table 2.2: Example of expatriate flexible benefits structure (Mercer, 2013)

Policy	Core/Flex Elements	
Compensation	Home-country compensation guideline	Core
Benefits	Home-country compensation guideline	
Work authorisation	Temporary visas/work permits; no permanent ones	
Healthcare	International Health-Care Plan	
Tax preparation	Core	
Dependent education	Core	
Emergency leave	Core	
Home auto loss on sale	Optional	Optional
Cost-of-living differential	Expatriate or EPI Index	
Tax equalisation	Optional	
Home leave	Optional – Economy Class	
Host-country transportation	Optional	
Cultural orientation	Optional/Online	

2.10 IMPACT OF EMERGING MARKETS ON EXPATRIATE POLICIES

Emerging markets are on a course of relatively rapid economic growth, where Gross Domestic Product (GDP) growth is set to overtake that in the "developed" world radically in future decades. It is also expected that emerging markets will have most of the world's population growth, while the workforce in the developed world will be decreasing. Factors such as the current capital flights and currency instability in some of the emerging markets propose that the development road for these countries may be a rough one.

2.10.1   Developing a new mobility mind-set

Where organisations are cutting back on full expatriation packages motivated by the need to control costs, reports of their demise are greatly exaggerated. Mercer's 2012 *Worldwide Survey of International Assignment Policies and Practices* discovered that most employers projected an increase in most assignment types in the coming years, namely.

- 70% anticipate increasing short-term assignments.

- 55% anticipate increasing long-term assignments.

- 49% anticipate increasing developmental/training assignments (this is more than half compared to European companies.

- 48% anticipate increasing locally recruited foreigners (these percentages were slightly higher in Europe and in the Asia-Pacific region).

In order to manage the costs of expatriate assignments in organisations in developed countries, employers are deploying cheaper options, such as transfers subject to terms and conditions in the host location. But in contrast, the growth of emerging markets warrants that traditional long-term assignments underpinned by a comprehensive benefits package are not vanishing. The continuing search for commodities and low-cost manufacturing destinations directs companies to hardship locations (Marsh & McLennan Companies, 2013).

A new generation of expatriates is entering from the emerging markets. The ongoing global war for talent spearheads new forms of assignment and a desperate search for talent. The new façade of expatriation is progressively focusing on how to locate engineers with the right skills mix in Kazakhstan and then assign them to projects in Africa or to relocate the talent from India to support operations in Indonesia, instead of being concerned about relocating American managers to supervise its business operations in China or Brazil (Marsh & McLennan Companies, 2013).

Some organisations presumed too quickly that Americans or Europeans who were on a couple of international assignments for a period of 10 years were known as global nomads and they were placed on international compensation structures disconnected from their home countries. (Global nomads are people of any age or nationality who have lived a significant part of their career years in one or more countries outside their passport country (Schaetti & Ramsey, 2014)). This approach backfired in some cases. For example, a German employee on assignment for 12 years may be branded a "global nomad" while the employee plans his retirement in Germany. When he returns, it may be discovered with total dismay that the savings in US dollars would be subjected to massive exchange rate losses when converted to euros. This would result in a fractured pension history, which would then create further complications. The frustrations would then be directed towards the organisation (Marsh & McLennan Companies, 2013).

By contrast, skilful assignees from emerging markets may fit the definition of global nomads better. because in many cases they have little intention of returning to their home country as there would be no suitable position available and no pension scheme which would present them with a happy retirement. In these cases, obtaining a "virtual home" for such employees or placing them on international salary structures and pension schemes is worth exploring (Marsh & McLennan Companies, 2013).

Analysts often simplify the values and aspirations of the new generations, which include Generation Y and the Millennials, and their enhanced willingness to move abroad. They expect the dawn of a new age of passionate globetrotters who will bring about a welcome reduction in incentive-heavy expatriate packages. The risk is that some people assume that employees will be willing to relocate even without generous expatriate packages, and even on local terms and conditions.

Although new generations are more willing to be more mobile than their predecessors, not all countries are equally appealing to international assignees. Normally there is an important disconnection of where the companies need to send their employees and where those employees aim to go. To illustrate this aspect, an example is where an employee needs to consider an offer of employment in New York or London or Singapore, where a favourable tax regimen exists and there is quality education and security. This will be much more lucrative to expatriates than an assignment in remote Western China, Africa, or Colombia (Marsh & McLennan Companies, 2013).

In order to manage the new generation aspiration for international assignments, employers need to align incentives with the different types of employees, where they will have *adventurers* who are willing to go to difficult locations; *traditional assignees* willing to move if incentives are attractive, and obstacles to mobility, such as family issues and dual career, removed; and lastly, the *hedonists*, who pursue a balance between career and lifestyle and will have a definite idea of where they want to relocate to (Marsh & McLennan Companies, 2013).

2.11 GLOBAL PHENOMENA: THE WAR FOR TALENT

It is known that millions of youthful professionals graduate from universities in emerging markets, but their employability remains low. For example, only 25 percent of Indian and less than half of Brazilian and Chinese professionals are deemed employable by global standards. The focus on and search for individuals with specific skills, such as engineers, also includes many other profiles, such as managers and marketing professionals with global business acumen, which makes the challenge to find this talent become an even bigger problem. In order to provide context, by 2030, the USA will need to provide 25 million workers, while Western

Europe will need to add 45 million. The reality is that this significant proportion of the new workers will be sourced from emerging countries. Simultaneously, out of the 214 million mobile workers worldwide, 40 percent of them transfer between developing countries. With this percentage growing, it is making the global war for talent even fiercer and positioning mobility at the heart of many employers' strategies (Marsh & McLennan Companies, 2013).

2.12 THE COMPLEXITIES OF PAY PRACTICES IN EMERGING MARKETS

It is a convoluted picture when one considers pay practices in emerging markets. The challenge is: how should organisations attend to pay discrepancies between low-paid (soft currency) employees being relocated from the emerging markets and (hard currency) employees in Western Europe or the United States?

In simple terms, an Indian employee earning US$5 000 could not be assigned to the United Kingdom (UK) without an extensive change to her remuneration package, while an American employee would not accept a job in India for such a low salary. This challenge was addressed by localising the Indian manager and letting the American expat remain on a home base traditional expatriate package. These approaches have limitations in that one of the main issues where the Indian manager is localised, is repatriation, which will result in a huge salary reduction which becomes problematic. At the same time, as for the highly paid American expat, the compensation level compared with that of peers in the host location is likely to be enormous, and the recipient organisation in the emerging market is expected to criticise the excessive costs of bringing in such a highly remunerated employee (Marsh & McLennan Companies, 2013).

In order to address these issues, more modern approaches have been developed, for example, peer allowances, or Mercer's International Spendable Income. These approaches focus on supplementing the spendable income part of the salary *(net salary minus savings and housing costs)* with an allowance for the period of the assignment as opposed to the normal process of fully localising the employee and integrating them into the host country salary structure (Marsh & McLennan Companies, 2013).

2.13 REVISITING EXPATRIATE PACKAGES: LOCAL HOUSING VERSUS EXPATRIATE HOUSING

Housing remains a costly part of the expatriate package. Multinational organisations have been initiating methods to control these costs either by paying only a housing differential that is the marginal cost of local housing over home-country housing, or, alternatively, by having a housing budget limitation. The objective is not to offer inferior accommodation but merely to bring housing allowances into line with rent for local people versus considering costly expatriate rental markets. A leading practice is to assess the quality of living and combine the degree of hardship to the provision of a housing allowance. In order to illustrate the practice, for locations such as the United States and Western Europe, a local level of housing is a consideration, while for countries such as Nigeria or Algeria, paying the full housing costs in a safe expatriate compound is justified (Marsh & McLennan Companies, 2013).

2.14 REVISITING EXPATRIATE PACKAGES: COMPLETION BONUSES AS A MOBILITY INCENTIVE

As an emerging consideration, employers have introduced completion bonuses when they want to attract employees to accept specific assignments and difficult locations. Mercer reported that completion bonuses are paid by 30 percent of organisations underpinned by a policy, and an estimated 60 percent of emerging countries pay completion bonuses on an *ad hoc* basis. This is particularly essential to close the growing gap between desirable and hardship locations (Marsh & McLennan Companies, 2013).

2.15 CALCULATING EXPATRIATE RETURN ON INVESTMENT (ROI)

2.15.1 Organisational variables impacting on ROI

When considering the return of investment for organisations on expatriate assignment, the largest number of variables having an impact is at the organisational level in terms of organisational internal activities and practices. According to the research conducted by McNulty (2009), expatriates identified twelve organisational variables likely to influence changes in expatriate ROI. These are outlined in Table 2.3.

Table 2.3: Organisational variables impacting on ROI of expatriate assignments (McNulty, 2009)

Organisational variable	Contextualisation
Planning the assignment	Administratively and strategically, where clear assignment objectives need to be defined with a long-term orientation with regard to the assignment and its expected benefits to the organisation and the expatriate. The importance of having an appropriate and flexible assignment policy, managing economic *volatility* (such as that which was experienced by the global financial crisis) which can regularly lead to ambiguous planning, and the cost-cutting measures that often result from it.
Selection	Relates to the selection of suitable candidates and determinations regarding when to use expatriates versus locals and/or external versus internal appointments.
Support on assignment	Where the assignee need to overcome certain language and communication barriers, managing extreme business travel, lack of incorporation support to the new workplace for the first few weeks, absence of adequate and appropriate training for the assignment, and poor top management support for the vision and expected outcomes from the assignment, particularly for senior management roles.
Quality of HR support	Refers to the practical support provided by HR division to undertake a transfer to a new country including HR's attitude towards assignees.
Non-work and family support	This factor is underpinned by finding proper education facilities for children, and managing spousal and dual career issues.
Performance management	The focus on customising performance appraisals to the context of an international assignment.
Repatriation	Is concerned with developing a plan to leverage an expatriate's knowledge and experience and how an assignment integrates into an employee's overall career development. (Illustrates expatriate's views that career planning should be an integral part of overall assignment planning.)
Retention	The purpose of retaining critical talented employees, and managing expatriate turnover.
Career management support	Involves career planning, talent management, and knowledge transfer capabilities

Organisational variable	Contextualisation
Organisational structure	The size of an organisation's operations, joint-venture activities, and centralised versus decentralised versus flat operational structures. Issues involve effectively co-ordinating regional activities on a global basis, and managing and adapting to new management structures in joint venture activities.
Organisational culture	Organisational culture is defined by expatriates as the underlying attitude an organisation adopts towards its employees, which is exhibited in how the organisation treats them on a day-to-day basis. The level to which expatriates accept or disapprove of a culture that takes care of either a supportive and inspiring work environment or one in which cost-cutting and an "old boys' network" impacts on the manner in which vital personnel decisions are made and communicated.
Fulfilment of the psychological contract	A question of whether expectations have been met, the extent to which promises have been fulfilled by both the organisation and the expatriate, and the possible impact of both fulfilled and unfulfilled expectations.

2.15.2   The calculation of expatriate ROI

There is a lack of consensus on what ROI from expatriation should be and not much tracking of career outcomes for repatriates. In most cases, organisations focus on the "hard" costs, as these are much easier to measure (Doherty, 2012). There are estimates that suggest that the costs of expatriate staff can be between three and, in exceptional cases (depending on the location), up to ten times as much as a domestic employee (Doherty, 2012). It is therefore of critical importance that organisations direct their focus on determining all the costs of expatriation and clearly define all the benefits as a result of the investment. Table 2.4 illustrates the differences between different types of expatriate costs as an input to determine the return on investment.

Table 2.4: Organisational hard cost versus less tangible cost

Organisational hard cost	Less tangible costs

• Base salary
 	
• Foreign service inducement/hardship premiums
 	
• Allowances and benefits including special vacations and leave
 	
• Travel expenses
 	
• Costs in preparing the individual to work abroad
 	
• Administrative support for expatriates provided inside the organisation which is predominantly outsourced
 	
• Taxation and other advice provided to the expatriate
	• *Home organisation*: Replacement and on-boarding costs
	   Knowledge creation, knowledge transfer and exploitation issues that impact on employee morale
	
	• *Host location:* Reaction of locals, including the issue of legitimacy, the potential perception of career ceilings, the impact on the host country, relations and reputation
	   Knowledge creation, knowledge transfer and exploitation issues that impact on employee morale

Table 2.4 above represents only an overview of the cost, but in order to contextualise the cost of an employee for an international assignment, the outline in Table 2.5 below of the total value represents a monetary value of the cost.

Table 2.5: Monetary value of the cost

Total compensation	• Contributions to home and/or host country pensions and saving plans. If your organisation is on a **pension holiday**, the employee should report the **underlying contribution value** of payments • Health care packages (e.g. medical insurance premiums), long-term disability coverage, accident insurance • Life insurance and death benefit contributions
Expat allowances	• Company cars/car allowance: include all running costs, lease costs, and depreciation charge incurred, but **not** purchase prices • Mobility allowances, home leave allowances, shipping of personal goods, temporary and long-term storage • Rent and/or accommodation allowances

Expat allowances (continued)	• Schooling or tuition fees • Hardship premiums, location allowances, provision of drivers and/or security • Cost of 'look-see' trips prior to assignment • Tax equalisation costs (i.e. the difference between host-country tax cost born by employer less hypothetical tax withheld from employee • Many organisations offer a lengthy menu of benefits items, including flexible benefits packages. Our definition gives details of only the most common examples, but you should report the cost of all assignment-related expenses applicable under your relocation programmes
Expat management employees	• The number of employees in the organisation who are primarily engaged in the management and administration of international assignments • Employees who spend less than 50% of their time on expatriate management and/or administration
Expat management costs	• Total compensation and benefits costs for expat management employees • All expat outsource costs • Investment in learning and development • Internal charges from other business units or functions for support to the expat management function • Overheads, e.g. facilities, materials, rent, equipment and depreciation charges for purchases • For total compensation and benefits costs for those involved in the management of expats, capture similar compensation and long-term benefits figures
Expat outsource costs	• All fees paid to external parties for expatriate management activities, i.e. relocation services, immigration, house search, cultural training, tax services, payroll preparation • Excludes VAT, sales taxes or other similar value-added tax charges applicable to fees paid to third party providers

Assignment-related learning and development (L&D) investment	• Cost of pre-assignment cultural training (either internally resourced or provided externally) • Cost of language training • All fees paid to external parties for assignment-related learning and development • Training costs relating to the delivery of technical training activity for example the use of overseas systems • Exclude expats who have transferred between two or more assignments over the course of the year but who have not returned to their home country

* Corporate Leadership Council (2002) defines hardship factors as including:

Housing Climate and physical conditions Disease and sanitation Educational facilities Infrastructure Physical remoteness Political violence and repression Political and social environment Crime Communications Availability of recreation facilities Availability of goods and services.

Measuring the return-on-investment (ROI) of expatriates has been debated for years, but according to a recent survey of expatriate practices conducted by the Society for Human Resource Management (SHRM) Global, there is no "universally understood and accepted" definition for the term. It raises the question as to why is it difficult to define expatriate ROI. The costs of sending an expatriate are instant and tangible, while the return or value created by the expatriate is insubstantial and stretches over time (Shearer, 2004).

Shearer (2004) made reference to two schools of thought measuring expatriate ROI, which focus on the financial model and strategic model.

2.15.3 Financial model

The financial model is defined by the principal that the expatriate pays back the incremental costs of the assignment. An expatriate is treated as an investment and it leads to the assumption that any benefits or losses in organisations are attributable solely to the performance of the employees – this is *quite a leap of faith* (Shearer, 2004).

The calculation of expat ROI involves converting qualitative behaviour into quantitative measurements, which is not a simple task and is concerned with an agreement between both HR and line management. In the process, the organisation needs to gauge the impact the expatriate makes on the financial performance of the organisation by quantifying the expatriate's performance on specific tasks and weighing the achievement of these performance measurements against variances in the financial performance of the organisation. According to Mike Schell, CEO of RW3, there are five steps involved in using the financial model, namely:

1. Define the assignment objectives.

2. Agree on quantifiable measurements for the assignment.

3. Evaluate the expatriate's performance against these measurements.

4. Develop an equation that converts qualitative behaviour into quantifiable measurements.

5. Calculate the ROI where it could be a complex cost accounting or a simple calculation to see if the expatriate covered the cost of keeping them on assignment (Shearer, 2004).

One of the noticeable challenges to the financial model is getting all the costs linked with an expat assignment. Where organisations require assistance, several accounting firms and HR consulting firms have the necessary software at their disposal to gather and organise these costs. There are many questions raised concerning an expat assignment, but they only emphasise that an organisation requires a clearly defined framework with regard to measuring ROI that focuses on when and how it is calculated and whether the calculation will focus on short-term or long-term perspectives (Shearer, 2004).

2.15.4   Strategic model

The strategic model is not as scientific as the financial model, but it influences organisations to critical assess the reasons why they are sending an expatriate. The strategic model is a non-numerical method of assessing the value of an expat assignment. Pivotal to this model are the answers to two basic questions: *"Who do you have on assignment, and why are they there?"* according to Paula Caligiuri of Rutgers University and Caligiuri and Associates (Shearer, 2004).

This model observes how effective the expatriates have been at accomplishing what the organisation has set out for them. If the assignment is developmental in nature, it needs to be determined whether the expatriate has gained the desired competencies. With every assignment, an organisation needs to be able to provide substantive evidence of what would have happened if the expat had not been there to perform a specific task or to kill a fire. Where the assignment is for developmental purposes, the organisation must establish what the long-term effect would be if they did not have globally trained senior managers in the future. Therefore, the selection of the correct employee for the assignment and clearly clarifying the expectations of the assignment are vital in the strategic model (Shearer, 2004).

2.16 REFERENCES

Corporate Leadership Council (CLC). 2002. *Compensation and benefits practices for expatriates*. [Online]. Available: http://www.corporateleadershipcouncil.com. [Accessed 14 July 2014].

Doherty, NT & Dickmann, D. 2012. Measuring the return on investment in international assignments: An action research approach. *International Journal of Human Resource Management*, 23(16):3434–3454.

Marsh & McLennan Companies. 2013. *Mastering the challenges of global mobility in a rapidly changing world*. Mercer. [Online]. Available: http://www.imercer.com/uploads/Europe/.../emc_booklet_final_low_res.pdf. [Accessed 20 July 2014].

Mcnulty, Y. 2009. *Measuring expatriate return on investment in global firms*. Caulfield East Victoria, Victoria, Australia: Monash University.

Schaetti, FB & Ramsey, SJ. 2014. *The global nomad experience – living in liminality*. Transition Dynamics. [Online]. Available: http://www.transition-dynamics.com/liminality.html. [Accessed 27 July 2014].

Shearer, C. 2004. *Calculating expatriate ROI*. Expatica.com. [Online]. Available: http://www.expatica.com/hr/story/calculating-expatriate-roi-10527.html. [Accessed 14 July 2014].

CHAPTER 3
INTERNATIONAL CRUCIBLE ASSIGNMENTS
Dr Mark Bussin and Mack Moey

3.1   INTRODUCTION

As the war for talent rages on, there is an acknowledgement that the pool of top talent is not sufficiently large to meet the growing demand for global leaders. It therefore makes business sense for organisations to grow and groom their own global talent pools. International assignments can serve as critically significant development opportunities for leaders and often form the pinnacle of leadership development programmes. They undoubtedly help leaders develop global business acumen and cross-cultural competence, but the costs attached are significant (Stahl, Chua, Caligiuri, Cerdin & Taniguchi, 2007).

To ensure that organisations reap the benefits of their investment in global mobility, they need to ensure that the assignments provide sufficient growth, stretch and scope for talent and leadership development goals to be met. The assignments should be Crucible Experiences. 'Crucible' refers to an intense, meaningful, and often transformational, experience which shakes and shapes your life. The Corporate Leadership Council (2012a) coined the term 'International Crucible Assignment' (ICA) and defined it as an expatriate experience that places leaders in challenging or unfamiliar situations and fast-moving environments (CLC Human Resources, 2012a).

This chapter will focus on the nature of the ICA and present the results of lessons learnt. The aim of the chapter is to allow you to plan and scope the nature of international assignment(s) to ensure that they result in sufficient and significant growth for both the organisation and the assignee.

3.2   BACKGROUND

The premise of the ICA is that organisations should focus on providing leaders with development experiences that push them outside of their comfort zones and into unfamiliar environments. There are ways to provide such experiences which do not include global mobility, such as exposing employees to:

- Experiences outside of their area of expertise
- Experiences in a new market

- Experiences in a new business
- Turning around an underperforming project
- Managing an underperforming team
- Managing a critical project on a fast cycle (CLC Human Resources, 2012b).

While these types of development experiences are useful and important, no others, individually or collectively, have a greater impact on global leader effectiveness than international assignments. The Corporate Leadership Council asserts that going on an ICA can increase the chances of becoming a Great Global Leader by 21 percent (CLC Human Resources, 2012a). The qualifier here is the crucible nature of the assignment.

Since international assignments are becoming the norm rather than the exception in leadership development, Deloitte (2008) suggests that organisations adopt an approach that makes global mobility a standard operating practice that is designed to be fast, flexible, efficient, and repeatable. When these demands are combined with the necessity to provide crucible experiences, it becomes necessary to tailor a company's talent management programmes, strategies, and practices to the different needs of each participant (Deloitte, 2008).

Although there is no room for a one-size-fits-all approach and strategy to ICAs, reviewing lessons learnt can help organisations to maximise efficiencies and leverage best practice.

3.3 ADOPTING A LEARNING AND DEVELOPMENT APPROACH TO INTERNATIONAL ASSIGNMENTS

If learning and development are accepted as key goals for an international assignment, a structured and deliberate effort should be made to ensure that leaders successfully transform their experiences into learning that will enhance their global leadership effectiveness. The focus of the assignment therefore needs to shift to include performance indicators based on learning effectiveness in addition to traditional work effectiveness.

Ng, Van Dyne and Ang (2009) pose two critical questions in this regard:

1. How do global leaders learn from their international assignments to become better global leaders?

2. What attributes of global leaders enhance their learning while on international work assignments?

In response to the first question, Ng et al (2009) propose that an experiential learning approach should be adopted. Experiential learning views learning as a continuous and dynamic process where new knowledge, changing existing ideas and perspectives, relearning, and integrating old and new ideas are all incorporated. Kolb (2005, in Ng et al, 2009) suggests that experiential learning must consist of four bases – experiencing, reflecting, thinking and acting – in order to turn an experience into learning effectively. In other words, it is not sufficient merely to have an experience. Having an experience must lead to transformation (of thought and action) in order to gain maximum developmental benefit.

How does this translate into best practice on the ground for international assignees? First and foremost, assignees need to have concrete experiences. Organisations should encourage their assignees to get involved in the host culture to gain these concrete experiences (Ng et al, 2009). It can be tempting for assignees to avoid the incredible learning opportunities that ICAs offer by isolating themselves in expatriate communities. In some countries it is common practice to stay in expatriate compounds, to use private transport with dedicated company drivers, and even to socialise only at expatriate restaurants, bars, and clubs.

Organisations should structure international assignments to facilitate interdependence with locals. These concrete and meaningful interactions with locals should increase their involvement and interaction with the local culture. In addition, organisations can reward leaders for learning foreign languages and increasing their knowledge of the local culture during their assignments. Each of these should facilitate and encourage cultural involvement (Oddou, Mendenhall, & Ritchie, 2000).

Experiential learning also requires reflective observation. International assignees are often placed under pressure to deliver large pieces of work within tight timelines. Their workloads are heavy and since they are not rewarded for learning and development objectives, they tend to focus on traditional areas of work performance. Assignees should be given structured time to reflect on the cultural, social and leadership value of their experiences on a regular basis. While the use of a personal journal could accomplish this with no cost implication, the chances of assignees keeping journals is remote. Individual coaching sessions with qualified and experienced coaches should be integrated into the assignees' schedules while on assignment. These sessions will guide the assignees to reflect on their experiences and can provide immense value to leadership development and ICA success.

The final stage of experiential learning involves active experimentation. Organisations can provide incentives and resources that encourage assignees to set specific and measurable developmental goals for exploration and experimentation. They also can make sure that reward systems do not contradict the importance of development (Ng et al, 2009).

In response to Ng et al's (2009) second question on what attributes of global leaders enhance their learning while on international work assignments, the answer is cultural intelligence (CQ). This is defined as an individual's capability to function effectively in culturally diverse contexts (Ng et al, 2009). One of the most significant predictors of CQ is self-efficacy – the belief of the assignee that they will be able to perform specific leadership roles effectively in culturally diverse settings.

Cross-cultural training programmes can be used to increase assignee self-efficacy by equipping assignees with the capability to engage in abstract conceptualisation that can help them make sense of novel and paradoxical situations. To achieve this, the cross-cultural training programmes should include leadership development skills such as inductive logic and reasoning as well as the usual concrete components of learning about the new country and culture. Leadership development skills help assignees to make sense of, as well as translate, their concrete experiences and reflections into more abstract understanding of the culture (Earley & Peterson, 2004, in Ng et al, 2009).

3.4 THE CONTENT AND CONTEXT OF THE INTERNATIONAL ASSIGNMENT ROLE

To achieve the objectives of growth and development during an ICA, it makes sense to provide assignees with the opportunity to learn new content areas and skills. In this way, they cannot rely on existing knowledge and past experiences to guide their work success. **Changing the content** of the role an international assignee adopts can increase the effectiveness of the assignment by as much as 11 percent (CLC Human Resources, 2012a).

When the content of the role is changed, the assignee is forced to leverage personal networks to identify and influence others, who in turn assist with the completion of key tasks. The benefit is that the assignee is encouraged to collaborate to develop a new network, resulting in greater interdependence with locals. In addition, the assignee is exposed to different parts of the business, increasing his/her knowledge and understanding of the organisation (CLC Human Resources, 2012a).

The context of a role refers to the environment in which an assignee operates. It can be changed either by changing the geographic location or the type of stakeholders with whom the leader must interact. CLC Human Resources (2012a) asserts that **changing the context** of an international assignment can increase the effectiveness of the assignment by as much as 8%.

The change of role content and context can be encapsulated in the construct of "frame-shifting". An ICA provides the assignee with the challenge of learning to shift their perspective and leadership methods to fit the different circumstances better. Frame-shifting requires the cognitive and behavioural agility to alter both your leadership style and your strategic approach. Successful global leaders are agile enough to take on new frames of reference and to modify their approach to various environments without losing sight of their primary business objectives (Gundling, Hogan & Cvitkovich, 2011).

Assignees whose roles change in content and context have to adapt their communication style, leadership style, and strategy in order to bridge the gap between the familiar and the new. The ability to "frame shift" is a key determinant in both the success of the international assignment and the assignee's leadership development (Gundling et al, 2011). We all have deep-rooted patterns of behaviour which are associated with past successes. It is difficult to disregard these tried and tested behaviours and venture into environments and situations where success is not easily assured. It is this opportunity to frame-shift that helps define an international assignment as crucible.

3.5 THE SCOPE OF THE INTERNATIONAL ASSIGNMENT ROLE

One of the milestones of leadership development is the increased scope of influence and responsibility. This may not always entail an increase in the number of direct reports or even budget authority. The critical driver of increased scope is an increase in the number of stakeholders the leader must manage. Stakeholders can be considered even more difficult to manage than direct reports as the basis for your sphere of control is influence and not power.

CLC Human Resources (2012a) reports that changing the scope of an international assignment can increase the effectiveness of the assignment by as much as 16%. Increased responsibilities accompany increased scope and in international assignments are mostly characterised by less direct authority. In these situations assignees are required to make decisions more quickly with less information, which develops their prioritisation skills (CLC Human Resources, 2012a).

Scope changes can include:

- An increase in the number of stakeholders an assignee must work with

- An increase in the assignee's responsibilities across markets or functions

- An increase in the assignee's decision-making accountability

- Responsibility for the same product, but in multiple geographies

- Management of a significantly larger process

- Management of a substantially larger team

- Management in a more matrixed environment (CLC Human Resources, 2012a).

**The Big 5 Personality Characteristics that Predict
the Success of International Assignees**

Within the general research literature on personality, five factors have been identified as a useful typology or taxonomy for classifying the personality characteristics that predict the success of international assignees. Labelled "the Big Five", this set of personality factors includes:

1. Extroversion
2. Agreeableness
3. Conscientiousness
4. Emotional stability, and
5. Openness or intellect.

These characteristics are linked to the four drivers of success during international assignments:

1. To be open and receptive to learning the norms of new cultures.
2. To initiate contact with host nationals.
3. To gather cultural information.
4. To handle the higher amounts of stress associated with the ambiguity of their new environments.

Source: Caligiuri, Tarique & Jacobs (2009).

3.6 THE TIMING OF THE INTERNATIONAL ASSIGNMENT

The selection of individuals to fill international assignments is the subject of many research studies. Personality traits (see the information block above), gender, language skills, previous international experience, family situation, and career stage, among others, have all been studied to understand their impact on the successful selection of international assignees.

While leadership development can take place at any age, persuading leaders between 36 and 45 years of age to accept international assignments is difficult. Leaders in this age group are significantly less mobile than others (CLC Human Resources, 2012a).

Family commitments, specifically regarding children, are likely to make leaders less available at a time when ironically, they could add the most value to the organisation by taking on international assignments. Leaders should be encouraged to consider ICAs during this age range.

Special efforts need to be made to facilitate successful ICAs for assignees who have children or partner complexities. The 2013 Ernst and Young Global Mobility Survey found that 65% of respondents cited personal issues such as lack of adequate schools, insufficient housing or inadequate work opportunities for spouses as reasons for failed assignments and early repatriation. It is widely accepted that a happy family situation leads to a happy international assignee.

3.7 THE TOTAL NUMBER OF INTERNATIONAL CRUCIBLE ASSIGNMENTS

How many ICAs should an assignee be given? Do they become more effective leaders with every new assignment or does the theory of diminishing returns apply? CLC Human Resources (2012a) proposes that the greatest development benefit for global leaders is moving from the first to the second assignment. After the third assignment, the value of each additional assignment for global leader development diminishes because many of the key development activities have already taken place.

There is a cohort of assignees who become career expatriates. These assignees are useful to send to countries where there are specific problems or to assist in upskilling new international teams, but rarely become top global leaders (CLC Human Resources, 2012a).

3.8 THE DURATION OF INTERNATIONAL CRUCIBLE ASSIGNMENTS

Duration is an important factor in driving the crucible nature of the assignment. Assignees that stay in one place too long no longer experience the same challenges as they assimilate to the host country. Those who stay for too short a duration do not receive the opportunity to resolve the challenges effectively. First assignments should last between 18 and 36 months; after this period the value of additional months diminishes, eventually lowering the overall value of the assignment. For subsequent assignments, after the 12th month the incremental value of each additional month diminishes (CLC Human Resources, 2012a).

3.9 CONNECTING THE ICA ROLE TO PAST AND FUTURE CAREER CHOICES

As discussed in Chapter 20, Repatriation and Reintegration, it is essential that the ICA is structured to form part of an assignee's career path to promote retention and promote business and personal benefit. The crucible nature of the assignment will change the assignee and these changes need to be acknowledged and appreciated to maximise organisational return on investment. Assignees should be told how their role and assignment(s) fit into the organisation's global strategy and this dialogue should be maintained throughout the assignment (CLC Human Resources, 2012a).

Insights into Attraction and Retention of International Assignees

At the April 2013 Mercer EMEA Mobility Conference, attended by more than 120 senior mobility professionals from some of the largest global organisations, Mercer asked and received replies to the following questions:

- **What are the three things international assignees say they appreciated most during their international assignment (how to increasingly attract international assignees)?** Answers revolved around enabling international assignees to acclimatise better to their new culture through family support, relocation support, networking with other international assignees, and ongoing communication with the home company base.

- **What do international assignees who stay in the organisation say are the three greatest advantages they've gained from an international assignment (how to increasingly retain international assignees)?** Answers focused on career development in the form of personal growth, professional growth, wider professional opportunities, and new mind-sets.

- **What are the top three activities that, if done in advance of an assignment, would most help international assignees prepare (how to increasingly attract and retain international assignees)?** Answers covered matters like "hygiene" factors and cultural issues: well-communicated terms and conditions, well-planned pre-assignment trip, orientation programme, and insight into host countries' habits and customs.

- **What are the three reasons for departure most often given by international assignees that leave the company following repatriation (how to increasingly retain international assignees)?** Answers related to lack of career advancement: jobs do not meet expectations, a better offer is made by another organisation, remuneration is below expectations, and an overseas experience is not valued by the home company.

- **What are the top three issues of dissatisfaction raised by international assignees while they are out in a host location (how to increasingly retain international assignees)?** Answers point to cultural issues and a lost sense of purpose: poor support for adjusting to the host location, insufficient link with the home organisation, intercultural issues, and poor family support in the host country.

Two underlying themes of the responses above were the issue of communication and the management of expectations. Having the right policies around compensation (given different pay levels across the worldwide platform) and family arrangements, especially in the growing context of dual-career households, can go some way towards improving the host-country experience and smoothing repatriation. These policies need to be clearly and consistently communicated.

A second theme revolves around the need for familiarisation with the culture to which the assignees are going – principally for the individual assignee but also for their families. Assignees need to know what awaits them – the likely behaviours of those operating in the host country. They also need to know what the host country expects of them, including how management in the host country is likely to view them given the assignees' natural preferences and ensuing behaviour.

Even if international assignees are simply "experts", sent to fulfil a technical role that the host nation cannot fill, those experts can accelerate and amplify their effectiveness and their ability to transfer knowledge if they approach their assignment with greater awareness of themselves – how they naturally behave at work and the effect that that is likely to have on others in the host nation – and the working culture in that host nation.

Source: Rathbone, 2014.

3.10 THE FUTURE OF INTERNATIONAL CRUCIBLE EXPERIENCES

The perceived value of ICAs is growing. Not only has the number of international assignees increased by 25% over the past decade; but PricewaterhouseCoopers (PwC, 2013) predicts a further **50 percent** growth in mobile employees by 2020. The nature of the assignments, however, is poised to change. There is a realisation and acknowledgement that when a directed and structured effort is made to ensure that assignments are crucible in nature, long-term (3- to 4-year) assignments are no longer necessary.

The duration of ICAs has reduced and **20 percent** of assignments now last less than 12 months, compared with **10 percent** in 2002 (PwC, 2012). The goal of cost containment linked to international assignments is likely to drive this trend going forward.

As organisations are increasingly using global mobility as a tool of learning and leadership development, there is a trend to send more junior and younger employees on international assignment. This trend is indicative not only of the learning and development value organisations place on ICAs, but also of their willingness to invest in global leader development. Early exposure to global environments can accelerate leadership development, and younger assignees often have less complexity in terms of children and spousal issues (Ernst & Young, 2013).

Sending younger employees on international assignment is also starting to constitute a key element in attracting, retaining, developing and engaging emerging talent in the millennial generation. Research conducted by PwC in 2012 found that **71 percent** of employees from the millennial generation say they want *and expect* an international assignment during their career.

Another trend that is predicted to increase over time is the number of women being sent on ICAs. The number of female assignees has doubled in the past 10 years from **10 percent** to **20 percent**, and PwC (2012) projects that this will rise to **27 percent** by 2020.

The objectives of international assignments are also evolving to reflect the value of the crucible experience. This is evidenced in the approach being applied to many assignments. In the past, employees were traditionally sent on international assignment to bridge a skills or capability gap in the host country. The future of ICAs will see a wider range of assignment objectives including:

- The development of global leaders with enhanced understanding of the global business environment

- The development of global leaders with cultural adaptability and cultural intelligence (CQ)

- The attraction, engagement and retention of top talent

- The creation of career opportunities that offer depth, breadth and diversity

- The two-way transfer of skills where there is an acknowledgement that the parent company has much to learn from the host country and that knowledge sharing is not a one-way process (PwC, 2012).

Alternatives to relocation are also set to redefine the future world of global mobility. The fact that crucible experiences can be designed as part of international assignments, without necessitating long-term relocation, will significantly lower costs and increase the willingness of employees to participate. Some alternatives to relocation include:

- *Project-based assignments* – Relocation and/or frequent travel may be required only for the duration of the project and may not be continuous

- *Commuting and extended business travel* – The availability and decreasing cost of travel has made business travel a viable alternative to relocation

- *Rotational employee programmes* – Short rotations of top talent or high-potential employees can provide crucible experiences without necessitating relocation

- *Reverse transfers* – Where top performers from emerging markets are moved into developed markets, usually on a short-term assignment, to gain experience and skills (PwC, 2012).

3.11 CONCLUSION

In a world where globalisation is fast becoming the norm, a new breed of leaders is required. To become a global leader one needs to have a personal and significant understanding not only of the different countries in which the organisation operates; but also of the people and cultures within these countries. To lead effectively, leaders need to understand the differences fuelled by cultural diversity and by the characteristics of the different nation-states (Caligiuri, 2009).

There is a paradigm shift occurring within the field of global mobility which is affecting both talent management and leadership development. The use of international assignments to provide crucible experiences, with the aim of enabling learning and development competencies, has changed the rules of the game. The ICA constitutes a critical tool in the endeavour to produce truly global leaders to meet the demands of globalisation. The next challenge is to how to identify talent most likely to experience the developmental gain (Caligiuri, 2009).

3.12 REFERENCES

Caligiuri, P. 2009. The necessary collaboration between global mobility and talent management for developing global leaders. *Mobility Magazine*. [Online]. Available: http://www.worldwideerc.org/Resources/MOBILITYarticles/Pages/1109-caligiuri.aspx. [Accessed 24 August 2014].

Caligiuri, P, Tarique, I & Jacobs, R. 2009. Selection for international assignments. *Human Resource Management Review*, 19:251–262.

CLC. 2012a. *International crucible assignments: Research brief*. Corporate Leadership Council Human Resources. The Corporate Executive Board Company, Washington, DC.

CLC. 2012b. *The global leader*. Corporate Leadership Council Human Resources. The Corporate Executive Board Company, Washington, DC.

Deloitte. 2008. *Smart moves: A new approach to international assignments and global mobility*. [Online]. Available: http://www.deloitte.com/assets/Dcom-UnitedStates/Local%20Assets/Documents/IMOs/Talent/us_talent_smartmoves_062410.pdf. [Accessed 12 August 2014].

Ernst & Young. 2013. *Your talent in motion. Global mobility effectiveness survey 2013*. [Online]. Available: ey.com/GlobalMobilitySurvey2013. [Accessed 16 August 2014].

Gundling, E, Hogan, T & Cvitkovich, K. 2011. *What is global leadership?: 10 key behaviors that define great global leaders*. Boston, MA: Nicholas Brealey Publishing.

Ng, K-Y, Van Dyne, L & Ang, S. 2009. From experience to experiential learning: Cultural intelligence as a learning capability for global leader development. *Academy of Management Learning & Education*, 8(4):511–526.

Oddou, G, Mendenhall, M & Ritchie, JB. 2000. Leveraging travel as a tool for global leadership development. *Human Resource Management*, 2–3:159–172.

PwC. 2012. *Talent mobility 2020 and beyond*. PricewaterhouseCoopers. [Online]. Available: http://www.pwc.com/en_GX/gx/managing-tomorrows-people/future-of-work/pdf/pwc-talent-mobility-2020.pdf. [Accessed 24 August 2014].

Rathbone, CLH. 2014. *The symbiotic nature of leadership development and mobility*. Mercer. [Online]. Available: http://www.mercer.com/content/dam/mercer/attachments/global/Talent/Develop-SymbioNatureLdrshpDevMobility.pdf. [Accessed 24 August 2014].

Stahl, GK, Chua, CH, Caligiuri, P, Cerdin, JL & Taniguchi, M. 2007. *International assignments as a career development tool: Factors affecting turnover intentions among executive talent*. Faculty and Research Working Paper. Insead: France. INSEAD 2007/24/OB.

CHAPTER 4
BENEFITS
Nazlie Samodien

4.1 INTRODUCTION

4.1.1 Look, See, Decide (LSD) Trip

The LSD trip is a critical part of the employee's decision in accepting an assignment. The family should accompany the employee as part of the decision to accept the assignment abroad. The employee needs to also decide if the working environment challenging and acceptable.

The trip is usually a few days and the family is shown housing, shopping, schooling, recreation and religious worship facilities, as well as the working environment.

4.2 ALLOWANCES IN LIEU OF BENEFITS

Some companies provide allowances instead of benefits. This is to ease the management and administration in the company. These allowances in lieu of benefits typically include:

- Housing allowance

- Education allowance for children and the spouse

- Home trip allowances

- Car allowances – if they do not provide a fully-paid-for vehicle in the host country. In first world countries, where the public transport system is reliable, they may provide a travelling allowance, to cover trains, underground tubes or buses.

These allowances are part of the total package paid to the assignee, and need to be included in the total cost to company for each assignment. Benchmarked data should be used when paying these allowances, to ensure that the assignee is being equitably remunerated for all of these benefits.

4.3 ACCOMMODATION

Most companies provide accommodation for assignees, especially in countries in Africa, as factors such as road infrastructure, security, utilities and the like need to be taken into account. In first world countries, a house may not be an option based on costs, whereas apartments could be an affordable option. Companies often rent these premises for assignees, or simply provide a housing allowance for each assignee to source his/her own apartment. It is necessary to ensure that the quality of the housing is of a good standard and that the maintenance is kept up if the company has signed the rental agreement. Most companies also pay for utilities but not for fixed line and ADSL line costs.

4.4 SCHOOLING

Schooling is always a concern for parents as children will certainly need to be reintegrated in the home country schooling system at the end of an assignment. Most companies pay for American or British international school fees and these institutions are available in many countries in Africa. Some schools require entrance exams to be written – which is best done during an LSD trip, so that the parents know before accepting the assignment whether their children will be able to attend school in the host country.

4.5 ARRIVAL IN HOST COUNTRY

On arrival, many companies make sure that there is someone to see the family through the process of getting through customs, getting their luggage and transfers to their accommodation. It is also preferable to have someone meet the family the next morning to take them wherever they need to go, to get to work, school, to shop or to arrange work permits etc. It is also a good practice to arrange for the family to meet other expatriate families so that they can start to set up a social circle as soon as possible. Activities such as these enable the family to settle down in the host country.

4.6 TRANSPORT IN THE HOST COUNTRY

The type of transport provided will be according to company policy. Most companies provide company vehicles in Africa because of poor public transport systems, security and road infrastructure. The vehicle should be available on arrival, so that the family can assume independence as soon as possible. School children should have some form of company transport to get them to and from school. A spouse is usually not provided with company transport.

4.7   HOME FLIGHTS

Many companies provide at least one flight home every year. Depending on the host country's living conditions, these may be as many as four a year. Some companies insist that the home trip be to the home country. Others permit any destination, provided that the cost is no more than that of the cost of a home trip – or the assignee pays in any additional costs.

4.8   STORAGE OF PERSONAL EFFECTS IN THE HOME COUNTRY

Most companies permit storage of household goods in the home country. Some pay for the storage and insurance, while others work on an average per household, and pay an allowance so that the assignees can arrange their own storage.

4.9   SCHOOLING IN THE HOME COUNTRY

For various reasons assignees may elect to leave their children in school/boarding school in the home country. Some companies do not pay at all for home country schooling, whilst others will pay only for boarding fees, and others will pay for schooling, but no more than the costs would have been in the host country. Another decision for policy is whether or not the company will pay for trips to the host country for the children in the home country to visit the family in the host location. It is important to place some limitation on the age of these students.

4.10 MEDICAL TESTING

Companies need to ensure that the whole family is considered when sending assignees to a foreign country.

It is vital that all medical affairs and concerns of an assignee are taken into account. The assignee and the family must feel that their wellbeing is considered by the employer. Depending on the host location, companies are advised to have a medical specialist go to the host country and establish what facilities exist in that country, and to draw up a medical management and evacuation plan for the company if required. Companies should also ensure that all assignees are insured by the company for medical evacuation in the event of an emergency.

4.11 LANGUAGE AND CULTURE TRAINING

With expatriates, technical skills are not the major consideration. A global skills set, resilience and adaptability are all key. Of major importance is the ability of an assignee to deal with foreign cultures, as well as to operate effectively in an environment where there may be turmoil and ambiguity. The emotional wellbeing of the employee and the accompanying family is essential to the success of an assignment. As such, many companies offer language and culture training to ease the settling in of the assignee and family and thereby a more successful assignment.

4.12 OTHER FAMILY CONSIDERATIONS

Family considerations need to be part of the selection process as they may result in a failed assignment if they are not part of the screening process. The dual income of a family and a spouse's career needs to be considered when sending an assignee abroad. One of these may have to be put on hold for the duration of the assignment, as it is not always feasible for the spouse to work in the foreign country. Most companies do not compensate for the loss of a spouse income but do assist with integrating the spouse with other trailing spouses and volunteer work in the home country.

Ageing parents or in laws may influence productivity as the assignee may be required to travel home frequently to see ailing parents. These costs not only inflate the cost of the assignment, but result in loss of productivity.

4.13 HOME COUNTRY ACCOMMODATION

Many companies do not get involved in the selling or renting of property in the expatriate's home country. If a company does assist, it would be necessary to define clear lines of responsibility to limit any losses that may be experienced.

Home country accommodation becomes a concern for the employer on repatriation, as the assignee may not have a place to stay on return from an assignment. Some companies do provide interim housing in the form of Bed and Breakfast (B&B) or furnished apartments for a limited period.

4.14 IMMIGRATION FORMALITIES

Companies need to understand the immigration obligations and ensure that the correct permits are applied for. Any other requirements, such as quotas, need to be factored in to ensure compliance.

On a practical level, it is important that the move to the host country be smooth. All visa's and work permits need to be finalised before the family leaves for the host country. All inoculations need to be administered and all the legal paperwork is in the possession of the family before they leave.

4.15 COST CONSIDERATIONS

4.15.1 Legal considerations

Contracts of employment may be with the host country company or a company in a third country may be established. This will depend on the company structure and policy. In these instances, the jurisdiction must be clearly stated in each contract.

If the employment is with the host country, then it is important that the secondment contracts be drafted in accordance with host country labour laws. A typical secondment arrangement indicates the host country employer will remain the legal employer for the duration of the assignment.

4.15.2 Security

Security is an important factor to consider and in some countries in Africa, Middle East and South America – the company pays for security at the home and whilst the employee is driving.

4.15.3 Payroll considerations

The company structure will dictate how the income tax will be treated. Some companies suspend the assignee from the home country payroll for the duration of the assignment while others keep the assignee on the home country payroll, and pay the assignment allowances only in the host country. There is no right or wrong way – this structure must be discussed with the Finance and Tax departments to ensure that the income taxes are aligned to the corporate tax structures.

Employers should seek professional advice on these issues, as they are a critical area of assignment management, and if not addressed from legal and tax perspectives, can be minefields for the company and the individuals to manage.

The most common area of concern is the operation and administration of the expatriate payroll. In the case of inbound expatriate employees, certain and specific variables are included in the pay elements. In certain instances, the expatriate may continue to be remunerated via the home country payroll, albeit with recharge of costs to host country.

This creates significant challenges for the payroll administrator to customise the local payroll to accommodate for the specific pay elements linked to expatriate assignments.

However, if certain salary costs are being recharged to the host country and certain benefits are provided locally, operating a shadow payroll may be necessary in the host country to allow for deduction of PAYE. In this instance, Double Taxation Treaties need to be analysed and considered.

Expatriate payroll management contains specific input data parameters aligned with distinct taxation methodologies. Assessment of the respective expatriate pay elements is essential to ensure correct payroll output.

4.15.4 Assignment termination

When an assignment comes to an end, this usually occurs in one of two ways, either localisation or repatriation.

4.15.5 Repatriation and post-adjustment

No assignment is successful until the assignee is successfully repatriated and integrated into the company, and the family has successfully reintegrated into their social and school environment. Around 40 percent of repatriates leave the company within the first year of returning home. This is usually due to poor repatriation processes and policy.

Repatriation is very often ignored, as the company deems that the individuals are returning home. But over the years, many things may have changed in home country, and reverse culture shock can take place. This makes moving back to the home country after an assignment disruptive and unsettling for the employee and the family.

The company needs to address this from a physical work perspective, as well as the emotional and mental perspective, ensuring that a holistic approach is taken to repatriation. There are specialists that focus on this service, assisting companies and their staff to adjust to the return of employees.

It is therefore advisable for companies to have a repatriation processes to enable retention. Personal development plans, coaching and counselling are interventions that can ensure integration back home. Most companies pay for airfares and for the relocation of household effects and pets when repatriating the assignee and the family.

If the employee is made redundant during or upon conclusion of the assignment, the employee will qualify for the retrenchment benefits of the home location company, unless the employment or assignment agreement states differently.

A repatriation allowance enables the employee to find interim accommodation for the family whilst their household goods are being transported from the host country.

Before repatriating an assignee, knowledge transfer to local employees in critical. It is also advisable for the employee to have a performance review is completed prior to departure.

4.15.6 Repatriation salary

Many companies do not guarantee employment in the home country on the termination of the assignment.

Some companies record the pre-assignment salary which is adjusted annually by the average increase in the home country, so that it does not stagnate while away.

However, often the assignee is promoted while on assignment, or the job that he or she takes up on assignment is a higher grade than he or she filled prior to assignment. The repatriation salary should therefore be aligned to the market at the point at which the assignee fills the position.

4.15.7 Localisation

Localisation will occur when the company and the employee agree that the assignment has come to an end and that the employee will remain in the host location.

Where localisation occurs, the following usually applies:

- The host country salary and benefits will be applied.

- A once-off gross lump sum is paid (the employee must bear the tax).

- A return home trip is provided for the employee and accompanying family members to finalise personal affairs.

- House sale and house purchase assistance is provided if costs of sale or purchase are incurred within 24 months of the employee's localisation. This assistance consists of reimbursement of transaction costs on the sale of the employee's house in the home location and purchase of a house in the host location. The reimbursement is usually capped and includes expenses incurred for stamp duty, legal/conveyance fees, and agent/marketing fees.

- Tax briefings are provided in the home and host locations.

- The employee should transition to the host location retirement scheme.

- Necessary visas/work permits in the host location for the employee and accompanying family members will be arranged. Work permits for spouses will be arranged where possible (depending on host location immigration rules).

- Post-assignment medical examinations may be provided.

4.16 INTEGRATION WITH TALENT MANAGEMENT

The integration of a global mobility programme with the company's talent management programme represents the highest level in a global mobility maturity model. Aspects include:

- Policies are aligned on a global level.

- A global talent pool is identified and tracked.

- Remuneration and reward are managed on a global level.

- Post-assignment retention strategies are developed and applied.

In summary, the treatment of benefits is company- and country-specific. One universal truism is the notoriously poor track record of repatriation across all continents.

CHAPTER 5
GROWTH STATISTICS FOR AFRICA
Ian McGorian

5.1 INTRODUCTION

This chapter seeks to summarise various factors that are both historical and predictive in the economies of sub-Saharan Africa (SSA). It is included because of the high GDP growth rate of the continent, a growing young workforce, the fact that it contains high amount of arable land and a lot of the world's minerals – making it a highly sought-after economic destination. Remuneration considerations take place in the context of the company, but also in the context of the company in the wider economy.

5.2 ECONOMY

The African economy undoubtedly lagged significantly in the 1980s and early 1990s, with some commentators calling these "the lost decades". However, since the middle of the 1990s, there has been a sharp turn-around in the fortunes of African economies. Adding to the optimism is that the global financial crisis of 2008–2009 had little effect on sub-Saharan African countries. A number of recent studies suggest that the most significant factors contributing to growth in Africa have been increases in the share of the working age population, capital appreciation, and total factor productivity (Cho & Bienvenue, 2014).

Resource-rich countries have benefited from an increase in Foreign Direct Investment (FDI) (EY, 2014). There is a noticeable divide between FDI trends in North Africa versus sub-Saharan Africa (SSA). While FDI projects in North Africa declined by nearly 30 percent, projects in SSA increased by 4.7 percent, reversing the decline of 2012. This further widened the gap between the two sub-regions, with SSA's share of FDI projects exceeding 80 percent for the first time. Foreign Direct Investment grew 16 percent to $43b in 2013 in SSA. FDI was boosted by new hydrocarbon findings in countries including Angola, Mozambique and Tanzania.

Foreign Direct Investment in SSA has increased over thirty-fold in the last twenty years. This is 7.5 times faster than high-income countries and 10 times faster than global GDP.

While the UK remains the lead investor into the continent, intra-African investment continues to rise steadily. Investors are also looking beyond the more established markets of South Africa, Nigeria and Kenya to expand their operations, as well as moving into more consumer-related sectors as Africa's middle class expands.

According to the *Business Monitor International* (BMI) and The Economist Intelligence Unit (EIU), Africa as a continent is expected to experience a continued growth in FDI given the positive economic outlook in major countries, some of which are highlighted below:

- Investment in Ghana is expected to continue to increase over the medium term driven by the country's stable political environment and investment opportunities in the oil and gas industry. Real GDP is expected to average of 10.7 percent over 2013 to 2016. This growth is predicated on the expectation that the oil and gas boom will continue and will attract foreign participation.

- Investment has continued to pour into Nigeria, as investors recognise the immense growth potential of Africa's largest consumer market. The EIU has estimated an annual net direct investment of Nigeria at US$ 11 billion by 2016.

- In Côte d'Ivoire, the improvement in the security, strong leadership from an investment-friendly government and the expectation of a US$20 billion investment in infrastructure is expected to support rapid economic growth. Also, the discovery of light crude oil offshore of the country in June 2012 by Tullow Oil PLC is expected to trigger foreign investments in the near to mid-term.

- Angola's growth is predicated on the rebound in the oil export industry in the foreseeable future. The growing opportunity in the oil and gas industry is expected to increase FDI flow into the country. The EIU has estimated an annual net direct investment of US$ 14 billion in the country by 2016.

- Ethiopia's forecast real GDP growth is expected to be at least 7 percent annually up to 2016 as the dominant agriculture sector continues to perform well, electricity supply improves and export demand picks up.

- After reaching 7.4 percent in 2012, Mozambique's economic growth is forecast to average 8 percent a year between 2013 and 2017, owing to the minerals boom and investment in the gas sector.

- FDI inflows into Zambia have increased steadily since 2009 increasing at a CAGR of 18 percent, driven by recent foreign participation in major sectors of the economy. This improvement is strongly linked to the performance of the mining industry, which has been a major recipient of capital, technical input and managerial know-how in the past few years.

The SSA economy is expected to grow by 7 percent on average between 2012 and 2016, based on the following:

- Sustained macroeconomic stability.

- Increase in foreign investment and expansionary fiscal policies, driven by the government's plan to increase infrastructure expenditure.

- Planned diversification of the economy, which is expected to reduce the dependence of the Zambian population on copper.

- Tanzania has emerged as one of Sub-Saharan Africa's top foreign investment destinations, attracting over US$700 million in 2011. The outlook for the Tanzanian economy is positive, with sustained strong economic growth. The EIU estimates that average real GDP will be greater than 7 percent between 2012 and 2016. This favourable outlook is based on the following:

  - High gold prices and increase in exports which will boost foreign exchange earnings

  - Increased investment in infrastructure which is expected to support growth and boost productivity

  - Continued implementation of key economic reform

  - Tighter monetary and fiscal policy aimed at stabilising inflation and exchange rates.

- Congo's mining sector continues to attract strong international interest, particularly for iron ore.

- Data from the United Nations World Tourism Organisation shows that tourist arrivals in SSA grew by 5.2 percent in 2013 (36 million tourists).

- South Africa should not be discounted, though. Where FDI can be quite volatile from one year to the next, the decline experienced in FDI to South Africa in 2012 does not necessarily represent a permanent trend.

For instance, in the past, much of South Africa's export trade has been within the Eurozone, which was hard hit by the 2008/9 recession and in many respects is still recovering. The reduced trade within the Eurozone over this period enabled inter-BRICS export trade between South Africa and the rest of BRIC (Brazil, Russia, India and China) to increase from 6 percent of total exports in 2005, to close to 20 percent in 2012. These new trade partnerships helped shield both South Africa and many other African countries from the downturn in the global economy (KPMG, 2013).

Of course, SSA does not operate in a vacuum and obvious analogies could be made, the two that resonate most significantly are the Asian Tigers in the 1960s and the BRIC 1990s success stories. Although there are indicators that Africa could be on a growth trajectory this will dependant on any number of variables including political stability, policies to attract capital, amenability to foreign trade and a progressive human capital framework.

While economic activity remained strong in 2013 supported by strong domestic demand and in particular investment growth (as an example, the JSE All Share Index grew 26.7 percent in the last year), downside risks remain from low commodity prices and capital inflows. The World Bank predicts global output growth at 3 percent in

2014, while the projection for SSA is 5.2 percent in 2014 and 5.4 percent in 2015. This is positive sentiment coming off actuals of 3.5 percent in 2012 and 4.7 percent in 2013.

Juxtaposed to this is the theory of the "Fragile Five", as witnessed in the summer of 2013. Brazil, Indonesia, Turkey, India and South Africa were most affected by the sharp sell-off in the equity and bond markets in this period. The exchange rates of these countries declined by 12.2 percent. Reserves declined by 6.4 percent and stock prices by 5.9 percent.

5.3   SOUTH AFRICA AND NIGERIA

Possibly the biggest change in the recent past has been Nigeria overtaking South Africa in GDP terms. The first point to take into consideration is that these calculations are computed from a base year. In the case of South Africa this base is reset every five years as the calculation becomes less accurate with the passage of time. In the Nigerian instance the base year is 1990, so the economy has not grown by 80 percent overnight. Rather, the figures we are seeing are an adjustment to reality.

It is as important to recognise that the South African economy is at a very different place in the development curve. The infrastructure, financial systems, manufacturing capabilities, quality of services, retail markets, income levels, sophistication of the work force, to name but a few, are simply incomparable to Nigeria.

Having introduced this perspective, Nigeria has outperformed South Africa consistently in GDP growth (Open Data for Africa, 2014):

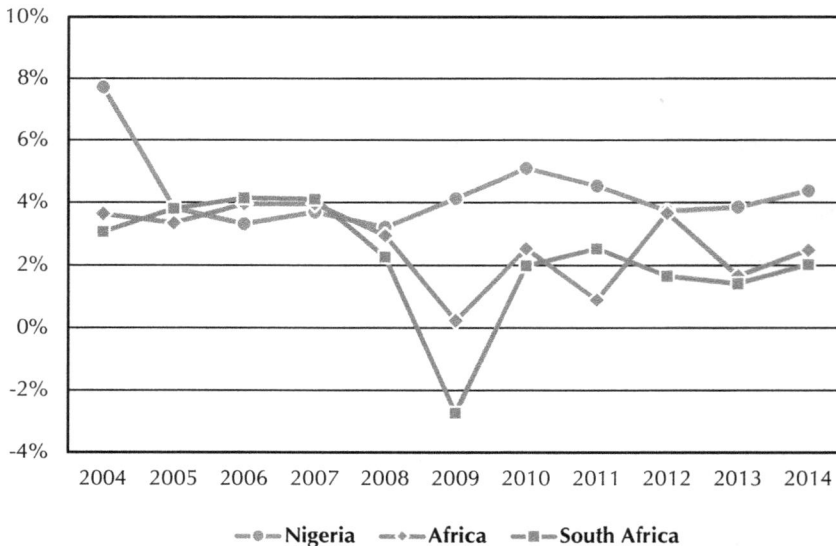

Figure 5.1: GDP growth 2004 – 2014

However, the relative size of the economies cannot be overemphasised (GDP at constant market price), as shown in Table 5.2:

(Adjusted to constant market price, 2005)

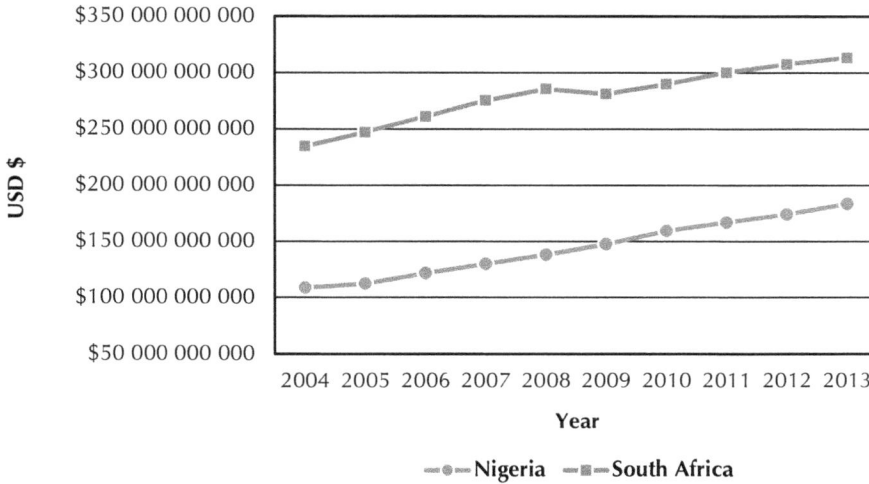

Figure 5.2: Gross Domestic Product (GDP) (Kim, 2014)

A sense of perspective is required when viewing these data. The differences between Nigeria and South Africa are so vast that one metric unit (GDP) supplies a small piece of the puzzle.

5.4 THE GLOBAL FINANCIAL CRISIS

Much research into the crisis has focused on the macro cause and results of the crisis. What remains interesting is the speed with which SSA recovered. There are several reasons for this.

SSA had a very different behaviour pattern in the decade leading up to the crisis. As an example, the government debt-to-GDP ratio improved dramatically, while that of the advanced countries deteriorated (see Table 5.1, below).

Table 5.1: General government gross debt, advanced economies, and sub-Saharan countries, 2000–2010 (IMF, 2012)

	Advanced economies	SSA
2000	72.47	70.01
2001	72.39	73.07
2002	73.47	66.60
2003	75.55	60.42
2004	79.67	53.91
2005	79.32	45.08
2006	76.66	34.24
2007	74.04	29.73
2008	81.02	28.69
2009	94.66	31.96
2010	100.71	32.09

This behaviour enabled expansionist government spending and tax alleviation after the crisis.

In addition to this, oil prices fluctuated significantly, benefiting Angola, Nigeria, Equatorial Guinea, Gabon and Congo (Campos & Dulci, 2014). In addition, the establishment of the East African Community in 2000 led to rapid growth for its member countries.

Finally, external debt had been massively downscaled in the decade leading up to the crisis (see Table 5.2, below).

Table 5.2: External debt (IMF, 2012)

SSA (Year)	Total external debt as a percentage of GDP
2000	63.22
2001	63.92
2002	60.63
2003	51.52
2004	43.46
2005	34.24
2006	25.58
2007	24.58
2008	22.48
2009	24.82
2010	23.61

These factors, combined with other factors, meant that SSA was able to recover significantly faster than the developed countries in the period after the third quarter in 2009.

5.5   THE IMPACT OF ECONOMIC GROWTH

Economic growth is not necessarily a cure-all. In fact, rapid economic growth has implicit problems in that inflation risks, regional inequalities and income inequalities could worsen in the short term. The instability in a growth curve can be compounded by fluctuating trade agreements and low investment appetite. Political instability in SSA has declined considerably in the last decade, a factor which has no doubt contributed to the economic turn-around. The events in North Africa over the past several years cannot be ignored as SSA countries that could devolve into civil war within very short timeframes still remain.

There is little doubt that corporate governance has improved in general, but pockets of stubborn resistance remain where corruption is the order of the day. The rule of law as applied to property rights, civil rights, political stability and social harmony needs to backed by an infrastructure that addresses the needs of the population. There can be little doubt that a number of SSA countries fall short in this regard.

Furthermore, a failure to move away from primary product exports does not help the cause. And even this intransigence has not reaped any benefit. In 1950 SSA accounted for 3 percent of world exports; by 2000 this percentage had halved (Mills, 2010). As another example, oil exports from Nigeria increased by 885 percent over 35 years, but over the same period, the number of people living on less than $1 a day increased by 535 percent.

For SSA to prosper in these changing times macro-economic and social policy needs to reflect the global perspective. This will require sophisticated and long-term strategies that reflect local dynamics but take cognisance of the broader environment. Short-term interventions like those imposed by the IMF did not take into consideration the operability and impact of the measures and were therefore to a large extent failures.

5.6   GENDER DISCRIMINATION IN AFRICA

Gender discrimination remains a global problem. The International Labour Organisation (ILO) estimates the gender pay gap to be 22.9 percent. Put another way, females earn 77.1 percent of what men earn. Of course, this statistic would vary by region, skill level, and group of workers, and also over time. For example, the World Economic Forum's 2013 paper reports a staggering 33 percent differential between male and female pay in South Africa. The recognition of gender discrimination is by no means new, the ILO having recognised equal pay for work of equal value as early as 1919. African approaches to the gender gap are varied.

In South Africa, the Employment Equity Act 55 of 1998 requires income-differential statements as part of the annual employment equity reports submitted to the Department of Labour. The remuneration data supplied is broken down into occupational category level, disaggregated by race and gender. If "disproportionate differentials" are reported, employers are expected to take appropriate measures in their employment equity plans to reduce or eliminate these differentials.

The General Labour Act in Angola specifically defines equal pay for work of equal value. Chad takes it a step further in that the Labour Code states that the different elements of remuneration should be determined according to identical standards for men and women. The criteria for promotion, job categorisation and classifications should be the same for both genders.

The Kenyan Employment Act provides that for any allegation of remuneration discrimination, "the employer shall bear the burden of proving that the discrimination did not take place as alleged". Labour inspectors are tasked with establishing equal pay for work of equal value using standard statistical methodologies.

Uganda is a little more vague on the subject, with a statement in the Employment Act that:

"the Minister [of Labour] and the Labour Advisory Board shall, in performing their duties, seek to give effect to the principle of equal remuneration for male and female employees for work of equal value".

The Guide for Inspections in Morocco prepared by the Ministry of Employment and Vocational Training (in collaboration with the ILO) specifically refers to Gender discrimination when inspecting conditions of work and remuneration.

Gender discrimination is not restricted to remuneration, it manifests in various guises. A 2013 World Bank and IFC report (Kim, 2014) finds legal and regulatory barriers to women's economic inclusion have decreased over the past 50 years globally, but many laws still hinder women's participation in the economy. Laws restricting women's economic activity are currently most prevalent in the Middle East and North Africa, Sub-Saharan Africa and South Asia. During the 50-year period following 1960 more than half the restrictions on women's property rights and ability to conduct legal transactions were removed in the 100 economies studied. The Middle East and North Africa remain the least reformed regions in the world. The same can be said for legislation covering domestic violence and sexual harassment. These two regions have the thinnest legislation pertaining to these issues.

The Social Institutions and Gender Index (SIGI) compiled by the OECD (OECD, 2014) indicates that 9 of the bottom 10 countries in the world are from sub-Saharan Africa.

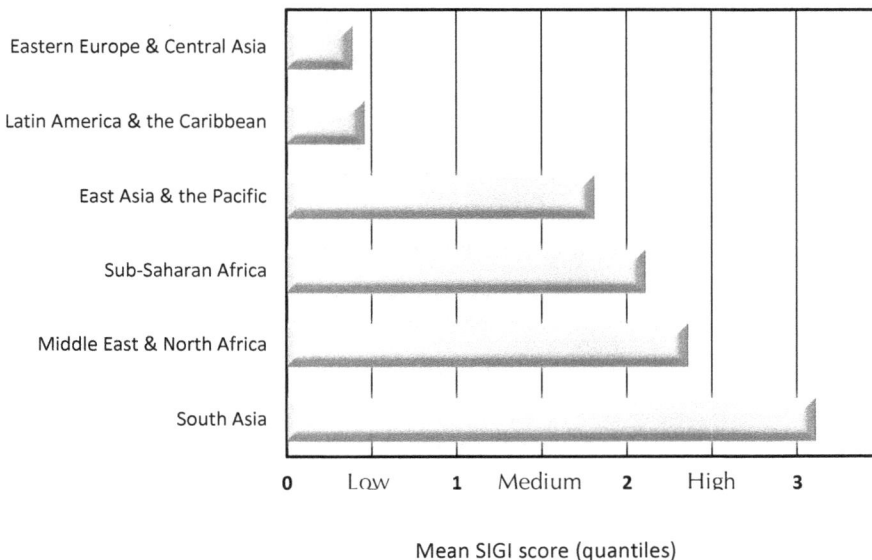

Figure 5.1: SIGI by region (OECD, 2014)

Remarkably, South Africa is ranked at number 4 in the top 10. All is not doom and gloom, however. In 2010 Kenyans voted for changes to the Constitution that would grant women equal rights in the family, marriage and property rights. The age of consent for marriage has been increased to 18 in Botswana, Madagascar and Mozambique. Land Administration Committees in Ethiopia are required to have at least one female member. Finally, Rwanda passed the Law on the Prevention, Protection and Punishment of any Gender-based Violence in 2009.

Clearly, however, there is still much work to be done to reduce and eradicate gender discrimination in Africa.

5.7 CONCLUSION

Sub-Sahara Africa stands poised to experience economic growth at rates unprecedented for the region. Realisation of this goal will depend on multiple factors. As an allegory of sorts Abraham Wald (an Austrian Mathematician) joined the Statistical Research Group in America during the Second World War. One of the problems he tackled was the optimum balance in armouring fighter planes. Obviously armour is required but it has a significant weight and therefore performance cost. Developing an optimum armour ratio as well as determining which parts of a plane to armour was therefore critical.

The Americans had tracked their planes that returned from Europe and produced data sets for Wald detailing the number of bullet holes and where they were placed, the concept being that they would increase armour ratios in the areas of the plane that displayed the greatest need. The data would surely indicate where the greatest concentration of bullet holes was located and therefore provide direction to plane designers.

Wald confounded Military Intelligence by stating that the armour should not go where the bullet holes were; it should go where they were not, his groundbreaking theory being that although the engine area suffered the least number of bullet holes per square foot, the missing bullet holes were on the missing planes! In other words, the missing bullets per square foot were in the planes that had been shot down. Aeroplanes ripped to shreds in the fuselage still made it back to base, whereas a single strike to the engine or cockpit could be catastrophic.

I present this allegory simply to suggest a new way of thinking for the SSA economy. We can certainly learn from the past, but should we be ever vigilant for the missing bullet holes?

5.8 REFERENCES

Campos, TLC & Dulci, OS. 2014. *Trajectories of development and responses to crises: South America and sub-Saharan Africa in comparative perspective*. [Online]. Available: web.isanet.org/...ISA%20BuenosAires%202014/.../55baa8c1-c886-4fdd. [Accessed 11 October 2014].

Cho, Y & Bievenue, T. 2014. *Sub-Saharan Africa's recent growth spurt: An analysis of the sources of growth*. [Online]. Available: http://go.worldbank.org/2PAA968JG0. [Accessed 5 September 2014].

EY. 2014. Africa attractiveness survey: Executive growth. [Online]. Available: http://www.ey.com. [Accessed 19 November 2014].

IMF. 2012. *World economic outlook database*.

Kim. Y. 2014. Societies dismantle gender discrimination. *Worldbank News*, September. [Online]. Available: http://www.worldbank.org/en/news/press-release/2013/09/24/societies-dismantle-gender-discrimination-world-bank-group-president-jim-yong-kim. [Accessed 8 September 2014].

KPMG. 2013. Overview of foreign direct investment in Africa. *KPMG Africa Blog*. [Online]. Available: http://www.blog.kpmgafrica.com/overview-of-foreign-direct-investment-in-africa/. [Accessed 22 August 2014].

Mills G. 2010. *Why Africa is poor and what Africans can do about it*. Johannesburg: Penguin.

OECD. 2014. *Poverty reduction and social development. The OECD social institutions and gender index*. [Online]. Available: http://www.oecd.org/social/poverty/theoecdsocialinstitutionsandgenderindex.htm. [Accessed 29 July 2014].

Open Data for Africa. 2014. *AFDB socio-economic database*. [Online]. Available: http://opendataforafrica.org/dqcelid/afdb-socio-economic-database-jan-2014. [Accessed 16 September 2014].

CHAPTER 6
CONDUCTING BUSINESS IN AFRICA – UNVEILED
Vishal Nundlall

6.1 INTRODUCTION

Interest in expanding into Africa has rapidly increased over the years, and Africa is capturing the attention of organisations all over the world. Although not necessarily true for Asian investors, many organisations are interested in expanding into Africa to embed their organisations in future growth markets since home markets are stagnating, or shrinking, in many instances.

The fundamental question is how to conduct business in Africa successfully and what factors must remain top of mind for potential investors. It is important to provide guidelines and a considered solution to this question.

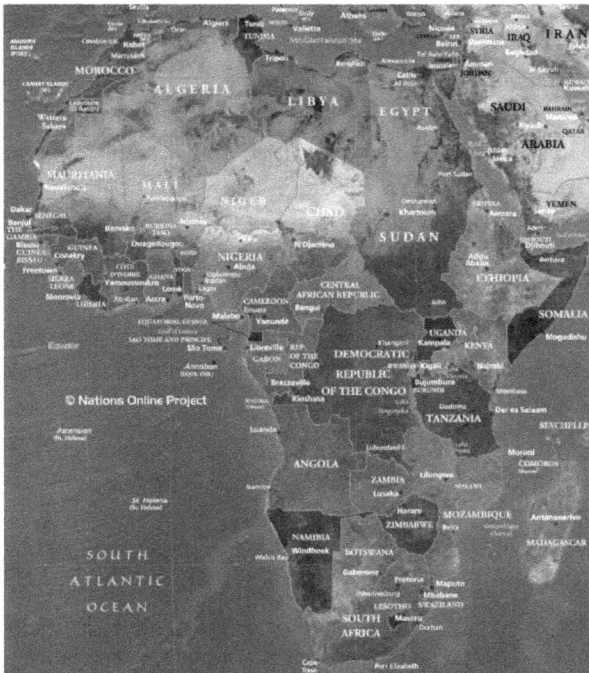

Figure 6.1: African landscape map (Google images)

6.2 KEY FACTORS TO CONSIDER WHEN CONDUCTING BUSINESS IN AFRICA

Key factors to consider include work and traditional cultures, languages, laws and regulations and understanding the market. This article explores the more prominent factors in brief but their importance in the success or failure of the business cannot be underestimated.

6.2.1 Work and traditional cultures

A common error when considering business investment in Africa is that comparisons are made with countries like Brazil, China or India that may have a shared ancestry and culture. Africa, on the other hand, is not homogeneous and is made up of a diverse mixture of traditions and cultures. Often organisations do not understand the work and traditional cultures of the people in the country in which they wish to operate.

In order for organisations to succeed in Africa, it is important for organisations to embrace cross-cultural traditions, management and communication styles. This involves understanding the role African culture plays in social interactions, management styles, organisational behaviour and business practices, and applying this to each specific country.

6.2.2 Language

There are over a thousand indigenous languages spoken in Africa. Many executives assume that since an African country was a Portuguese or English colony, the population in that country speak the relevant European language as a first language. This misconception makes conducting business in Africa extremely difficult. As it is impossible to be able to speak and understand all the different languages and dialects across Africa, it is crucial to have a person or people on your team who speak and understand the language(s) in the country. Many countries have ten or more local African languages that are spoken. Business and communication can falter if the question of language is not factored into one's business strategy.

6.2.3 Laws and regulations

Africa, like every other continent, has laws and regulations that vary from country to country, and therefore special consideration should be given into understanding these parameters before considering expanding into the country. This involves in-depth research and consultation with local experts on the different laws and regulations that govern conducting business in the specific country.

Considerations include the type of legal entity that is required to conduct business, as well as any regulatory approvals that are required. In some countries there may be industry-specific business licences that organisations need to apply for prior to being able to operate in the country.

The corporate establishment of an entity, and any relevant legal registrations and business licences, can take anything from one to six months to be completed. This is an important factor as it impacts directly on when an organisation can start operating in the country and may restrict the type of business that the investor is legally allowed to conduct.

Terminology may also have a different meaning and functionality in different countries across Africa. This makes consultation with local experts crucial.

6.2.4   Understanding the market

Understanding the market is vital to success. Organisations should research and have an in-depth knowledge of the market. Sourcing the right customers in the African market, and marketing one's products and services, can take a long time and is a challenging task. In this respect, organisations can consult with the Chambers of Commerce, the respective embassy, or traders in the country of interest.

Organisations should also visit the location in question if they intend establishing a company or representative office – desktop research simply does not work on its own.

6.3 GUIDELINES FOR CONDUCTING BUSINESS IN AFRICA

- **Research** the relevant country prior to conducting business in Africa and always take the time to understand the culture, language, laws and regulations and market of the country. Before starting up a business, send a staff member in the country to build a network of advisors and **learn from the operational difficulties** of others.

- **Planning** is important to the success of conducting business in Africa and an organisation can never plan enough. Planning involves **understanding the requirements, costs and timelines** required to implement and sustain the business.

- Organisations should **partner with seasoned experienced advisors**, such as Deloitte, to help them with   planning and the development and implementation of a **sound business strategy**. It is important to partner with an advisor who has experience and an established footprint in Africa.

- A good approach is to **apply local knowledge with a tested global methodology**. In this way, you leverage local experience while using innovative global methodologies to enhance your business dealings.

- **Build a network of resources** in the country and maintain a relationship with them. Building relationships is important to the success of conducting business in Africa.

- **Ongoing evaluation** is important, and organisations must equip themselves to be flexible and respond swiftly to change.

6.4   CONCLUSION

Deloitte takes a strategic approach to conducting business in Africa, using a combination of consultation with seasoned local and global expertise, a sound strategy, and applying project management methodologies in planning and implementation. Our approach involves partnering with our clients to provide them with an innovative, customised solution designed to enable them to penetrate the African market successfully.

CHAPTER 7
EXPATRIATE ASSIGNMENTS
Dr R Nienaber, D Trompetter and Dr M Bussin

7.1 INTRODUCTION

Many researchers agree that the ultimate success of a global assignment mostly depends on the expatriate's ability to adjust to the host country. This adjustment relates to not only the expatriate, but also the accompanying family. The expatriate to an extent still has some stability – they go to work, socialise with their colleagues, and continue to build their careers. For the spouse, this is very different: they probably do not (and mostly no longer) have a job, have no friends, can't speak the language, and cannot find a suitable church where they are welcomed. Ultimately: their favourite brand of dishwashing liquid is not available in the grocery store of their new town.

According to Black, Mendenhall & Oddou (1991), between 16 percent and 40 percent of all expatriates return prematurely from international assignments, costing their organisations at least one and often up to ten times the annual remuneration. In addition to these costs, approximately 30 percent to 50 percent of expatriates stay in their host locations but are considered ineffective or only marginally effective by their employers – a good enough reason for employers to gain better insight into what the factors are that contribute towards successful assignments.

The three common criteria for determining expatriate success have been identified as:

- Completion of the foreign assignment
- Cross-cultural adjustment
- Performance while on the foreign assignment.

In an EY (2013) mobility survey, it was cited that 65 percent of respondents indicated personal and family-related issues as the primary reason for their failed assignment or early repatriation. Personal and family-related issues included lack of adequate schools, insufficient housing, or inadequate work opportunities for the spouse. Assignments need to work for the company and the employee, and employers need to remind themselves continually not to forget the family.

Although personal and family-related issues are cited as the most frequent reason by far for failed expatriate assignments, other factors have also been highlighted, namely (Trompetter, Bussin & Nienaber, 2014):

- Expatriates' inability to either adapt to the location or the work environment

- Job not meeting expectations

- Expatriate is not technically competent

- Relationship issues with the new line manager.

The factors impacting expatriate assignments and therefore contributing to successful assignments can, according to Black (1988), be categorised into three dimensions:

- *General adjustment*, which includes adjustment of the expatriate and the accompanying family to the host culture and the host country's general living conditions

- *Interaction, cultural or social/socio-cultural adjustment*, indicating the ability of the expatriate and accompanying family to engage in a comfortable manner with host country nationals and the ease with which they manage everyday situations, including language barriers, and

- *Work adjustment*, which entails fitting into a local culture including the performance and competence expectations, workplace standards and requirements associated with working in the foreign environment.

Adjustment within the host location contributes significantly to the expatriate's performance, reduces chances of the premature return of the expatriate, enhances the investment in the assignment for the employer, and also creates examples of successful assignments for other employees who may not ordinarily be interested in such an adventurous work experience, despite perhaps having the potential to succeed.

If adjustment in the host location is one of the primary reasons for assignment failures, it goes without saying that the expatriate and the accompanying family have to adjust well on all levels, to ensure a successful assignment.

7.2 GENERAL ADJUSTMENT: THE EXPATRIATE FAMILY

Recent statistics indicate that between 70 percent and 90 percent of expatriates on long-term assignments, defined as a period in excess of 12 months, are accompanied by a spouse and, if applicable, minor children (Lee, 2007). While expatriation is common practice in most multinational organisations, there seems to be a high failure rate because neither the expatriate nor the family wishes to deal with the level of uncertainty that is associated with the process. The successful adjustment of the family falls under the category of *sociocultural* and *general* adjustment types which are both significant contributors towards successful assignments.

Issues that families experience when they accompany the expatriate to a host location have been identified by Grove and Hallowell (1997) (see Table 7.1).

Table 7.1: Family issues contributing to successful/failed assignments

Adjustment issues for the spouse	Adjustment issues for children
New country	Insecurity
New community	Loneliness
New language	Identity crisis
New customs	Visibility
New school systems	Conflicting values
New job status or unemployment	Unresolved grief
New personal status (or lack thereof)	

In addition to the family issues that are experienced, it is estimated that in 30 percent of cases, the spouse is not involved in the decision to relocate, 36 percent are involved only after the decision was made, and 28 percent are involved during the process of decision making.

When considering family matters and personal circumstances of expatriates prior to making the final selection, employers should not only look at dual career families – the definitions of spouse, dependent children and family have become quite complicated, both in social terms as well as from a legal point of view. Same-sex couples, adopted children and dependent children over the acceptable age of 25 years are becoming the norm that many organisations have to deal with in an equal, non-discriminatory and transparent manner.

In particular, family support, as it pertains to cross-cultural adjustment, is an important factor in determining the success of an international assignment.

According to Lee (2007), the family's support of the expatriate significantly increases the risk of an assignment being successful. Family support is therefore important for the following reasons:

- A failed assignment will mostly result in a premature return of the expatriate, which is very costly for the employer (and often also for the employee).

- Premature return of expatriates to the home location can have a damaging effect on the employer's reputation and lead to loss of business opportunities or loss of trust in the company as an employer.

- The expatriate's self-esteem and self-confidence is likely to be negatively affected if they elect to return home sooner than planned as they have to face colleagues, friends and family back at home.

- Reduced self-esteem and self-confidence levels often result in decreased levels of engagement.

- The expatriate's health may be affected negatively. In a study conducted by Sanchez, Spector and Cooper (2000), a comparison was made between a group of expatriate executives and a similar group of executives who remained in the home location which revealed a significant increase in the stress-sensitive hormone prolactin, reduced mental health, and an increase in cigarette and alcohol abuse for the group of expatriate executives.

- Seeing the impact of a failed assignment on employees could negatively influence other employees in terms of their decisions to take on such a venture.

7.3 INTERACTION, CULTURAL OR SOCIAL/SOCIO-CULTURAL ADJUSTMENT

Socio-cultural adjustment has in simple terms been defined as the expatriate's ability to "fit into" the host culture. This ability is measured in terms of the amount of difficulty experienced by expatriate in managing everyday situations (Selmer, 2006). One of the factors contributing to the ability to adjust is whether there are language differences between the host and home countries. In many countries language can in fact be seen as a significant obstacle to adjust to and should therefore receive specific attention in the pre-departure training of the expatriate as well as the accompanying family. For example, for a US citizen to be expatriated to the United Kingdom can be a lot easier than for a US citizen to be expatriated to Korea. Not only are there language barriers, but the culture, religion, food, economic, social and political factors all present additional stressors for the expatriate.

Coping with highly ambiguous and stressful situations requires a high level of emotional intelligence. It has also been proved that expatriates who demonstrate a great interest in and who are motivated to explore and experience diverse cultures, while having greater self-confidence in their ability to adapt to new environments, adjust better to work–life and social demands required in the host location. A high level of behavioural cultural intelligence also allows for an employee to be more flexible in his/her verbal and non-verbal communications with others enhancing his/her ability to adjust.

7.4 WORK ADJUSTMENT

In addition to general and social cultural adjustment, work adjustment is also a very important factor contributing to the successful assignment. Black (1988) quotes two specific factors that influence work adjustment, namely:

- *Individual factors*, including the individual's desire to adjust, technical or managerial competence, a person's social orientation or ability to build relationships, individual tolerance for ambiguity (also referred to as open-mindedness) and the individual's self-confidence.

- *Job-related factors*, including previous work experience, discretion, pre-departure knowledge of the new environments, role ambiguity, role conflict, and work–life balance.

Black et al (1991) also identified the following categories of pre-departure variables that significantly influence adjustment:

- Previous experience
- Pre-departure training
- Candidate selection.

The relationship with the line manager in the host location, and the line manager's willingness to coach the expatriate also plays an important role.

The U-Curve Adjustment Theory (Black et al, 1991) is a popular model to explain to expatriates the process of adjustment that they and their families will go through while on assignment.

7.5 THE U-CURVE OF CROSS-CULTURAL ADJUSTMENT

Of the three dimensions of adjustment stated, *cultural adjustment* or *social cultural adjustment* has been indicated to be the most difficult area of adjustment as it has the biggest impact on the expatriate and the accompanying family. In terms of the U-Curve Adjustment Theory, the expatriate goes through four phases of adjustment. The initial period is also termed the "honeymoon phase", which is followed by "culture shock", "adjustment" and then finally the "mastery phase". Figure 7.1 (Black et al, 1991) shows the different phases experienced by the expatriate and the accompanying family, before finally settling down and adjusting to the new environment.

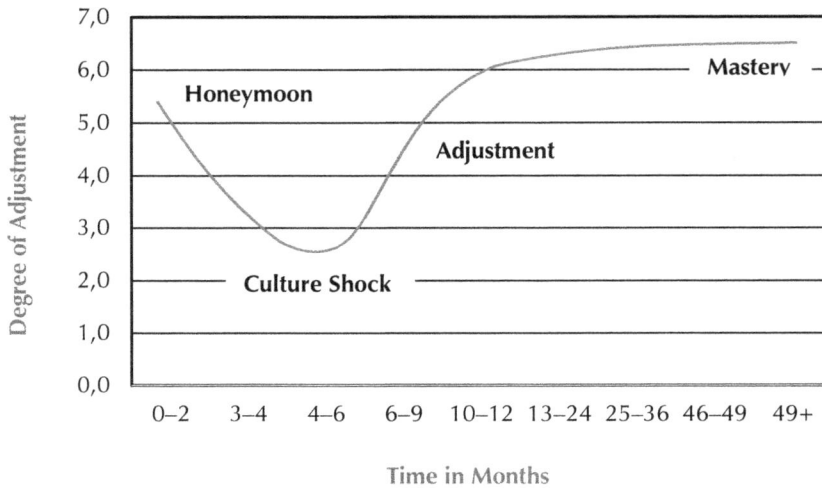

Figure 7.1: The U-curve of cross-cultural adjustment (Black et al, 1991)

The top left of the U-curve, in the "honeymoon phase" refers to the first few weeks of the expatriate and family spending time abroad, where they feel excited, almost fascinated, with their new surroundings.

On the downward slope, the expatriate spends more time engaging with the new social, business and cultural environment and starts to experience the loss of family and friends, in the form of either a support structure or a circle of friends. Many expatriates start to feel a genuine sense of disillusionment about what they thought they were going to experience versus what the actual experience entails. The expatriate is no longer treated as a new employee or a guest in the office and is expected to start making a significant contribution despite not necessarily understanding the new environment yet. Cultural faux pas are made; an irritation is experienced with the unfamiliarity both inside and outside the workplace; side-line comments are made about the "handsome and generous reward packages of expatriates"; and the expatriate and family are starting to encounter everyday problems such as traffic congestion, undrinkable drinking water, and different food preferences. This is typically the period where the expatriate/family members experience "real culture shock" and start to understand that they are in the journey for the long haul and that it is not just a short holiday for the adventurous.

Counselling or coaching during this period may be very valuable for the expatriate and the spouse/children, teaching them the ropes in the foreign environment and making them more conscious of differences and similarities in their immediate environment. If there is a trust relationship with this person, they will feel confident sharing some embarrassing experiences and also ask questions about matters about which they feel unsure.

Just when the expatriate/family members become a bit desperate in their new environment, and feel they are never going to adjust to the host location, they move out of the "culture shock" phase into the upward rise of the U-curve towards the "recovery phase", where the expatriate and the family gradually start to understand the new cultures, the new environments and ways of working, and they learn how to behave appropriately within their new context. The initial unknown environment becomes more familiar; friendships are formed inside and outside the office environment; the employees start to find favourite shops and restaurants; short cuts to avoid traffic congestion are identified; and often the public transportation system is used on a frequent basis. As this phase is typically from 10 months into the assignment, the anticipation of returning home after a 12-month assignment could also support the employee in adjusting during the last few months.

Lastly, people who are in for the long haul typically reach the "mastery or adjustment " phase after about 24 months in the new location and are ready to localise in the host environment, return home, or move on to the next assignment. The expatriate is considered to be effective both inside and outside the work environment. Twenty-four months can be a very long time, if the expatriate or the spouse/children find it impossible to adapt and end up wanting to return home.

The extent to which "highs" and "lows" are experienced by the expatriate during the different phases, or the timeframes attached to each of these phases, are mostly dependent on the expatriate's own ability to adapt and cope in a foreign business and social environment, the expatriate's level of competence, the extent of socio-cultural differences between the host and home countries, the opinion of the host nationals about the appointment, general levels of job satisfaction and also the degree of contact with host nationals which typically enhances the expatriate's ability to adjust more quickly in the foreign environment.

Although the expatriate may experience different timeframes in the respective adjustment phases, this is merely indicative of their resilience to change or innate ability to adapt to the new cultures and social circumstances. Many organisations include an "adaptability" assessment in their battery of assessment tests completed as part of the assignment process, which provides excellent input into understanding how difficult the move to the host environment will be and the type of support that will have to be given to both the expatriate and the accompanying family.

7.6   EXPATRIATE SELECTION

Technical skills, family situation, relational skills and motivational state all play a significant role in the expatriate's ability to adjust to the host location. Technically qualified candidates are not always capable of easily adjusting to critical cultural differences, such as those involving social status and emotional intelligence.

Mendenhall & Oddou (1985) define four dimensions of adjustment which could be handy for organisations when they go through a selection process, namely:

- **Self-orientated dimension:** Activities and attributes that reinforce the expatriate's self-confidence. This dimension includes three specific factors: reinforcement substitution, stress reduction, and technical competence, of which the last is the most relevant from an organisational perspective.

- **Others-orientated dimension:** Activities and attributes that improve the capacity to interact in a positive way with the host nationals. The dimension consists of two specific factors: relationship development and willingness to communicate with host nationals.

- **Perception dimension:** Capacity to understand the behaviour of host nationals. The well-adapted expatriate makes less rigid assessments about host nationals' behaviour.

- **Cultural toughness:** The culture in some countries seems to be less adaptable to the culture of others – this also depends where the expatriate comes from and which location they go to.

The last dimension stated, namely *cultural toughness*, is one of the few non-work factors that significantly contribute towards adjustment. The more culturally distant or different a host culture is from that of the expatriate, the more difficult it will be to adjust. Taking into consideration the U-curve model, the first two years of the assignment tend to be the most difficult, after which expatriates who remain in the host country overcome the culture toughness dimension.

It is widely accepted that for an expatriate to be successful on assignment, there is a need to have the required technical skills as well as the ability to adapt in a foreign environment and culture.

The selection of the most appropriate person for the expatriate position, who will have the ability to adjust in the host location, should take a number of factors into consideration, namely:

- Organisational socialisation
- Career transition and sense making
- Work role transition
- Relocation/domestic transfers

7.7   CONCLUSION

Globalisation and internationalisation of markets and economies have led to a significant increase in expatriate assignments around the globe. Despite the increase in the number of expatriates living and working in host countries, and learning from these assignments, the percentage of failed assignments has not reduced over the past 20 years. The most important reason cited for expatriate failures is the excessive emphasis on technical skills during expatriate selection without considering personality traits, as well as the expatriate's family situation. Expatriates are removed from their comfortable home environment where they are familiar with the language, culture, ethics, politics and social structures and placed in unfamiliar territory, which can lead to feelings of hopelessness, lower engagement, higher stress levels, and often deteriorating relationships at home, as well as in home and host countries.

Openness to a profound personal transformation is probably the most important indicator for readiness for an expatriate assignment and ultimately a successful assignment. Core personality traits forecasting success include high levels of emotional intelligence, willingness to take risks, courage, self-confidence, adaptability and flexibility, and should be considered in the selection of expatriates. It therefore speaks for itself that the selection process as well as the pre-departure training of expatriates and the accompanying family is of crucial importance in ensuring successful expatriate assignments and positive return of investment for the company as well as the expatriate.

7.8   REFERENCES

Black, JS. 1988. Work role transitions: A study of American expatriate managers in Japan. *Journal of International Business Studies,* 19(2):277–294.

Black, J, Mendenhall, M & Oddou, G. 1991. Towards a comprehensive model of international adjustment: An integration of multiple theoretical perspectives. *Academy of Management Review*, 16(2):291–317.

EY. 2013. *Your talent in motion. Global Mobility Effectiveness Survey, 2013*.

Grove, C & Hallowee, W. 1997. The trailing family: An overlooked key to successful relocation. *Benefits and Compensation Solutions*.

Lee, H. 2007. Factors influencing expatriate failure: An interview study. *International Journal of Management*, 24(3):402–413.

Mendenhall, M & Oddou, G. (1985). The dimensions of expatriate acculturation: A review. *The Academy of Management Review*, 10(1):39–47.

Sanchez, JI, Spector, PE & Cooper, CC. 2000. Adapting to a boundary-less world. A developmental expatriate model. *Academy of Management Executive*, 14(2).

Selmer, J. 2006. Adjustment of business expatriates in Greater China: A strategic perspective. *International Journal of Human Resource Management*, 171(2).

Trompetter, D, Bussin, M & Nienaber, R. 2014. The relationship between family adjustment and expatriate performance. Unpublished Masters dissertation: University of Johannesburg.

University of Maryland. *Education abroad – the U-curve of adjustment*. [Online]. Available: http://www.international.umd. [Accessed 23 February 2014].

CHAPTER 8
CAREER MANAGEMENT OF EXPATRIATES
JC Nel

8.1 INTRODUCTION

Expatriate assignments play a critical role in the execution of international business strategies and the development of management and core business specialised skills for global deployment (Mendenhall, Kuhlman & Stahl, 2001). Despite the strategic importance of international assignments, it does not necessarily enhance the careers of those involved. leading to reluctance to accept the assignments and often resulting in early termination of assignments (Stahl, Miller & Tung, 2002; Zhou, 2014; Vogel & Van Vuuren, 2008).

Managing the career paths of the individuals involved often becomes a dilemma for organisations as the individuals involved in expatriate assignments often view them as unattractive (Selmer, 1998). It is therefore important to explore the purpose of both expatriate assignments and career path management within organisations to ensure that employees' career opportunities are well managed.

8.2 CAREER PATH MANAGEMENT

8.2.1 Historic background

Understanding the origins of and reasons why organisations have embraced the concept of career paths will assist the organisation in decide the role of the specialist/professional path into the future.

8.2.2 Traditional career path management systems

Most job evaluation systems were designed over 50 years ago. The systems generally worked well in the era of hierarchical organisations, where managers were powerful. They generally graded managers higher than everyone else. The typical graded hierarchy is illustrated in Table 8.1.

Table 8.1: Typical graded hierarchy

Grade	Organisational level
1	Global management
2	Top management
3	Senior management
4	Management
5	Professionals, specialist 2
6	Supervisors
7	Technicians, artisans, specialist 1
8	Advanced operational
9	Operational
10	Primary

The hierarchical career path system actually prevented professionals/specialists from moving up the levels because their contribution was undervalued by the job evaluation rules, and many of the rules were weighted to management positions. This approach had certain problem areas, which included:

- There was no clarity on the exact requirements for movement as the descriptions were not detailed enough, and usually a time factor was applied. Instead of promoting the growth of ability, the system became an automatic promotion device, and only those staff with significant performance problems did not receive their promotions.

- The system encouraged staff to focus on promotion rather than the growth of ability, and staff still perceived their futures to be controlled by management decision.

- Staff pressure for promotion to the next milestone resulted in many cases where management promoted too soon, thereby devaluing the positions over time. For instance, it was found that in certain organisations/institutions, systems analysts were actually doing the work of analyst programmers.

In the hierarchical system, expatriate assignments were focused on management positions, with little emphasis on specialist/professional positions. With the implementation of dual career path systems, organisations have recognised the need for specialised/professional skills required within the expatriate assignments.

8.2.3   Dual career path systems

With the relatively quick rise of the specialist/professional, these old job evaluation systems put organisations at risk in terms of:

• Promoting the top specialists/professionals to retain them in the organisation without the necessary management competence.

• Specialists/professionals defecting to management in order to be "promoted".

• Specialists/professionals leaving the organisation for more money and status.

• Losing organisational talent and intellectual capital due to resignation or promotion of specialists/professionals.

• Dissatisfied specialists/professionals due to fulfilling management roles.

• Deploying managers into expatriate assignments without the prerequisite competence and therefore focusing not on management of the organisation but rather on operational issues.

Organisations are now designed to acknowledge this phenomenal growth in specialists/professionals, and dual career paths are offered to counter the risks mentioned earlier (Bussin, 2011). Job evaluation systems with dual career paths were also designed in response to this, as illustrated in Table 8.2.

Table 8.2: Dual career path grading system

	Management/operational	Specialist
1	Global management	Global expert/Manager of technology
2	Top management	National expert, technology strategist
3	Senior management	Expert specialist
4	Management	Advanced specialist
5	Supervisors	Operational specialist
6	Advanced operational	Senior technicians/artisans
7	Operational	

The implementation of dual career path systems has resulted in the selection process for expatriates changing from the initial management positions only to include specialised/professional positions (Ntshona, 2007).

Using specialised/professional expatriates, although at a high cost of remuneration, may reduce the eventual transactional cost because skills transfer can take place at a more rapid rate and at the same time provide the host organisation with a competitive advantage (Zhou, 2014).

8.3 MOTIVATIONS FOR EXPATRIATE ASSIGNMENTS

Although candidates for expatriate assignments acknowledge the various risks of international assignments, they still value opportunities for international assignments, mainly for the following reasons (Stahl et al, 2002; Ellingsbo & Thorell, 2003):

- Personal challenges
- Professional development
- Job importance
- Opportunities for skills acquisition
- Personal development
- Career enhancement
- Status upon return to the country of origin
- Future opportunities for advancement
- Geographic location of the assignment
- Monetary considerations
- Fear of restricted career opportunities within home office.

Research has, however, proved that international assignments limit career progression after repatriation, yet this has not served as a deterrent for taking up such opportunities (Vogel & Van Vuuren, 2008).

8.4 CAREER MANAGEMENT OF EXPATRIATES

8.4.1 The expatriate cycle

Organisations realise the need for expatriate deployment to ensure that they obtain and maintain the competitive edge within their foreign operations. During the selection of expatriate candidates, the most prevalent criteria are qualifications, skills, experience, and personal qualities to succeed in expatriate assignments (Mehegan, 2004).

> *"It is essential that the successful international businesses of today become aware of the competitive advantage of thorough preparation of their expatriate managers and the impact it is going to have on their overall profits. To ignore its importance is tantamount to managerial neglect."* (Hawley, 2000)

South African companies are not immune to the globalisation phenomenon and therefore need to ensure that the right employees are deployed on expatriate assignments, taking cognisance of their different career stages. This requires sound planning with refined selection processes, as illustrated in Figure 8.1.

Strategic
Planning

Repatriation   Selection

Performance   Preparation
Measurement

Figure 8.1: Strategic expatriate cycle

8.4.1.1 Strategic planning

The strategic planning phase requires the organisation to clearly link foreign assignments to strategic operational requirements (Ntshona, 2007; Zhou, 2014). This includes strategic assessment of whether an expatriate is the best and most cost-effective sourcing solution.

8.4.1.2 Selection

During selection there are some major selection characteristics to consider when choosing an individual for an expatriate assignment. Typically, these are as follows:

- Technical and decision-making skills
- Managerial skills
- Intercultural competence
- Adaptability
- Diplomacy
- Language proficiency
- Emotional intelligence

- Personal characteristics
- Adaptability of the candidate's family, and
- Age profile.

Liu (2002), for example, indicates that careers are generally divided into four stages: the exploration stage (<30 years old); the determining stage (from 30 to 45 years old); the maintenance stage (from 45 to 55 years old); and the declining stage (>55 years old). During these stages, the success of deployments depends on the psychological contract of the employee and possible commitment to an expatriate assignment and the success of repatriation.

Ronan in Chew (2004) identified five categories of attributes of success to ensure effective deployment of expatriates and their families. These are illustrated in Table 8.3.

Table 8.3: Categories of attributes of expatriate success

Job factors	Relational dimensions	Motivational state	Family situation	Language skills
Technical skills	Tolerance for ambiguity	Belief in the mission	Willingness of spouse to live abroad	Host country language
Familiarity with host country and headquarters operations	Behavioural flexibility	Congruence with career path	Adaptive and supportive spouse	Non-verbal communication
Managerial skills	Non-judge mentalism	Interest in overseas experience	Stable marriage	
Administrative competence	Cultural empathy and low ethnocentrism	Interest in specific host country culture		
	Interpersonal skills	Willingness to acquire new patterns of behaviour and attitudes		

During the selection process, each candidate should be assessed against the selection criteria to ensure a best fit for the assignment. This should include the possibility of repatriation after the conclusion of the assignment (Mehegan, 2004).

8.4.1.3 Preparation

Although many organisations deploy expatriates across the globe, very little attention is paid to the preparation of the expatriates and their families (Hawley, 2000; Hodge, 2009; Ntshona, 2007; Reiche, 2012). It is therefore essential that close attention is paid to the preparation of both the assignees and their families.

8.4.1.4 Pre-departure training

Upon conclusion of the selection process, it is critical that the pre-departure training is completed to ensure effective and successful deployment abroad. The most important preparation includes career planning, spouse and family counselling, and cross-cultural training (Hodge, 2009; Ntshona, 2007).

8.4.1.5 Performance management

Literature indicates that between 16 and 40 percent of all expatriates end the assignments prematurely because of either poor performance or inability to adjust to the foreign environment, while as many as 50 percent of those who do not return function at a low level of effectiveness (Hawley, 2000).

Expatriates often feel isolated in the host countries while also being of the opinion that their reputation is under threat back in their home countries (Hodge, 2009; Reiche, 2012). It is therefore important to manage their performance in the host country from the originating country.

Performance measurement can be achieved only by analysing the strategic objectives for the expatriate assignment. Using the strategic objectives, the strategic deliverables, time schedules, and outputs need to be formalised in a performance contract as per the performance management system deployed in the originating country (Chew, 2004).

Consistent coaching, performance tracking and performance measurement need to be applied to ensure effective engagement in the expatriate assignment. This includes preparation for repatriation.

8.4.1.6 Repatriation

Expatriate assignments have become more commonplace in multinational companies/corporations (MNCs), which correlates with international trends. This includes the recognition of the importance of the role they play in the organisation's internationalisation strategies (Zhou, 2014).

Some expatriates quit in their expatriation period, which brings risk and disadvantage to their multinational organisations. On the other hand, some expatriates are repatriated as scheduled, but finally find there is no longer any job fit in the origination organisations, which causes disappointment and declining motivational levels, according to Yan, Zhu & May (2002) in Zhou (2014) and Reiche (2012).

Therefore, the challenge for organisations is to view repatriation as reverse expatriation, posing many of the same problems and warranting many of the same solutions (Zhou, 2014; Kraimer et al, 2009; Aguilera, 2006).

8.5   REPATRIATE AGREEMENT

Successful assignments begin with repatriation planning at the time of expatriation. Several researchers indicated that at the onset of an overseas assignment a repatriation agreement should be agreed upon between the employee and the employer in order to develop a repatriation process to help manage the employee's goals and expectations.

The elements of a repatriation agreement are very likely to include provision of a specified period – research indicates three years (Zhou, 2014; Hodge, 2009) – of the assignment, and a return incentive payment.

On return, the expatriate should have the assurance of a job that is mutually acceptable (that is, one equal to or better than the one held before leaving), and a provision of re-entry training combined with a repatriation programme to support the repatriate and help the family readjust back into their home country (Hodge, 2009).

Relocation benefits such as arranging pre-repatriation home country 'house hunting', school registration, and the shipment of personal goods, would further reduce the problems associated with a return home (Ntshona, 2007; Vogel & Van Vuuren, 2008).

8.6   REPATRIATION PROGRAMMES

According to Zhou (2014), the effectiveness of a repatriation programme rests on its ability to address the certain questions:

- "Will I get a good job when I return?"

- "Will my career be enhanced and will my newly acquired skills and perspective be valued and well utilised in the home organisation?"

Repatriation programmes consist of activities that provide a comparable position or a promotion from the job held before repatriation and assistance for the employee and family in re-assimilating their home culture on their return. These programmes are crucial in demonstrating supportiveness to the returnees. The repatriation strategies are likely to improve repatriation success rates by emphasising the commitment of the organisation to its expatriate staff and may encourage expatriates to feel that their best interests were a priority, leading to enhanced expatriate commitment to the parent firm. In addition, it helps to develop commitment to the new local work unit, thereby facilitating the retention of these strategic human resources (Reiche, 2012; Vogel & Van Vuuren, 2008). Repatriation programmes could include the following:

8.6.1 Mentorship

Mentorship has proved to be one of the most effective means of reintroducing the expatriate into the originating/parent organisation. The main function of the mentor is to facilitate the expatriate's reintroduction into the parent company and to provide information on changes to the company such as restructuring and changes in organisational culture or positioning (Ellingsbo & Thorell, 2003).

8.6.2 Family counselling

Counselling of expatriate family members is important when assisting them to readjust to the home country. Cross-cultural adjustment is required in many cases to adapt to the home country owing to changes in the socio-, economic- and political environment (Els, 2007). This may lead to tension within the household, especially if the spouse attempts to re-establish his/her personal career. Counselling is required to facilitate the reintroduction process.

8.6.3 Career management

A large number of expatriate assignees are dissatisfied upon return from the expatriate assignments. This is caused by factors such as loss of authority granted during the expatriate assignment, the changes in organisational structure, and not fitting into the "new" parent company-assigned position (Hodge, 2009; Reiche, 2012). This may be eradicated by means of proper career management.

Career management is about taking a longer-term view. This strategy provides customised coaching to ensure that assignees succeed in carrying out the demands of their daily work, and achieve the stated objectives of the expatriation, thereby contributing to the success of their organisations in their global endeavours and understanding their role in the parent organisation upon repatriation. It is a known fact that many expatriates run into difficulties in achieving their objectives and return home to face a career cul-de-sac, or no job at all (Hodge, 2009; Hawley, 2000).

Pre-expatriation counselling and coaching is therefore required prior to the expatriate assignment. The expatriate assignee needs to understand and participate in the expatriate and repatriation career planning.

8.6.4   Repatriation planning list

The importance of repatriation can be facilitated by actions such as those illustrated in Table 8.4. This planning list is not exhaustive but merely an indication of the possible planning actions that can be introduced to facilitate a smoother repatriation and to reduce loss of expatriate employees upon their return to their home countries.

Table 8.4: Repatriation planning list

Number	Repatriation action
1	Pre-departure repatriation briefing
2	Career planning sessions before departure
3	Career planning sessions 6–8 months prior to repatriation
4	Parent company mentoring
5	Continuous career related communication
6	Assigned organisational unit providing career guidance
7	Home visits during expatriate assignment
8	Pre-repatriation training
9	Guarantee of position prior to expatriate assignment
10	Reorientation programme about changes to the parent company
11	Coaching on expatriate self-responsibility for career planning

8.7   CONCLUSION

Expatriate assignments are utilised by most global organisations as a result of value add and contribution of the expatriate to the foreign assignment in terms of competence and experience. The management of the expatriate is therefore dependent on not only preparation for the expatriate assignment but also strategic planning to reincorporate the expatriate assignee back into the parent company after repatriation.

8.8   REFERENCES

Aguilera, RV. 2006. *International career management: Case: Catskill Roads.* College of Business & ILIR, University of Illinois.

Bussin, M. 2011. *The remuneration handbook for Africa. A practical and informative handbook for managing reward and recognition in Africa.* 1st ed. Johannesburg: Knowledge Resources.

Bussin, M. 2013. *The performance management handbook for emerging markets. A practical and informative handbook for managing performance for the world of work in emerging markets.* 1st ed. Johannesburg: Knowledge Resources.

Chew, J. 2004. Managing MNC expatriates through crises: A challenge for international human resource management. *Research and Practice in Human Resource Management,* 12(2):1–30.

Elingsbo, T & Thorell, J. 2003. Expatriate assignment: A means for career development. Unpublished Masters thesis: Luleå University of Technology.

Els, S. 2007. *The success rates, and determinants, of South African expatriate managers in sub-Saharan African countries to first world countries.* MBL Research Report, Pretoria: University of South Africa.

Hawley, K. 2000. *Expatriate preparation.* [Online]. Available: http://www.expatprep.com/library/expatriate-management-in-africa-not-so-easy-no-room-for-complacency/. [Accessed 12 August 2014].

Hodge, S. 2009. *Global business news.* [Online]. Available: http://www.globalbusinessnews.net/. [Accessed 28 August 2014].

Kraimer, ML, Shaffer, MA & Bolino, MC. 2009. *Repatriate Retention,* 48(1):27–47.

Liu, J. 2002. The characteristics and model of psychological contracts. *Journal of Wuhan Economic Administration,* 16(4):30–33.

Mehegan, P. 2004. Selection and retention strategies for employees for expatriate assignments. [Online]. Available: http://blog.iese.edu/expatriatus/2012/08/28/international-itinerants-a-new-breed-of-expatriates. [Accessed 28 August 2014].

Mendenhall, M, Kuhlman, T & Stahl, G. 2001. *Developing global leaders: Policies, processes, and innovations.* Westport, CT: Greenwood Publishing Group, Inc.

Ntshona, BS . 2007. *Expatriate management within a context of best practice in the Africa division of a multinational bank.* Unpublished masters thesis, GIBS, University of Pretoria.

Reiche, S. 2012. *Blog Expatriatus.*IESE Business School. University of Navara. [Online]. Available: http://blog.iese.edu/expatriatus/about/#sthash.vZbB0HHO.dpbs. [Accessed 2 January 2015].

Selmer, J. 1998. Expatriation: Corporate policy, personal intentions and international adjustment. *International Journal of Human Resource Management,* 9(6):996–1007.

Stahl, EK, Miller, EL & Tung, RL. 2002. Toward the boundaryless career: A closer look at the expatriate career concept and the perceived implications of an international assignment. [216–227]

Vilet, J. 2012. The business of HR. *TLNT,* January. [Online]. Available: http://www.tlnt.com/2012/02/20/why-cant-organisations-retain-their-expatriate-employees/. [Accessed 12 August 2014].

Vogel, A & Van Vuuren, JJ. 2008. *Factors influencing the preparation, support and training of South African expatriates.* Pretoria: University of Pretoria.

Zhou, Y. 2014. The career path of expatriates at repatriation. *Journal of Economics, Business and Management,* 3(5):548–553. [Online]. Available: http://www.joebm.com/index.php?m=content&c=index&a=show&catid=43&id=536. [Accessed 11 August 2014].

CHAPTER 9
JOB SIZING – JOB EVALUATION
Laurika Fourie

9.1 INTRODUCTION

Having a consistent job evaluation system for global operations is imperative from an internal equity point of view. This section describes how this can be achieved using a web-based platform called JE[asy].

9.1.1 What is job evaluation?

The purpose of job evaluation is to determine the complexity level/value of a job. It is a systematic and objective process of comparing one job to another in terms of relative job content and complexity levels. Job evaluation can be a powerful tool in an organisation in terms of creating and defending internal equity, as well as a base for the measurement of external equity.

The purpose or uses of job evaluation provide a way to regain control over salary and wage administration and ensure a consistent rationale for pay structures. In addition, negotiation and collective bargaining are made easier by using a common language or defined point of reference.

Job evaluation can be used in the following circumstances:

- A variety of pay rates exist for a variety of reasons.

- Similar jobs are rewarded on different levels.

- There are demands for internal and external parity.

- There is little or no co-ordination of pay rates.

- There is no logical basis for pay rates.

- "Job values" are confused with "person values".

- Organisational structure reviews are required.

- Development of career paths is required.

Employers should scrutinise their pay practices to ensure that disparities in remuneration are objectively justifiable and are not grounds for claims of unfair discrimination.

Job evaluation can serve as a defence to an equal pay claim, where the employer will use the job evaluation results to prove that there is in fact a "difference" in complexity value or that work is of equal value or complexity.

This follows the inclusion of section 6(4) in the South African Employment Equity Act 55 of 1998 as amended by the Employment Equity Act 47 of 2013, with effect from 1 August 2014. Section 6(4) now expressly accommodates claims of equal pay for work of equal value in the general prohibition against unfair employment discrimination. Internationally, this concept has been regulated for over 30 years, and South Africa has now come into line with international practice.

The first step in proving fair pay differentiation is to prove work is or is not "of equal value", or in other words, equal complexity or worth. This can be proved only through the use of a logical, systematic, and objective job evaluation system.

9.2   JE^{asy} WEB-BASED JOB EVALUATION SYSTEM

JE^{asy} is a job evaluation tool. It is a web-based classification solution, ensuring valid and consistent job evaluation results without the complexities of normal job evaluation processes and methodologies. The web-based JE^{asy} system is used by 192 companies in Africa to evaluate jobs across various industries.

In summary, this is a job evaluation system that offers:

- Web-based access worldwide

- Validation of results (free for three months when you buy any of the range of products)

- Customisation to your unique environment.

The system allows clients to be totally flexible in that they can align factors to their business requirements as well as personalise the grade structure – they have the ability to add, edit or delete bands and sub-grades and personalise statements in order to reflect the organisation's terminology and environment.

The system offers sophisticated built-in validation criteria which validate and highlight inconsistencies in the job evaluation results between job evaluation panel members and within the hierarchy of jobs.

An automatic workflow process on the system guides the job evaluation co-ordinator on each step of the evaluation process from the initial input of data into the system to the finalised job evaluation report.

9.3   UNIQUE FEATURES

The unique features of JE^{asy} are:

- Integrated "job profiling" system

- Automatic workflow process on the system guides the job evaluation (JE) co-ordinator on each step of the evaluation process, from the initial input of data into the system to the final job evaluation report

- Ability to add records of information that are salient to the particular position and job evaluation session

- Sophisticated built-in validation criteria which validate and highlight inconsistencies in the job evaluation results between JE panel members and within the hierarchy of jobs

- Status of each job grade result is displayed on company-specific organisational charts set up on the system

- Panel members/JE co-ordinators communicate via email and cellular text messages through the system.

The factors that the system uses are set out below. They comply with international legislation governing pay for work of equal value.

The JE^{asy} system evaluates jobs by measuring five factors across three categories:

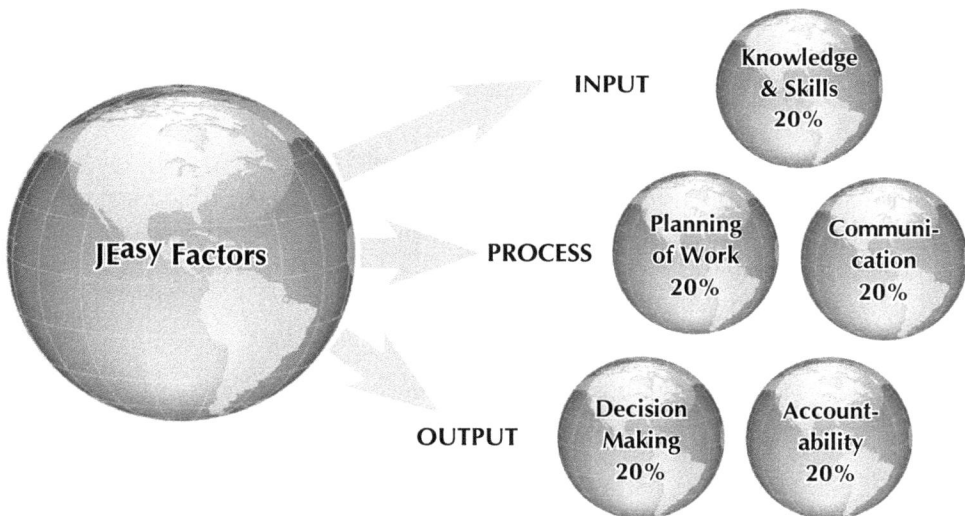

Figure 9.1: JE^{asy} factors

An automatic workflow process on the system guides the job evaluation co-ordinator on each step of the evaluation process from the initial input of data into the system to the final job evaluation report.

1	Create an online job evaluation panel
2	Assign permission and authority
3	Conduct the evaluation via email or on-line
4	Reference the attached documents
5	Identify relevant statement from customised set
6	Establish relevant band and sub-grade
7	Validate against a benchmark and work through deviations
8	Request free validation and finalise grade

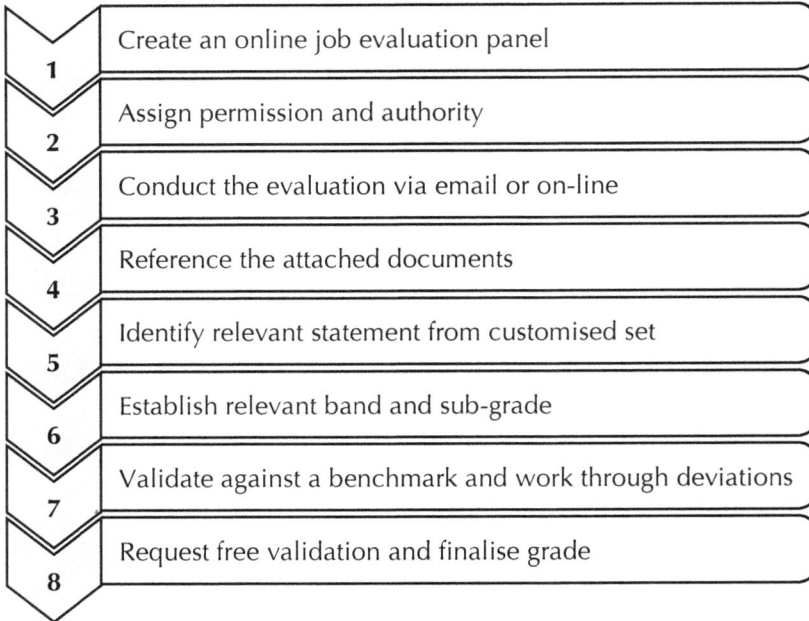

Figure 9.2: Job evaluation process

9.4   CONCLUSION

This is a sophisticated yet simple-to-use, flexible, web-based job evaluation classification solution, customised to your unique environment, which engages all stakeholders in a very robust job evaluation process.

You will be able to:

- Access the system, worldwide, at any time.

- Align the factors to your business requirements.

- Personalise the grading structure by adding, editing or deleting bands and sub-grades.

- Personalise statements to reflect your particular terminology and environment.

- Utilise the fully integrated profiling system.

- Benchmark your job grade results against grades in the market.

- Link to salary benchmarking information via our RewardOnline® website.

- Use the results to validate and highlight inconsistencies between JE panel members and within the hierarchy of jobs.

- Easily co-ordinate the evaluation process. The automatic workflow process will guide you, step by step, from the initial input of data through to the final job evaluation report.

Once one has the levels sorted out, the next step is to "price" each job according to market practice for the industry, country, or region. The next chapter covers market pricing approaches.

CHAPTER 10
JOB PRICING –
UNDERSTANDING REWARDONLINE®
Chirs Blair, Morag Phillips and Peter Karlak

10.1 INTRODUCTION

There are many reasons for conducting a salary benchmarking exercise. Whether the results are used to attract the best resources, to retain your labour force or for ease of mind that your organisation is paying market-related salaries, few would argue the importance of salary benchmarking.

Reliable and good market data is not only the cornerstone of salary benchmarking but is the cornerstone of expatriate pay as well. Therefore, when choosing the source of your data as well as the benchmarking tool to be used, the following factors should be considered:

- What is the source of the data influencing the benchmark results?

- What elements of pay are being compared? Are we comparing apples with apples?

- Who is the comparator group making up the data set?

- Do participants in the survey provide their pay data to the survey producer as part of the condition to participate?

- Does the survey provide only averages or salary ranges?

- Are jobs matched by title only or by capsule role description and grade?

- How is confidentiality of data handled?

- Are the data audited and vetted by an external party?

21st Century Pay Solution's RewardOnline® is a system that offers solutions to the above. RewardOnline is a web-based solution that will enable you to enjoy "real-time" functionality and data availability, in a format that is convenient and easy to use. The salary survey data has been audited and validated by EY.

RewardOnline offers remuneration benchmarks for over 1 000 roles at both executive and general staff levels. Benchmark data is refined to take account of a range of business metrics, including company structure and complexity, company size, industry and region. The survey contains roles that are current in the South African context, with current grades for each position. RewardOnline is also available for the market in Namibia, Botswana, and Kenya (live survey databases), as well as 23 other countries (referenced benchmark data).

For each position, data have been split to detail each element of pay using two different formats depending on regional applicability as follows:

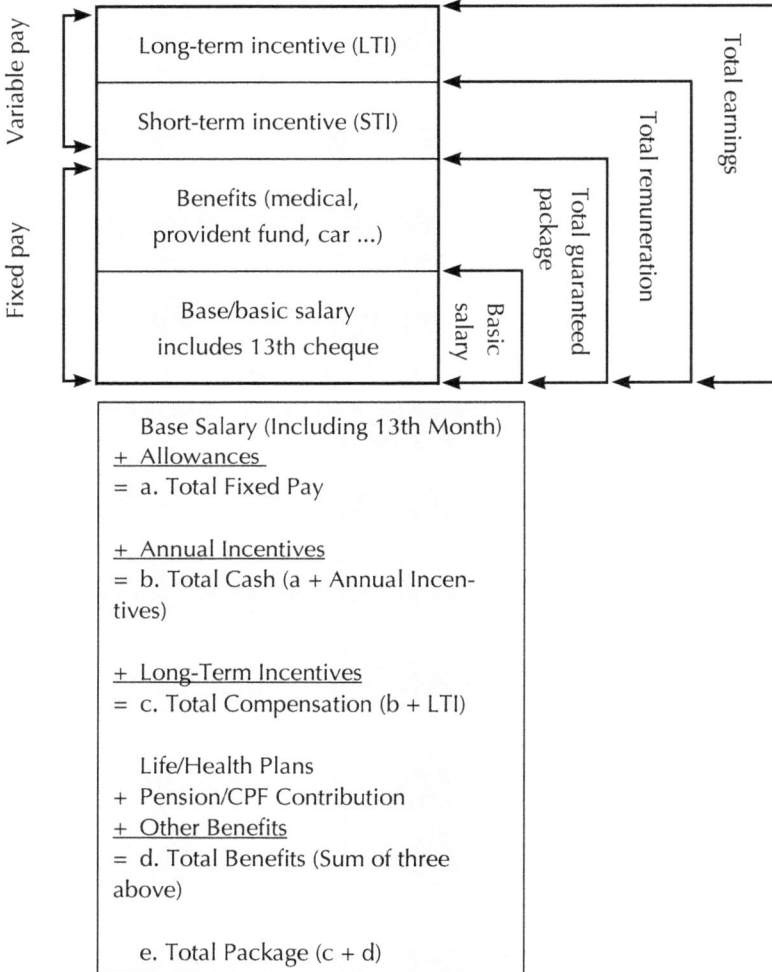

Figure 10.1: Typical elements of remuneration mix (format 1) and compensation (format 2)

By presenting fixed and variable pay separately, you are able to make a true comparison to the elements that make up the total remuneration mix in your organisation. LTI data are available only for executive roles.

With regard to differentiation between live and non-live data sources, 21st Century has developed a methodology to present salary data in countries where survey houses are not active. Conceptually, the existing data sets that 21st Century holds for various positions are used as an anchor to project pay rates reflected as "reference data".

The 21st Century Big Pay Index is an index which is used in order to reference the level of pay per grade and per job in other countries, relative to South African data. The benchmarks which are obtained using this methodology are referred to as "referenced benchmarks" as they are referenced against live, audited data in the South African market database.

The methodology for the 21st Century Big Pay Index is based on a blend of experience and science. This index has integrated our experience with the science of economics in order to produce a unique index which offers predictions of the highest quality in markets which otherwise would not have a credible point of reference regarding salary levels in those countries. The 21st Century Big Pay Index has been created from a multitude of data sources such as the United Nations, World Bank and International Living Index. The data sets which have been used include measures of purchasing power, pay relativity per grade, economic conditions and rankings, and lifestyle factors. The combination of factors which has been taken into account allows for an index which is indicative of the cost, standard and economic conditions of living within a country and adjusted to incorporate the reality of differing pay levels at each grade prevailing in each country.

10.2 CONCLUSION

This blend of experience and science delivers a dynamic, fresh new approach to remuneration and pay solutions in developing economies which are tailored to each country, taking into account their unique economic and social climates. This model has been tested for various countries against existing data sets and has proved itself to be robust in its results.

Other features of the RewardOnline (www.rewardonline.co.za and www.21century.solutions) system include:

- Access to over 1 000 positions

- Accurate market-related grades (including modal grades) and easily understandable job titles

- Detailed remuneration data for executives, in the Private Sector and State Owned Enterprises

- Fully integrated with the Organised Framework for Occupations (OFO) reporting standard

- Comprehensive information to reflect the remuneration elements per position and across all levels in the organisation

- Analytical capabilities (for example, view your own organisation's data in comparison with the market; conduct compa-ratio analyses)

- Customised reporting capabilities over a range of industries and locations, including the organisation's own customised grading systems

- Track record of your own data and benchmark history

- No additional fees per benchmark request (unlimited access for a full year)

- RewardOnline Library – contains articles reflecting current remuneration trends

- Access data for long-term incentives for executives

- Select the specific percentile results you would like to see

- Filter according to the jobs that exist in your company, or access the full database of jobs

- Compare remuneration data by job, by grade, and by job family

- Interactive graphing

- Access to premium reports, including niche reports on remuneration trends as well as a customised report where you can select the specific comparators against which you would like to compare your executives.

Once one has market data, the next step is to put together pay scales to further enhance defensible remuneration structures. The next section sets out international best practice when designing pay scales and salary structures.

CHAPTER 11
SALARY-STRUCTURING ANATOMY
Morag Phillips

11.1 INTRODUCTION

The design of a salary structure is a perfect example of how remuneration management is a blend of both science and art. On the one hand there are scientific "evidence" and benchmarks that describe pay in a selected market. On the other hand there is extensive research that defines typical best practice principles in pay scale design, with consideration of international practice and worldwide research. The end result is to use this best practice research and convert it to "best fit" for the organisation. In other words, every salary structure is unique – a guideline that is linked to your organisation strategies (both business and HR and reward strategies), your level of affordability, and your current pay pattern.

11.2 CORE COMPONENTS OF A SALARY STRUCTURE

The principle behind remuneration is that rewards must be equitable within the company **and** competitive within the market. This balance between internal and external equity is a delicate one.

A salary structure consists of a series of pay ranges, each attached to a grade and each containing a maximum and minimum rate. Jobs are grouped together in ranges which have similar internal and external worth. The midpoint value for the range represents the competitive market value for a series of jobs and is typically the point in the scale that is anchored to the external market. From there, a structure is created with a specific range, overlap, slope, and market positioning.

A salary structure is an administrative tool that is designed to manage pay levels and ensure that pay opportunities are internally fair, externally competitive, and cost-effective. They are created and administered to support an organisation's pay strategy.

In addition, a salary structure typically has three or five points, defined as shown in Table 11.1.

Table 11.1: Pay ranges per grade

Minimum	The bottom end of the pay scale; the point of entry per grade
Lower guide	The mathematical midpoint between the minimum and the midpoint
Midpoint	The midpoint of the proposed pay scale, aligned to a market reference point such as the market median
Upper guide	The mathematical midpoint between the midpoint and the maximum
Maximum	The top end of the pay scale; the exit point per grade

These five points become the pay range per grade, and all pay decisions are made within this range. One would expect a normal distribution of individuals across this range, based on individual characteristics that the organisation has identified as important. This pay scale is designed to align with the remuneration strategy.

In pictorial format, a salary structure draws a link between the market and your unique structure.

11.2.1 Market data

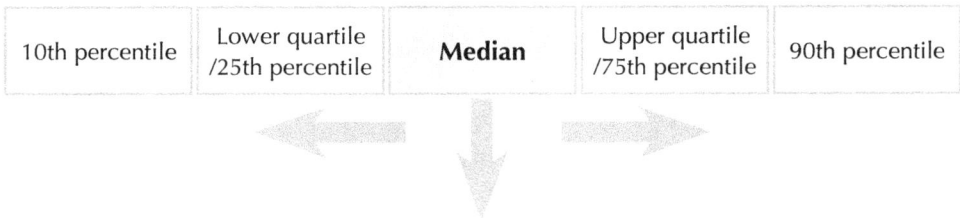

10th percentile	Lower quartile /25th percentile	**Median**	Upper quartile /75th percentile	90th percentile

11.2.2 Unique company pay scales

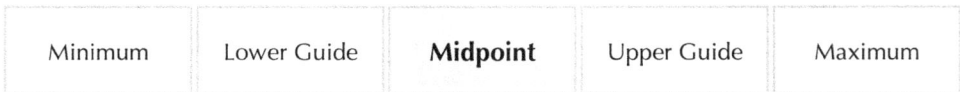

Minimum	Lower Guide	**Midpoint**	Upper Guide	Maximum

In this example the market median is used as an anchor around which the pay scale is built. In order to find a balance between the need to employ staff at cost-effective rates and the need to compete for scarce skills and top performers, the national market median is regarded as the most appropriate market reference point for many organisations, assuming this is affordable and aligns from a strategic perspective. The scales are also wide enough to allow differentiation based on performance and in line with remuneration strategy.

The definitions in Table 11.2 below are essential for understanding salary structures:

Table 11.2: Definitions

Term	Definition
Pay scale/Salary scale/Salary structure	The pay scale refers to the pay attached to grades/bands and the way in which these scales are structured; their range, their slope, overlap, differentials and market positioning.
Pay slope	The steepness or angle of the pay curve. The percentage difference across the pay scale.
Pay range	The pay range refers to the width of the pay scale, that is, the distance between minimum and maximum pay for each grade/band.
Pay overlap	The extent to which the maximum of the lower grade/band overlaps with the minimum of the next higher grade/band. It is dependent on both the pay range and pay slope.
Grade differential/ Midpoint differential	The difference between the midpoints of each grade/band.
Internal equity	The relative grade assigned to different jobs within the organisation. In addition, internal equity assesses how reasonable these grades are. Internal equity can be examined on two levels, namely horizontally (between departments) and vertically (within one department).
External equity	The competitiveness of the level of remuneration assigned to each grade and based on the need to compete in a free market for skills.
Job evaluation	The systematic and objective process of determining the relative worth of a job in the organisation utilising a structured process. The result of this process would be accurate job grades, which form the anchor for a salary structure.

11.3 WHAT INFLUENCES THE DESIGN OF A SALARY STRUCTURE?

The design of a pay structure is guided by a number of key "best practice" principles, as well as the reality of the history and context within which the organisation operates. One of the most difficult challenges in pay structure design is getting the balance right between affordability and competitiveness.

Pay structures are typically designed to support both internal equity and external competitiveness.

Internal equity refers to the relative grade assigned to different jobs within an organisation. The focus in external competitiveness is on external equity and is based on the organisation's need to compete in a free market for skills. Part of this competition is the management of labour costs – ensuring that the labour force is neither overpaid (leading to a higher cost than necessary for the organisation to provide its service) nor underpaid (possibly leading to a high turnover or labour unrest, which could harm productivity). Low turnover or a lack of competitors for labour is not an indicator of a lack of competitiveness in an industry or that the compensation system is working perfectly in the organisation, since turnover could be for a number of different non-pay-related reasons. However, once it is established that employees are leaving to move to other companies, data regarding these companies should be obtained.

11.3.1 Technical considerations

When an organisation is designing a pay scale, it will choose how best to use the market-related data to inform the design of a pay scale specific to their requirements. A pay scale design is always influenced by current pay practice. The end result is to create a scale that has defined points that have some relativity and link to the market, but should also be applicable to the organisation, its strategy, and its level of affordability.

11.3.2 Design of pay scales is influenced by several factors

The general factors influencing the salary structures of a company are shown in Table 11.3, below.

Table 11.3: Factors influencing salary structures

Factor	Applications
Corporate culture and values	An organisation's pay structure normally reflects the way in which employees' work is valued. The achievement of the company's goals, such as having the best workforce or encouraging risk-taking, can be reinforced by the pay strategy and structure.
Management philosophy	Management values and philosophy regarding the definition of jobs, development opportunities, promotions, and so on, are reflected in the pay strategy adopted by the company.
	Example: Narrow pay ranges and additional grades allow for more frequent promotions and the perception of greater growth and development opportunities than broader bands.
External economic environment	Factors to consider here include supply and demand for certain skills, inflationary fluctuations and cost-of-living indicators such as the Consumer Price Index (CPI).
External socio-political environment	Factors to consider here include the level of unionisation within an industry (organisation) and decisions regarding minimum pay and government scrutiny.
	Note: In addition, the culture and operation of a specific organisation may also constitute socio-political factors
Centralised remuneration policy	This factor relates to the association between strategy and remuneration. The pay strategy and resulting policy are part of the overall internal direction of the company, and one policy is applied to each separate business unit.
Decentralised remuneration policy	While the centralised policy focuses on internal strategy, the decentralised policy focuses on the company's overall competitive posture.
	When this is applied, the pay structures may be different for different segments/business units.

Pay structures undoubtedly help create a systematic and equitable base for remuneration management. However, they are only tools. Pay structures can even become a burden to the company unless certain specific factors are taken into account. Take account of the following factors before deciding on a pay structure.

Table 11.4: Implementation factors to consider

Factor to consider	Associated questions
Competitive posture	What is the competitive posture of the company? At what point in the market should the company pay?
Decision making	Who will make the critical decisions underlying the pay structure? How do I involve line management in implementing the structure and supporting it?
Monitoring	How frequently will the pay structure be monitored and assessed for validity and appropriateness?
Flexibility	Is the pay structure flexible enough to handle dynamic situations?

11.4 PURPOSE OF A SALARY STRUCTURE

The purpose of Pay Scales is to provide guidelines linked to grade. They provide a logical framework within which to base remuneration decisions. The application is shown in Table 11.5 below:

Table 11.5: Pay scale purpose

Guideline factor	Application
Recruitment	Managers can grade the job and offer a salary in the pay range (according to the remuneration policy).
Performance	Employees who demonstrate sustained superior performance could move through the pay scales more quickly.
Competence and skill demonstration	More and more company remuneration policies allow individuals who apply relevant competence and skill to move up the pay scales more quickly.
Contribution	Paying for contribution is a major trend which should be reflected in all leading companies' remuneration policies.

Guideline factor	Application
Business needs or scarcity of skill	This, together with scarcity of some skills, sometimes leads to "anomalies" in the pay structure, but these are defensible.

11.5 PAY SCALE DESIGN CRITERIA – DEFINING THE EXTERNAL MARKET COMPARISON

We need to consider the following before designing a pay structure.

11.5.1 Strategic issues

Strategy issues include matters such as:

• Whether the structure is able to support a company's business strategy

• Compatibility with total remuneration design strategy (including base, incentive and indirect remuneration)

• Guaranteed pay-to-variable pay ratio

• Competitive practices – specifically, external equity

• The organisation's job and workplace design approach to produce internal equity i.e. the grading structure

• Administrative policies of the organisation

• Funds available for salaries.

Companies usually survey comparators similar to them in all or some of the following characteristics:

• Size and structure

• Industry type (products, services)

• Geographic location

• Revenue/income size

• Required job skills.

11.5.2 How to obtain the data

The key methods of obtaining the required data are shown in Table 11.6.

Table 11.6: Key methods of obtaining data

Method	Considerations
Refer to published surveys	Ensure that these are reviewed before you use them for usefulness and applicability. If possible, examine the survey input document along with the output
Participate in a customised survey	Such surveys should involve other companies of a similar size and/or industry type
Conduct a survey	A number of survey options are available. To obtain urgent data conduct a telephone survey

Remember: The process is time consuming and is not recommended if you are surveying more than one job |

Important: Before deciding to conduct a survey, consider the following:

- Timing
- Costs
- Usefulness of data
- Survey purpose.

Ensure that you also take account of hidden concerns such as the difficulty in persuading peer companies to participate.

11.6 DESIGN OF A SALARY STRUCTURE

The following design issues need to be considered:

- Base pay policy line – which market are you comparing against, and which point in that market?
- Number of job grades/bands
- Midpoint to midpoint differentials
- Range spreads
- Range overlap
- Number of pay structures or bands.

The following broad process is recommended.

Step 1 – Validate the internal structure

The design of a salary structure relies on a solid structure of validated job grades and internal relativities. This forms the anchor for the salary structure design, and the accuracy of the interpretation depends on the accuracy of the grades. In other words, the internal equity is the first step in pay scale design. Important questions to ask are shown in Table 11.7, below.

Table 11.7: Internal equity considerations

Questions	Outcome
• Do any job evaluations appear to be "out of place" either vertically or horizontally? • Is the job description or questionnaire complete? • Is the job being compared to the correct peer group? • Is the rater evaluating the job or the person? • Does the hierarchy of positions make intuitive sense? • Is it possible to identify peer and subordinate/ superior relationships?	Confirmed structure; Confidence regarding job grades

Step 2 – Anchor the midpoint to market data

Table 11.8 indicates the important questions to ask.

Table 11.8: External equity considerations

Questions	Outcome
• Are the market numbers reliable? • Are the job matches appropriate? • How many open grades are needed to meet future needs? • Is it possible to keep the market comparisons current? • Do the market data need to be smoothed to achieve an ideal midpoint progression?	Incorporate market data

Step 3 – Determine the structure of the scale

Again, the questions in Table 11.9 are important with regard to design considerations.

Table 11.9: Design considerations

Questions	Outcome
• How wide should each pay range be? • Are the overlaps too big or too small? • How do my actual data compare with the proposed scale? • Is this an affordable solution? • Can you identify the outliers?	Finalise the salary structure design

In determining the structure of the scale, the main decision points are the **range**, the **overlap**, and the **slope**.

11.6.1 Pay range considerations

The following are typical range spreads for different positions found in an organisation:

Table 11.10: Typical pay ranges

Percentage spread	Typical jobs
20–30%	Lower level service, production and maintenance
30–40%	Clerical, technical, Specialist
40–50%	Higher level professional, administrative, middle management
50% and over	Higher level managerial, executive and technical

When choosing a pay range width, remember that the width of the range will determine the maximum and minimum salaries. As the range gets wider, maximums increase, minimums decrease, and midpoints remain constant.

Ranges should be designed with midpoints that reflect the "going rate" – your market anchor. Minimums and maximums should as far as possible be market related.

When minimums are too low, the company will be forced to pay the employee a higher amount in the range to remain competitive. Furthermore, this narrows the position's long-term earning potential. In turn, a high maximum may provide higher long-term earning opportunities which are more costly than is required for the company to be competitive.

11.6.2 Pay overlap considerations

It is normal for the minimum and maximum value of a grade also to fall into the adjourning range. The width of the range and the midpoint differentials determines the amount of overlap between adjourning grades. Grade overlap is significant when midpoint differentials are small and range spreads are large, but grade overlaps are small when range widths are small and midpoint differentials are large.

11.6.2.1 Applications in pay for performance

When using a pay for performance system, grade overlap allows high performers in lower pay ranges with a longer time within a grade to be paid more than a relatively new performer (or lower) performer in a higher pay range. Despite the benefits, too much overlap limits the difference between midpoints which then limits the earning potential of the staff and may cause compression problems between supervisor and staff pay. A typical overlap is 10 to 30 percent.

11.6.3 Pay slope considerations

Pay slopes are viewed in the steepness or angle of the pay curve. The percentage difference between the pay for one grade and another provides a useful tool for measuring and comparing pay slopes.

On the assumption that there is an equal increase in responsibility between each grade and the next one in a company, the "ideal" pay slope would have an equal percentage increase in salary between each grade and the next. This is referred to as a straight pay slope. However, it is sometimes impossible or impractical to implement a straight pay slope in an organisation. Reasons are as follows:

- Companies without a straight pay slope may have to pay exorbitant costs to straighten the slope.

- There may not be an equal increase in responsibility between all grades.

- Pressure on the minimum wage from unions.

- Negotiated pay scales reflect a compromise between union and management, not a theoretical ideal.

- A straight pay curve often conflicts with market trends.

11.7 CONSIDERATIONS FOR PROGRESSION WITHIN THE PAY SCALE

In designing a pay scale, it is expected that the majority of employees will fall within the ranges provided for by the pay scales. The pay scale is seen as a continuum and not notches. Only in exceptional circumstances will employees fall outside the scales. Movement within the scales would be based largely on performance and the employee's current comparison to market.

Pay progression is a process by which employees get higher levels of pay by achieving certain milestones. Pay progression is affected by pay grades, range of each pay grade, and levels of hierarchy within the structure. Pay progression can be based upon various factors, depending on the strategy of the organisation:

- Length of service of an employee in the organisation or experience

- Age-related increment

- Merit-/performance-based pay increase on the recommendation of the line manager

- Pay increase linked to team performance

- Pay progression based on organisational performance

- Pay increase based on individual competency or skills

- Pay increase due to change in market rates.

In terms of best practice, performance is being increasingly used as a criterion, rather than tenure or experience with no concomitant performance improvement.

The objective of pay progression is to retain the experienced workers or employees and to show that the company looks after the interests of loyal workers and employees, and the top performers.

We have set out below guidelines as to how the principles could be applied.

11.7.1 Minimum

This is the position in the salary range which is considered an equitable rate of pay for promotions or employees who meet only the core requirements in terms of competence and performance.

11.7.2 Midpoint

The midpoint in the range is the salary which is considered to be a fair and equitable rate of pay for an employee who is fully qualified from the standpoint of training and experience, and whose demonstrated performance on the job over a period of time (usually two to four years) is entirely satisfactory in all respects. In addition to this, employees who are deemed competent should be paid around the midpoint.

11.7.3 Upper Guide

The position which is considered an equitable rate of pay for an employee who has sustained an above-average performance over a long period of time, and who always exceeds requirements of the position. Supply and demand factors should be considered as shown by staff turnover levels or reputable salary surveys.

11.7.4 Maximum

The pay scale point that is reserved for administering the salaries of employees whose achievements are seldom equalled, whose performance is consistently rated excellent, and who consistently add value through exceptional contributions to the position. Extreme supply and demand factors are obvious.

Set out below is another example of the movement through pay scales.

11.7.5 Recruitment Level (Minimum)

• Recruitment level for entry into a job.

• Minimum entry qualification and competencies as inherently required by a job, for example, B-degree, N1 and so on.

• Basic understanding of the specified functional area.

• Authorisation or competence declaration requirement, for example, Trade test.

• Extensive training and development requirements.

• Potential to acquire competencies for the full scope of the job.

11.7.6 Development Level (Lower Guide)

• Basic understanding of policies, directives, and procedures applicable to the job.

• Functions without assistance on common/usual assignments.

• Functions with assistance on unusual/uncommon assignments.

• Narrow range of knowledge, skill, and application.

• Basic knowledge of theoretical elements applicable to the job.

• Basic knowledge and understanding of fundamental and/or widely-used methods.

- Basic core competence requirements are known and understood.

- Can interpret key indicators within own environment and recommend appropriate actions.

- Information and/or decisions regarding area of accountability that need to be shared with outside parties are reviewed by a superior prior to release.

- Functions within clearly specified guidelines.

- Training and development required to meet the requirements of proficiency.

11.7.7 Proficient Level (Midpoint)

- Meets all requirements as set in the basic level.

- Declared proficient in a specified role – mastery of full scope of job.

- Functions independently in terms of day-to-day tasks.

- Can give guidance/assistance to other colleagues regarding processes, tasks, policies, and directives.

- Can identify and interpret elements and their relationship without supervision/ assistance.

- Superior's functional input required only as a sounding board for tasks on hand – completes tasks without constant superior intervention.

- Identify, analyse and interpret information and/or situations and make usable/ workable recommendations.

- Good understanding of bigger scenario.

- Fully accountable and functions independently.

- Accredited, certified, authorised, and so on. for the performance of tasks of own duties.

- Performs outputs of a single function and additional projects of abnormal circumstances well.

- Proactive in development of own role/function.

- Recognised as a credible advisor in own function/role.

- Good theoretical and practical background and/or exposure in own role.

- Can represent a function or discipline with full knowledge and skill.

- Good understanding of customer base and requirements.

- Can develop short- and medium-term plans.

11.7.8 Advanced and/or Specialist Level (Upper Guide)

- Meets all requirements as set in the Proficient level.

- Competent and acknowledged as an expert within own job.

- Provides useable solutions (proactive exploration) based on a wide frame of reference.

- Opinion leader in own area.

- Can development short-, medium-, and long-term plans.

- Knowledge and skill influences strategic direction of own role and inputs beyond own functional area.

- Ability to establish new and own methods or systems – innovative.

- Can establish information networks impacting on own role, job, and functions.

- In-depth knowledge of own function and its relationship with other functions.

- Own work is accepted without or with minor alterations by the recipient – trends indicated and solutions proposed.

- Subject matter expert.

11.7.9 Movement within the pay scale

The pattern that should emerge where performance is appropriately managed is that movement in the pay scale is based on performance. Typically, where a sound performance management system is in place, progression in the pay scale is, for the most part, determined based on outputs and performance. Entry-level employees would therefore be paid at or near to the minimum of the pay scale, standard-level performers between the minimum and the midpoint, and high-level performers between the midpoint and the maximum.

11.7.10 Promotions

It is recommended that when an employee is promoted to a higher level, this should be treated as an appointment decision, with the same criteria considered.

11.7.11 Annual Increases

Best practice indicates that in the majority of organisations with a performance culture, fundamental criteria for movement within the scales is both market related and based on the performance of the individual in the job. Where there is a link between individual performance and guaranteed pay (that is, a performance increase is added to guaranteed pay), this is very effective for the purpose of attraction, retention, and motivating the right behaviours.

In other words, there are two types of pay opportunities:

1. At appointment

2. As an individual performs and progresses through the scale.

The anchor points for the appointment decision have been defined in order to ensure consistent practice and internal equity, as well as external equity and alignment with market. From that time on, pay progression is purely based on performance and a person could be positioned anywhere on the continuum between the minimum and maximum.

These guidelines should be developed with consideration of the remuneration strategy and more specifically the remuneration mix, in particular the portion and amount of variable pay.

One would expect a normal distribution in terms of the bell curve with the majority of staff at or near the midpoint, and a small percentage at or near both the lower guide and upper guide.

11.7.12 Management of outliers

Best practice in terms of addressing the management of "outliers" without increasing costs (without a corresponding increase in performance/productivity) suggests that the following guiding principles should be applied. "Outliers" refers to those employees who fall outside the guiding principles identified:

- Underperformers who are overpaid – gradually retard increases through the link between annual increases and performance

- Under-performers who are underpaid – pay at the minimum of the grade

- Over-performers who are overpaid – confirm that it is defensible to pay up to the pay range based on their performance history and the impact of that performance on the annual increases

- Over-performers who are underpaid – move at the fastest rate to the correct point through the reward of performance in the annual increase process

As an alternative, over time, the organisation could consider a stronger link between annual increases and performance. Furthermore, where there are market adjustments to be made, these could be linked to this annual increase performance review process.

11.8 SOME CLOSING THOUGHTS

The following sample checklist will assist with the process of design and implementation of a pay structure.

- Job grading is complete and grades are signed-off.

- Market benchmarks are available for each grade and for select jobs.

- Current individual salaries are available for each grade.

- Company remuneration policy and strategy is available and gives guidance on design issues such as:

  − Market stance

  − Fixed Pay − Variable Pay philosophy

  − Performance, contribution, and competence pay stance

  − Range, slope, overlap philosophy.

- Cost-benefit analysis of several options is done.

- An implementation project plan covering:

  − Timing

  − Communication plan

  − Dealing with anomalies (upgrades, downgrades, salaries above and below the proposed pay scales)

  − Stakeholder presentations complete for example, Remuneration Committee, EXCO, and Trade Union

  − Regular updating of scales

- Written policy and procedure document.

Once the pay scales are designed, specific cognisance needs to be taken of the expatriates. The next section discusses these in more detail.

> **Remember:**
>
> Remuneration and the development of pay structures is not an exact science. However, it must be defensible and based on sound logic.
>
> *Use best practice to get your own best fit.*

CHAPTER 12
EXPATRIATE REWARD MODELS
Dr Mark Bussin

12.1 INTRODUCTION

This chapter examines the different models that can be utilised for effective and a balanced, equitable, yet competitive reward and remuneration system.

12.2 REWARD AND REMUNERATION

Organisational reward systems – both financial and non-financial – are key elements in a company's strategic approach to human resource management, as these can influence a number of human resource processes and practices aimed at attracting and retaining high performing staff (Guthrie, 2007; Rubino, 2006). Research has shown that the types of rewards offered to employees reduces labour turnover, has a motivational impact, and positively influences the company's organisational culture and bottom line (Guthrie, 2007; Marchington & Wilkinson, 2008; Nelson & Spitzer, 2003). Remuneration or compensation also matters because money spent on salaries, benefits, and other forms of reward typically amounts to well over half an organisation's total costs. Reward and remuneration are therefore major determinants both of profitability and of competitive advantage for a company (Torrington, Hall, Taylor & Atkinson, 2009).

12.2.1 Purpose of reward and remuneration

Employers utilise employee reward and remuneration to achieve the following organisational goals (Gilman, 2009; Torrington et al, 2009):

- **Recruiting high-quality employees and retaining their services in the organisation:** Prospective employees compare pay scales and will most likely choose those jobs that offer the higher salary. Employees expect to be treated fairly by employers, and part of this perception of fairness is influenced by the equity (fairness) that exists in the compensation system.

- **Improving employee performance:** Employees expect to receive a certain level of remuneration for exerting a certain level of discretionary effort. They also expect that the compensation they receive for exerting a specified or determined level of effort will be fair. When the organisation recognises hard work and excellent performance, employees will be more willing to exert higher levels of discretionary effort in the expectation that this will also be rewarded in future.

- **Ensuring fairness:** Employees expect congruence between their effort levels and the compensation they receive. They also compare their own efforts and rewards with those of their colleagues as well as with those of employees in similar jobs in different organisations. When employees perceive incongruence between their effort levels and compensation, or that of their colleagues or other employees with whom they compare their situations, they experience dissonance and will react to that dissonance either by changing their effort, their perceptions of the reward, or the people with whom they compare themselves, or by leaving the organisation.

  Organisations establish fairness in the pay structure by ensuring internal equity through job evaluation and by ensuring external equity through salary surveys.

- **Ensuring legal compliance:** Compensation consists of more than money. All countries have specific legislation and regulation that affects components of compensation such as leave, overtime pay, and minimum pay levels. Unions often have a profound influence on employee compensation, and applicable union agreements must be considered in the determination of a compensation strategy.

- **Controlling labour costs:** Employee remuneration is often one of the main cost items in the organisational budget. Ensuring a sustained competitive advantage means engaging the best talent, but ensuring sustained profitability means creating and implementing a compensation strategy that gets the best value for money. Labour costs consist of the number of employees and the hours they work, the average cash compensation paid, and the average benefit costs (Milkovich & Newman, 2009). All three of these components can be controlled in order to keep labour costs in the affordable region, although the increased use of a variable pay component may make tight management of labour costs more difficult.

- **Motivating staff:** Reward and remuneration systems are often used to direct effort and enthusiasm in specific directions and to encourage particular types of employee behaviour that lead to improved organisational performance. People value and are motivated by different rewards for different reasons and therefore reward systems must be diverse to accommodate different and changing employee needs. Reward systems must be comprehensive and based on realistic analyses of employee needs and work situations. Intrinsic and extrinsic rewards influence an individual's motivation and job satisfaction (Weiss, 2001).

Studies show that non-financial reward initiatives which are aimed at strengthening employees' intrinsic motivation have a positive impact on performance (Peterson & Luthans, 2006). These non-financial rewards fulfil employees' need for challenge, responsibility, decision-making, variety, social recognition, and career opportunities, either alone or in conjunction with financial rewards (Armstrong & Murlis, 1994; Luthans, 2005; Odendaal, 2009). Additional research also suggests that whereas financial and other tangible incentives such as pay, benefits and praise may be more motivating in the short term, in the long run, non-financial incentives such as challenging and interesting tasks are more motivating (Arnolds & Venter, 2007).

Remuneration in Emerging Markets

Talent in emerging markets is not cheap. Constraints in the talent market drive salary inflation that works in tandem with the upward wage pressure already present in rapidly expanding economies. During 2011 workers in the United States, Canada, and Western Europe experienced some of the world's lowest base salary increases, around 3%, while some of their peers in emerging markets enjoyed average salary increases of twice that rate or more. According to the ECA *International Salary Trends Survey*, in 2011 Latin America was expected to see the world's largest average salary increases, as much as 27% in Venezuela. Salaries across Asia-Pacific were expected to rise on average by 6% during 2011, with the largest increases being awarded to employees in Vietnam, India and Indonesia, each with expected gains of 9% or more. In the Middle East, employees were expected to see salary increases of around 5% in Saudi Arabia and the United Arab Emirates. Eastern European workers saw average salary gains of nearly 5% as well, with employees in Russia, Romania and Bulgaria enjoying the region's largest gains (CTPartners 2011).

12.2.2 The impact of globalisation on remuneration

The emergence of the global marketplace is having a profound impact on the traditional ways in which work is managed, as well as how employees are remunerated, which raises the issue of global pay. More and more companies are doing business internationally, which implies that they have employees in various countries, but also implies a squeeze on profits caused by intensive local and global competition (Dessler, 2009).

So far there has been a strong perception that the way in which pay is determined and delivered constitutes a well-defined marketplace that reflects a common set of values unique to each country. This perception, however, has frequently not been based on reality, since pay practices vary widely, based on a number of variables, such as industry, geographical location, company size, location of the parent company, where a company is in its growth cycle, and the degree of creativity or risk-taking a company may exhibit in dealing with local traditional pay practices and statutory requirements (Coleman, 1999).

A number of progressive multinational companies have started to view the global marketplace within the context of the company's own strategic plans and response to competition on a global scale. Rather than focus on each country individually, these organisations look at the global marketplace and seek to develop synergistic approaches that maximise the best remuneration practices and apply them to the highest degree possible in local markets. Quality of products and services, increasing market share, and sustaining a competitive edge are core goals that trigger a high level of interest in creative approaches to remuneration (Coleman, 1999; Dessler, 2009; Torrington et al, 2009).

12.2.3 The reward system

Reward management is a key element in the strategic approach to human resource management. The actual remuneration system may require adjustment to develop employee motivation, effort and performance. The total reward system is essential to effective reward management and is a significant part of the company's financial strategy (Marchington & Wilkinson, 2008).

The reward practices and reward criteria must be linked with the organisation's performance appraisal system. Weiss (2001:117) stipulates the following criteria for an effective reward system:

- Rewards should be clearly defined and consistent with other rewards for comparable work and expertise.

- Employees should be informed about what exactly they are being rewarded for (for example quality or performance or innovation).

- Rewards should differentiate between different levels of performance.

- The criteria for giving rewards should be accurately and comprehensively communicated across organisations to ensure that employees perceive the rewards to be equitably distributed.

- The organisation's rewards must be comparable to those of the company's competitors.

- Rewards must fit individual needs, be high enough to provide personal satisfaction, satisfy high performers, be related to job satisfaction, be related to performance, and fit other organisational requirements (management style, structure, and strategy).

12.2.4 Reward strategy

The **reward strategy** of an organisation informs all employees of the direction the organisation wishes to take on reward management. It also describes the types of rewards that are offered to support implementation of the organisational strategy and accomplishment of organisational goals (Luthans, 2005). The strategy provides a well-reasoned and action-based framework for developing reward policies, practices, and processes. It also differentiates the components of total rewards and is based on the needs and values of the organisation and its employees. The reward strategy ensures that the organisation is directing its reward investments appropriately to achieve the greatest impact (Armstrong, 2006; Gross & Friedman, 2007).

The **total reward framework** evolves from the organisation's reward, human resources, and organisation strategy. Effective reward strategies positively influence employee behaviours by incorporating extrinsic and intrinsic motivators. Employees receive tangible and intangible rewards in return for their performance while making a meaningful contribution to the organisation. As the organisation succeeds, so does the employee, and vice versa (Luthans, 2005).

It is important that a reward system clearly states the company's value proposition (Barnes, Blake & Pinder, 2009). A **value proposition** is an analysis and quantified review of benefits, costs and value that an organisation can deliver to customers and other constituent groups within and outside of the organisation. It is also a positioning of value, where **Value = benefits – cost** (cost includes risk). The **value proposition statements** are not communicated externally. Rather, it is the **messages** created out of the value proposition statement that are communicated externally. These can be used in a variety of ways, such as in marketing communications material or in sales proposals (Kaplan & Norton, 2004). In the context of reward and remuneration, a company value proposition is generally used to position value to prospective employees when recruiting new people or for retaining and motivating existing employees. This is also sometimes called the **employee value proposition (EVP)**. Examples of marketing messages of several well-known organisations, communicated as part of EVPs, are included in Table 12.1.

Table 12.1: Examples of marketing messages communicated as part of Employee Value Propositions

Organisation	Marketing message communicated as part of the EVP	Impact
McDonald's (Singapore)	"Every crew member can be a manager"	Empowers restaurant employees who wish to make McDonalds a long-term career, and communicates career path and longevity as employee benefits.
Kotak Mahindra Bank (India)	• **F**ocus on results • **L**eadership • **A**ctive involvement/in-clusiveness • **M**aximum challenge • **E**ntrepreneurial creativity	The EVP is called "the FLAME" and is designed to "ignite the spirit within" employees. It communicates a workplace characterised by challenge, innovation and reward.
Hewlett Packard (global)	"Stretch, Strive, Succeed"	Communicates a workplace that is inspiring and challenging, and characterised by simplicity, clear direction, and success.

12.2.5 Reward categories

WorldatWork, the largest global not-for-profit professional association dedicated to knowledge leadership in total rewards, defines total rewards as containing five core reward categories which are illustrated in the following model:

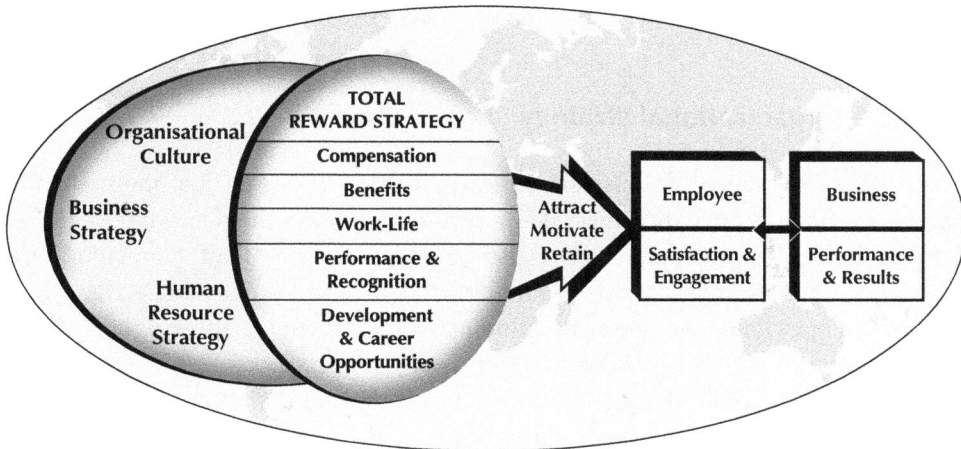

Figure 12.1: WorldatWork' s Total Rewards Model (WorldatWork, 2007:7)

Figure 12.1 not only positions the total reward strategy within the context of the business, the human resources strategy, and the organisational culture, but also illustrates the five core categories of a total reward framework, which also form part of the company employee value proposition (EVP):

- Remuneration (compensation)
- Benefits
- Work–life balance
- Performance and recognition, and
- Development and career opportunities.

Attitudes towards reward systems are changing. Employers realise today that remuneration is no longer used only as a currency in exchange for effort, time and skill. Reward programmes are increasingly used to attract, retain and motivate employees (Gross & Friedman, 2007). It has also been proved that where reward processes have been linked to key performance drivers in an organisation, employee morale, retention, engagement, and productivity have significantly improved. Furthermore, governance and compliance with organisational policies and regulatory requirements are enhanced (Luthans, 2005; Torrington et al, 2009). This confirms that although there appears to be a need for more flexible reward systems that align to employee needs, these systems should still be governed by policies, guidelines, and frameworks and should not lead to total flexibility at the expense of regulation.

12.2.6 Drivers of reward strategy

Four considerations contribute to making strategic reward and remuneration decisions. These include (1) organisational (business) strategy; (2) organisation product life cycle; (3) remuneration policy; and (4) employee reward preferences and needs.

12.2.6.1 Organisational strategy

The ultimate objective of the total reward strategy is to ensure that the company attracts and retains the right employees and that it motivates them to do those things that support the business plan, while also being legally compliant. Recognition for outstanding achievement is also an important part of the process. The **right** total reward strategy can deliver the **right** amount to the **right** people at the **right** time, for the **right** reasons (Gross & Friedman 2007).

The organisational strategy refers to the fundamental direction adopted by the organisation. The broader organisational strategy gives rise to specific questions at different levels in the organisation. At **executive management level**, the question revolves around the kind of business the organisation should be involved in. At the **functional level**, the question revolves around how the strategy should be implemented in order to achieve organisational goals. Where remuneration is concerned, the question is whether the existing reward and remuneration strategy will encourage employees to behave in a way that will lead to the achievement of organisational goals.

Organisations can choose to follow various business strategies. The strategies that are most commonly used are the innovator strategy, cost-cutter strategy, and the consumer-focused strategy. These strategies require diverse and even contrasting behaviours from employees, so the compensation strategies should vary in each case. The business that decides to have an **innovative business strategy** must develop a total reward strategy that will reward innovative behaviour and decisions. The organisation that follows the **cost-cutter approach** should focus on efficiency and emphasise productivity in the compensation of employees, while the **consumer-focused business strategy** should be supported by a compensation strategy that rewards employee behaviours that ensure customer satisfaction (Milkovich & Newman, 2009).

A reciprocal relationship exists between the business strategy and the total reward strategy. The organisational strategy informs the reward strategy, and the reward strategy enables employees to implement the business strategy by giving clear indications of the types of behaviour that will be rewarded. The **business plan** is used as a point of departure for developing the reward and remuneration strategy. This is followed by an assessment of how well the current total reward system supports the objectives of the business. Gaps and any areas that are over-funded are identified. A pay or remuneration strategy which forms the basis of the total reward strategy is then developed. The reward and remuneration philosophy is then updated accordingly and aligned with the business strategy.

12.2.6.2 Organisation product life cycle

Industry or product growth rate or life cycle stage has a significant impact on the remuneration strategy adopted. Figure 12.2 shows an example of industry maturity or product life cycle and sets out common organisational strategies that are used in each of these stages.

Common business strategies used in specific life cycle stages

Embryonic	Growth	Mature	Ageing
• Start-up • New product development	• Acquire market share • Find new markets	• Consolidate position • Find and protect market niches • Become low-cost producers	• Cost reduction • Withdraw from unprofitable market segments

Figure 12.2: Industry maturity or product life cycle

Each of these stages has a preferred remuneration strategy attached to it. Table 12.2 shows the most appropriate remuneration strategy for each stage.

Table 12.2: Common approaches to reward and remuneration in each life cycle stage

Embryonic	Growth	Mature	Ageing
• Less emphasis on salary, benefits and perks • Attention to share options and long-term incentives	• Continued emphasis on long-term incentives with increasing attention to ways in which to promote short-term results • Catch up with salary and benefits	• Most attention focused on keeping salary and perks competitive • Reduced concern for long-term incentives • Bonuses orientated to productivity improvement	• Benefits and salary are king • Very little attention given to long-term growth-orientated incentives

12.2.6.3 Remuneration policy

The remuneration policy indicates how the remuneration strategy will be implemented. It guides management decisions and should therefore be informative enough to ensure effective decision-making, but also be flexible enough to allow for individual differences in pay should this be necessary. Organisations can choose between several competitive pay policy options. The **match policy** pays employees' salaries similar to those of the competition. This approach ensures that the organisation's remuneration costs are approximately equal to that of the competition and therefore its ability to attract and retain talented employees will be similar to that of competitors.

When an organisation pays more than competitors in the market, it follows a **lead policy**. This approach allows the organisation to attract and retain talented employees, but also increases labour costs. An employer who pays below the current market rate follows a **lag policy**. This may hinder the ability to attract and retain talent, except when the low basic salary is enhanced with other forms of compensation such as share options or high-performance bonuses.

Table 12.3: Typical content of a remuneration policy

- Statement of intent and philosophy
- Employee value proposition (EVP)
- Purpose
- Application and scope
- Document control and versions
- Philosophy of guaranteed or fixed pay (GP)
- Philosophy of variable pay (VP)
- Remuneration mix
- Comparative benchmarking
- Links to performance management
- Communication and the extent of transparency allowed
- Annual remuneration reviews
- Remuneration committee scope and guidelines

The total rewards strategy and framework are integral parts of an organisation's **employee value proposition (EVP)** (CLC, 2008). When the framework is designed, the components offered by competitor organisations should be considered as well as the value that employees attach to the respective components (Harris & Clements, 2007). A sound reward framework positively influences the EVP, enhances the employer brand, and builds the organisation's reputation as an "Employer of Choice" for current and prospective employees.

Research (cited by Bussin, 2004 in Arnolds & Venter, 2007) shows that managers and employees tend to differ regarding their perceptions of a company's incentive scheme and their preferences for types of non-financial recognition rewards. In a study conducted by Arnolds and Venter (2007), frontline employees ranked paid holidays, retirement plans, cash incentives, wage increases, and job security as the highest individual motivators. On the other hand, Grigoriades and Bussin (2007) found bonus schemes to be mostly preferred by middle managers. It is recommended that organisations have the effectiveness of their incentive schemes evaluated by the people participating in the scheme (Armstrong, 2006; Grigoriades & Bussin, 2007).

12.2.7 Elements of remuneration

Once the mechanisms for determining rates of pay for jobs in an organisation have been settled, the pay or remuneration package should be constructed. As shown in Figure 12.3, the payment of an individual will be made up of fixed (or guaranteed) pay elements and variable pay elements. **Fixed or guaranteed pay elements** are those that make up the regular weekly or monthly payment to the individual, and which do not vary other than the exceptional circumstances. These include basic salary and employee benefits. **Variable pay elements** can be varied by either the employer or the employee (Torrington et al, 2009), and include short-term and long-term incentives.

12.2.7.1 Incentives

Short-term incentives (STIs) are defined as incentives that are applicable for up to one year, such as **incentive target**, **discretionary bonus**, and **profit share**, and are tied to the performance of the company, team and/or individual. The **incentive target** is a bonus that is related to the achievement typically of a financial target such as turnover or profit, as well as other objectives. The **incentive bonus** is typically a percentage of the total guaranteed package. The **discretionary bonus** is a discretionary amount that bears some relationship to the individual's performance. **Profit share** is a predetermined percentage of the organisation's profits, usually also dependent on the achievement of other objectives. **Long-term incentives (LTI)** refer to incentives that are applicable for over one year, such as a share option scheme, share grant scheme, share purchase scheme, or long-term cash incentive scheme. In pictorial format, the various forms of pay can be represented as follows:

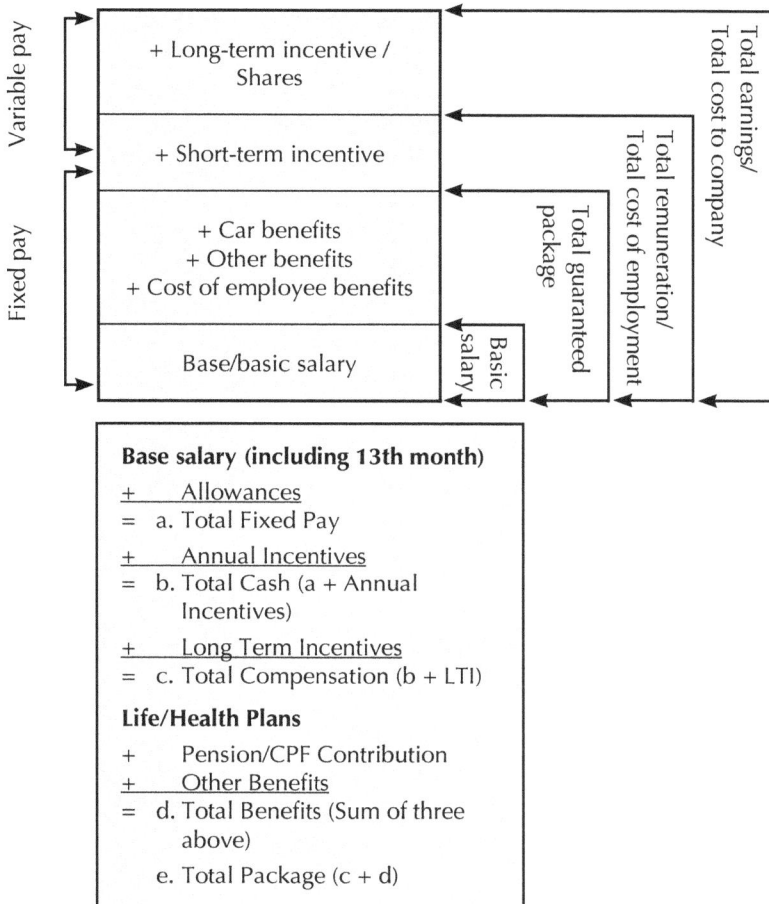

Figure 12.3: Typical elements of remuneration (option 1) and compensation (option 2)

Individual incentives reward individual performance. Sales commissions and once-off bonuses are commonly-used individual incentive methods. **Team incentives** focus on the performance of a work group or team. **Gain-sharing plans** are examples of a team incentive that are used, for example, when an employee team achieves specific goals such as reducing waste, reducing accident rates, or improving productivity. **Organisational incentive schemes** reward employees based on the performance of the entire organisation. **Profit-sharing schemes** and employee share ownership schemes are commonly-used organisational incentive schemes.

The incentive scheme should at least fit the organisational and reward strategies, reward the correct desired behaviours, and be managed effectively to ensure procedural and distributive fairness. The type of scheme implemented depends largely on what the scheme is supposed to achieve. It is a widely-held view that there is no one best type of scheme – the scheme has to be designed to drive the desired behaviours. There are vast bodies of research showing that organisations with financial incentive schemes outperform those that have none.

Most organisations implement incentive schemes to incite superior individual, team and company performance, align with shareholder thinking (agency theory), share some of the wealth created in the organisation, tie the onerous salary bill to the fortunes of the company, reward participants for a job well done, drive company strategy, and create more shareholder wealth. The best-of-breed organisations use both short-term and long-term incentives in their remuneration mix. The primary purpose of this is that it encourages the long-term viability of the company, and executives are encouraged not to harm the company for short-term gains, because they would have too much to lose in the long-term. A well-designed "total earnings" scheme should prevent this from happening (Bussin, 2002a).

The link between the performance management system and remuneration is most commonly experienced in 3 ways. The higher the performance score:

- The higher the fixed pay increase
- The greater the slice of the STI pie relative to the pool
- The greater the likelihood of receiving a larger amount of the share scheme pool and share top-ups.

12.2.7.2 Benefits

Benefits (fringe benefits) are indirect compensation that employees receive because they belong to the workforce of an organisation. These tend to be more prolific in emerging markets and in some countries the tax treatment is still favourable towards this. As shown in Table 12.4 below, these may be either cash or non-cash additions to an employee's pay and must be taken into account in calculating the total package.

Table 12.4: Examples of cash and non-cash benefits

Examples of cash benefits	Examples of non-cash benefits
• Car allowance • Entertainment allowance • Housing subsidy • Professional fees • Cellphone allowance	• Vacation leave • Sick leave • Pension/provident fund contribution • Medical contribution • Group life assurance • Accident insurance • Housing loan • Educational assistance • Travel abroad

Where trade unions are recognised, any changes to conditions of employment must be negotiated with the trade unions. Sometimes organisations are subject to regulation through bargaining councils, which means that their remuneration practices are prescribed by industry-specific needs. It is unlikely that an application for exemption regarding the total package structure can be successful.

12.3 INTERNATIONAL REMUNERATION

The remuneration of international assignees tends to be a rushed, last-minute decision. The implications often arise only after the assignee arrives in the host country, and when the assignment comes to an end, the new position in the home country, for example, pays less than the employee earned on assignment.

Few organisations spend sufficient time creating a well-designed international assignment remuneration strategy and policy, and this is a dangerous area to neglect, given the latest research, which indicates very high employee turnover at the beginning and end of international assignments.

Most large global organisations have established a clear policy for remunerating international assignees. However, it is a complex area of remuneration fraught with issues such as volatile exchange rates, weak and strong currencies, differences in cost of living between countries, and attractive and less attractive countries to work in. This is an area where clear principles and policy are required to ensure fairness, equity and retention. Hopefully this chapter will contribute to assisting in the management of international assignment remuneration.

Global, and increasingly regional, organisations understand the value placed and received from best practice international assignment remuneration, along with the role of human capital in an organisation's success. International assignment remuneration is no longer allocated to a human resources administrator, but is becoming a critical element in a total reward (TR) system and in reinforcing employees' commitment to organisation objectives.

12.3.1 Types of international employment

The question of what constitutes an international assignment is one of the first issues to be established. Based on the length of stay outside the usual country of employment and the effect on the employee's tax position, five common types of international employment are distinguished.

12.3.1.1 Business trip

A business trip is classified as such if it has the following characteristics:

- From one day to 30 days in one location
- Unaccompanied by family

- No change in tax position.

12.3.1.2 Project assignment

A project assignment has the following characteristics:
- From 30 days to six months in one location
- Unaccompanied by family
- Normally, no change in tax position.

12.3.1.3 Fly-in, fly-out assignment

A fly-in, fly-out assignment has the following characteristics:
- Pattern of employment in a foreign location with regular home
- Unaccompanied by family
- Change in tax position.

12.3.1.4 International assignment

An international assignment has the following characteristics:
- Between six months and three years in a foreign location
- Accompanied by family
- Change in tax position.

12.3.1.5 Permanent transfer

A permanent transfer is classified as such if it has the following characteristics:
- Indefinite international change in place of work
- Accompanied by family
- Change in tax position.

The focus of this chapter is international assignments. Employees sent on international assignments are referred to as international assignees or expatriates.

Today's competitive global business climate means that employees increasingly have to work in various countries and return to the home base. Business leaders have to understand and use all of the tools available to ensure success. An effective, equitable approach to internal assignment remuneration is one of these powerful tools.

12.3.2 Definitions and underlying philosophy

A common reason for difficulty in understanding the value of an international assignment remuneration policy is the lack of consistent definitions of each element of international assignment remuneration and the underlying philosophy. The following definitions are all key elements of an international assignment policy.

12.3.2.1 Home base salary

This is the salary the assignee is normally paid in his or her home country. It is consistent with the home-country market and the home-organisation pay scales.

12.3.2.2 Home net salary

This is the home base salary less hypothetical tax (the tax that the assignee would have paid in the home country).

12.3.2.3 Cost-of-living index (COL)

This is a figure that represents the difference in the cost of living between the two countries involved in an assignment (home country and host country). For example, the COL for an assignee sent to France from Africa may be 16. This information is based on the difference in the price of a similar basket of goods, and reflects that France would be 16 times more expensive than Africa. COL indices can be bought from consultants who specialise in the various areas.

12.3.2.4 Exchange rate

This is the currency exchange rate between the two countries involved in the assignment (home country and host country). The exchange rate is normally set at the beginning of the assignment and reviewed annually or when there is a change in the rate which is greater than 10 percent.

12.3.2.5 International Premium Index

This is a figure that represents the difference between the two countries involved in the assignment (home country and host country) in terms of factors such as economic system, political system, religion, standard of living, security, and climate. The exchange rate is normally set for the duration of the assignment and reviewed only if a major change occurs (for example, the host country may develop a serious economic or political crisis).

12.3.2.6 Employee currency election

The International Premium Index (IPI) is the percentage of the total assignment remuneration package which the employee elects to have paid in the host country and the home country.

Any discussion of an organisation's international assignment remuneration policy must take cognisance of the following underlying philosophies in the aims, which are to:

- Provide consistent equitable treatment for all international assignees, worldwide.
- Protect purchasing power against changed spending patterns.
- Recognise job size globally.
- Provide "reasonable gain".
- Offer flexibility within limits and where tax effective.
- Be competitive.
- Address spouse support issues.
- Save a simple structure to provide seamless coverage for different scenarios.

12.3.3 Approaches to international assignment remuneration

The application of the above philosophies has resulted in the emergence of three broad approaches to international assignment remuneration. These are the following:

- **Build-up method:** This method uses the home base salary as a base salary, minus hypothetical tax, and builds on this by adding an international premium, a cost-of-living index, and the exchange rate to deliver a net assignment package. The build-up method is used to maintain internal equity and to equalise the impact of host country tax.

- **Local market approach:** This approach uses the principle of applying the better of build-up or local market. It is used where a strong local market exists in the host country, and where the build-up method delivers less than the local market remuneration levels (for example, an assignee sent to a major first world country such as the United Kingdom or United States).

- **Internationally-mobile expatriate:** This approach is used by large global multinational organisations, which often have a large pool of permanent expatriates who move from one country to the next on assignments. The internally-mobile expatriate approach is used to put all expatriates on an equal footing, regardless of nationality.

12.3.4 Positioning international assignment remuneration in the total reward system

The following figure shows a typical positioning of the build-up method:

```
                    ┌─────────────────────────┐
                    │   Business objectives    │
                    └─────────────────────────┘
                                 │
                    ┌─────────────────────────┐
                    │      Total reward        │
                    └─────────────────────────┘
                                 │
      ○             ┌─────────────────────────┐
                    │   Home-based salary      │
                    │        750 000           │
                    └─────────────────────────┘
                                 │
      ○             ┌─────────────────────────┐
                    │  Less hypothetical tax   │
                    │       − 306 181          │
                    └─────────────────────────┘
                                 │
      ○             ┌─────────────────────────┐
                    │     Home net salary      │
                    │        443 819           │
                    └─────────────────────────┘
```

Essential spending (40%) 177 528	Home net balance (60%) 266 291
x Cost of living index 71 200	International premium (30%) 225 000
x Exchange rate 146	
= Host currency 1 845 439	= Home currency element 491 291

Host currency: Supa-Nova Peso   **Home currency: Rands**

TOTAL: 750 482

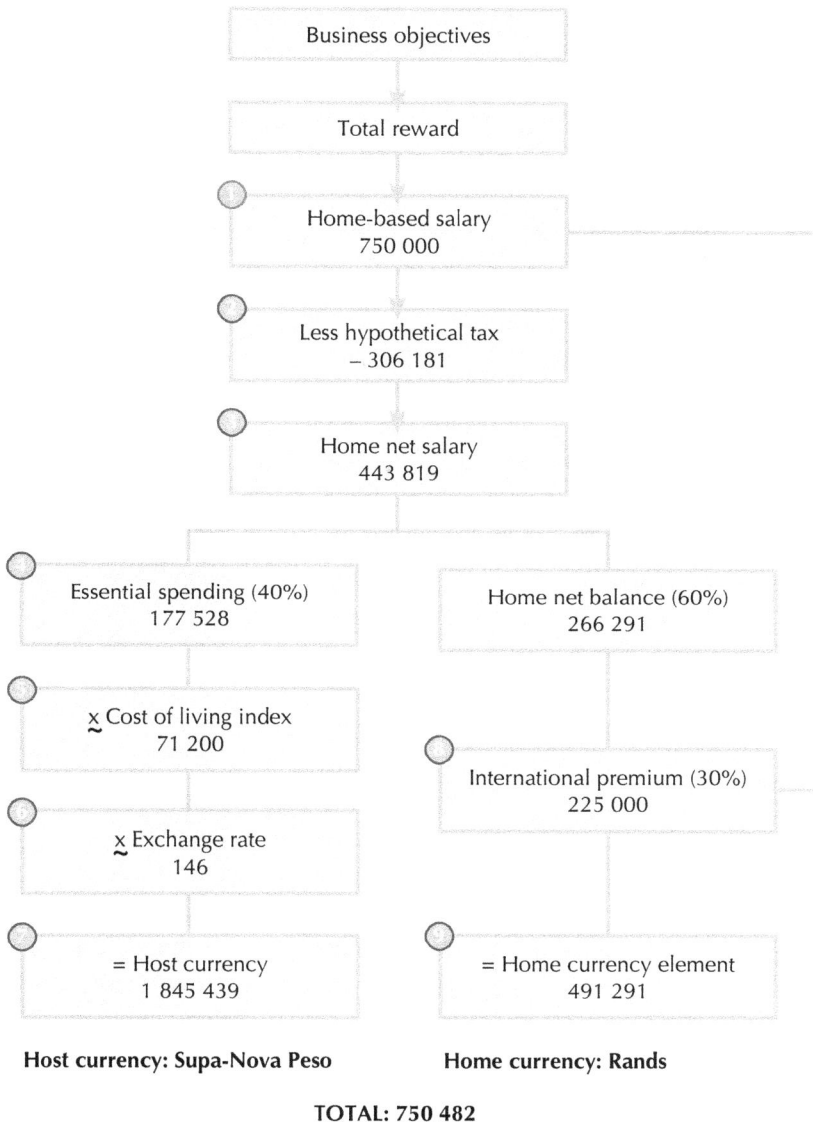

Figure 12.4: Build-up method

12.3.4.1 Design considerations

The approach to expatriate remuneration differs from one organisation to another, and within a single organisation, depends on a number of factors such as:

- Length of assignment
- Host country
- Level of assignee.

Designing an international assignment, remuneration policy should include the organisation's position on each of the elements reflected in Table 12.5. Typical applications of each element are shown for each of the three broad approaches:

Table 12.5: Comparison of approaches for international assignments (Bussin, 2011)

Remuneration	Build-up method (BM)	Local market approach (LMA)	Internationally mobile expatriate (IME)
Purpose	Used to maintain internal equity and equalise impact of host country tax. Used by approximately 70% of organisations.	Used where a local market exists and where the build-up method delivers less than local market remuneration levels. Used by approximately 20% of organisations, most often for First World assignees, for example, to Western Europe and the United States of America.	Used to put all group expatriates on an equal footing regardless of nationality. Employees resign from home country and relocate to group organisation usually in tax-free country. Used by fewer than 10% of organisations, usually only by large global groups with large numbers of assignees.
Market relationship	Home base salary in home country is market related. Typically basic plus cost of all benefits except car benefit (where car is provided in host country).	Host country market determines level of remuneration.	International base salary typically in US$. Benefits funded from group organisation in tax-free home country.

Remuneration	Build-up method (BM)	Local market approach (LMA)	Internationally mobile expatriate (IME)
Tax philosophy	Assignees neither lose nor gain as a result of tax treatment in host country.	Taxed in host country.Net pay depends on tax laws and structure of package.	Taxed in host country, taking advantage of tax-free home country status.
Hypothetical tax	Generic model used to calculate home net salary.	N/A.	Generic model used to calculate home net salary.
Home net salary	Result of home base salary less hypothetical tax.	N/A.	Result of home base salary less hypothetical tax.
Cost of living (COL)	COL is used to neutralise the effects of COL differences between the home and host country. Applied to essential spending only (typically 40% of home net salary).	N/A.	COL is used to neutralise the effects of COL differences between the home and host country. Applied to essential spending only (typically 40% of home net salary).
Exchange rate	**COL is linked to exchange rate.** COL exchange rate used to deliver local amount of assignment salary.	Paid in local currency or US$ if allowed.	Paid in local currency or US$ if allowed. **COL is linked to exchange rate.** COL exchange rate used to deliver local amount of assignment salary.

Remuneration	Build-up method (BM)	Local market approach (LMA)	Internationally mobile expatriate (IME)
International premium	Reflects amount of premium needed to compensate for assignee living conditions.	N/A.	Reflects amount of premium needed to compensate for assignee living conditions.
Car benefit	Excluded from assignment salary calculation and provided in host country in line with local host policy where appropriate.	In line with host country policy.	Excluded from assignment salary calculation and provided in host country in line with local host policy where appropriate.
Housing	Housing typically provided in host country, often furnished, and includes utilities, water, lights, and housekeeper, depending on host country policy. No involvement by organisation in home country housing arrangement, but caution against selling.	Housing typically provided in host country, often furnished, and includes utilities, water, lights, and housekeeper, depending on host country policy. No involvement by organisation in home country housing arrangement, but caution against selling.	Housing typically provided in host country, often furnished, and includes utilities, water, lights, and housekeeper, depending on host country policy. No involvement by organisation in home country housing arrangement, but caution against selling.

Remuneration	Build-up method (BM)	Local market approach (LMA)	Internationally mobile expatriate (IME)
Assignment salary quotation	Two elements: (1) Local spendable (host currency); (2) Home base element (home currency).	Local host country currency only. Can remit an elected amount back to home country.	Two elements: (1) Local spendable (host currency); (2) Home base element (home currency).
Employee currency election	Assignee elects once a year a mix of specific amounts in host and home.	Assignee elects once a year a mix of how much in host and home.	Assignee elects once a year a mix of specific amounts in host and home.
Variable incentive bonus	Remain on home country scheme **based on home base**, but in line with host country and individual performance. Variable pay is designed to ensure that TR is competitive within home country.	Participate in host country scheme. **Based on host base** in line with host country and individual performance. Variable pay is designed to ensure that TR is competitive within host country.	Remain on home country scheme **based on home base**, but in line with host country and individual performance. Variable pay is designed to ensure that TR is competitive within home country/ international market.

Remuneration	Build-up method (BM)	Local market approach (LMA)	Internationally mobile expatriate (IME)
Retirement benefits (Overall approximately 80% of assignees remain on home country retirement plans)	**Remain on home country retirement scheme.** Basis of retirement funding is home base as assignee is expected to return and retire in home country. The most typical rate for approximately 67% of organisations is: Employer 15%, Employee 0% of home base salary.	**Remain on home country retirement scheme**, where possible. Basis of retirement funding is home base as assignee is expected to return and retire in home country. If the assignee converts to local by resigning from the home organisation, retirement funding reverts to the host country.	**Remain on home country retirement scheme.** Basis of retirement funding is home base (US$) as assignee is expected to return and retire in home country.
Medical benefits	**Half of organisations allow assignees to remain on home country medical scheme, and half provide offshore medical cover** The majority of organisations provide assignees with emergency evacuation cover.	Medical cover and benefits are provided locally in line with host country policy. The majority of organisations provide assignees with emergency evacuation cover.	**Half of organisations allow assignees to remain on home country medical scheme, and half provide offshore medical cover** The majority of organisations provide assignees with emergency evacuation cover.

Remuneration	Build-up method (BM)	Local market approach (LMA)	Internationally mobile expatriate (IME)
Guaranteed 13th cheque	A 13th cheque is paid if it is part of the home salary structure policy. If paid, it is paid based on the gross home country base salary. Less than 10% of organisations pay a guaranteed 13th cheque. In the majority of cases 13th cheques are built into the build-up model and incorporated in the total package so as to simplify administration.	A 13th cheque is paid if it is part of the host salary structure policy. If paid it is paid based on the gross host country base salary.	A 13th cheque is paid if it is part of the home salary structure policy. If paid it is paid based on the gross home country base salary. Less than 3% of organisations pay a guaranteed 13th cheque for IMEs.
Disturbance allowance	Outward disturbance allowance of one month's net home base salary. Return disturbance allowance of one month's net home base salary.	Outward disturbance allowance of one month's net home base salary. Return disturbance allowance of one month's net home base salary.	Outward disturbance allowance of one month's net home base salary. Return disturbance allowance of one month's net home base salary.

Remuneration	Build-up method (BM)	Local market approach (LMA)	Internationally mobile expatriate (IME)
Relocation allowance (Approximately 80% of organisations pay for the storage costs of household effects that the assignee does not take to the host country)	Relocation is generally paid for household effects and personal items, but only half of organisations pay for the removal of luxury/general items.	Relocation is generally paid for household effects and personal items, but only half of organisations pay for the removal of luxury/general items.	Relocation is generally paid for household effects and personal items, but only half of organisations pay for the removal of luxury/general items.
Education policy	Provide appropriate education support for assignees' children, in order to minimise the disruption to their education caused by an international assignment.	Local education policy applies.	Provide appropriate education support for assignees' children, in order to minimise the disruption to their education caused by an international assignment.
Partner support policy	No attempt to compensate for loss of income of spouse. May provide partner support e.g. budget to study or find a new job.	N/A.	No attempt to compensate for loss of income of spouse. May provide partner support e.g. budget to study or find a new job.

Remuneration	Build-up method (BM)	Local market approach (LMA)	Internationally mobile expatriate (IME)
Flights	Two flights per year for unaccompanied assignees.	Two flights per year for unaccompanied assignees.	Two flights per year for unaccompanied assignees.
	One flight per year for accompanied assignees.	One flight per year for accompanied assignees.	One flight per year for accompanied assignees.
	Additional flights are provided on compassionate grounds, typically on the death of a family member or next of kin.	Additional flights are provided on compassionate grounds, typically on the death of a family member or next of kin.	Additional flights are provided on compassionate grounds, typically on the death of a family member or next of kin.

Bussin (2011)

Rigorous and careful benchmarking is often required in advance as the "expat community" is sometimes small, and very often detailed notes are exchanged.

12.3.4.2 Critical success factors

As important as international assignment remuneration is to an organisation, management often continue to undervalue the impact it has on assignees' morale, motivation and financial performance. The critical success factors to good international assignment package design involve the following:

- Include current and former assignees in the design process.
- Make use of research information and current best practice.
- Make use of tax experts regarding tax in both host and home countries (reciprocal tax agreements make this essential).
- Research shows that three- to five-year assignments provide optimum ROI.
- Candidates' soft-skill abilities (EQ) should be assessed before the candidates are assigned.

- Typically utilise international assignments as developmental opportunities for high-potential employees.

- Companies should invest time and effort in managing employee and spouse expectations.

- Companies should track employee career development over 10 to 15-year horizons.

- Most international companies use home country base salary to calculate the international assignment package.

- Increasingly, companies try to outsource the international assignment administration function.

- Companies should double their repatriation efforts, as many assignees stay longer than required on high levels of assignment remuneration.

12.4 BENCHMARK FINDINGS, AND LESSONS LEARNT

When doing the research on best-of-breed schemes, one often comes across the following as typical benchmark findings. This could serve as a lessons-learnt checklist for your scheme design:

- Companies generally assist with tax compliance.

- Companies strive to put international assignee on equal footing with that at home.

- Most companies use external consultants for overall design, COL and parity.

- Half the companies allow the international assignees to complete "location ranking questionnaires" (typically 16 to 20 factors).

- Conversion to local conditions ranges from immediate to three years.

- The parent organisation is still responsible for the international assignee's career.

- Equity is managed by home base and job.

Other important design considerations include:

- Soft issues such as the spouse's loss of employment, repatriation, and re-skilling

- Volatile currency such as the and against the major currencies in the past

- Selling houses in the home country at a loss

- Provision of a car benefit in the host country

- COL index, particularly in high-inflation countries.

12.4.1 Current issues

Any international assignment remuneration policy must always take into account the fact that there are a greater number of dynamics involved with expatriate pay than with that of local employees. Many issues are still being grappled with by organisations who have been managing international assignees for many years. Some of the current issues being debated are the following:

- Hard-currency trend is on the decline (used only in highly unstable markets).

- Assignees from low cost-of-living/low-paying countries will always tend to earn less than assignees doing the same job in a host country and who come from higher cost-of-living/higher-paying countries, using the build-up model.

A few solutions to "trailing spouse" issues are the following:

- Help the spouse to find a job.

- Assist with the choice of a career by:
  - Preparing a résumé
  - Obtaining a work permit
  - Organising career counselling
  - Reimbursing for tuition.

In addition, the following continue to cause problems:

- There is a significant trend towards a dual or hybrid approach to compensate compensation.

- Home needs (to cover country commitment and incentive allowances, and fixed currency in home country) are often overlooked or neglected.

- Host needs (to cover local day-to-day living costs and fixed currency in local situation) are not adequately compensated for.

- Expatriate remuneration continues to be in a state of flux in response to the changing world in which we work.

The statistics of expatriates returning home and leaving the organisation within a few years is high. Organisations often do not take the time to focus on a repatriation programme. It is assumed that because the person used to live here, "he (or she) will be fine". Suggestions to ensure a smoother repatriation and secure longer tenure include the following:

- Ensure that the person reintegrates into a real job of equal or higher complexity and status than was the situation when the person left.

- Ensure that the spouse and family are thoughtfully integrated back into the community.

- Avoid saying anything such as: "Things here are different now. Where have you been?"

- Be open to new thoughts and ideas the person may have learnt while away.

- Induction back into the organisation, focusing on what has changed, new strategies, and new focus areas, is of the utmost importance.

Many methods of paying expatriates exist, and this issue is a huge debate within remuneration committees. Whether to pay them in home base pay or host-based pay must be decided on. A combination is often best. How to pay them often depends on their job, status and personal commitments. As a rule of thumb, expatriates should be neither better nor worse off.

To this end, the next chapter covers cost-of-living calculations and what needs to be considered in the formula to calculation whether the expatriate is indeed in the same position and not worse off.

12.5 REFERENCES

Aamodt, MG. 2007. *Industrial/organisational psychology: An applied approach*. Belmont, CA: Wadsworth, a part of Cengage Learning.

Appelbaum, SH, Roy, M & Gilliland, T. 2011. Globalization of performance appraisals: Theory and applications. *Management Decision*, 49(4):570–585.

Armstrong, M. 1995. *A handbook of personnel management practice*. 5th ed. London: Kogan Page Publishers.

Armstrong, M. 2006. *A handbook of human resource management practice*. 10th ed. Cambridge, United Kingdom: Cambridge University Press.

Armstrong, M & Baron, A. 2003. *Performance management: The new realities*. London: Chartered Institute of Personnel and Development.

Armstrong, M & Murlis, H. 1994. *Reward management. A handbook of remuneration strategy and practice*. 3rd ed. London: Kogan Page Publishers.

Arnolds, CA & Venter, DJL. 2007. The strategic importance of motivational rewards for lower-level employees in the manufacturing and retailing industries. *SA Journal of Industrial Psychology*, 33(3):15–23.

Barnes, C, Blake, H & Pinder, D. 2009. *Creating and delivering your value proposition: Managing customer experience for profit*. London: Kogan Page Publishers.

Braddick, CA, Jones, MB & Shafer, PM. 1992. A look at broad banding in practice. *Journal of Compensation and Benefits*, 27:28–32.

Briscoe, DR & Claus, M. 2008. Employee performance management: Policies and practices in multinational enterprises.In A Varma, PS Budhwar & A DeNisi (eds). 2008. *Performance management systems: Global perspective*. London: Routledge. [15–39]

Bussin, M. 1993. Broad banding, multi-skilling, skill based pay: Any connection? *Human Resource Management*, 9:26–27.

Bussin, M. 2002a. *Choosing the right incentive scheme – guide 9*. The Nuts & Bolts Business Series – Remuneration Series. Johannesburg: Knowledge Resources.

Bussin, M. 2002b. *Retention strategies – guide 10*. The Nuts & Bolts Business Series – Remuneration Series. Johannesburg: Knowledge Resources.

Bussin, M. 2004. *Total remuneration strategy*. Paper presented on 27 February. [Online]. Available: http://www.sara.co.za/library/eventdocuments/eventdocuments2004/. [Accessed 23 April 2005].

Bussin, M. 2010. *The remuneration handbook for Africa*. Johannesburg: Knowledge Resources.

Bussin, M & Botha, J. 2010. Performance evaluation. In M Coetzee & D Schreuder (eds). 2010. *Personnel Psychology*. Cape Town: Oxford University Press. [328–367]

Cascio, WF. 2006. Global performance management system. In GK Stahl & I Bjorkman (eds). 2006. *Handbook of research in international human resource management*. Cheltenham: Edward Elgar.

Chiang, F. 2005. A critical examination of Hofstede's thesis and its application to international reward management. *International Journal of Human Resource Management*, 16(9):1545–1563.

Chingos, PT & Marwick, KP. 1997. *Paying for performance – a guide to compensation management*. New York, NY: John Wiley & Sons, Inc.

Coleman, NK. 1999. Global pay and results. In H Risher (ed). 1999. *Aligning pay and results: Compensation strategies that work from the boardroom to the shop floor*. New York, NY: AMACOM Books. [259–273]

Corporate Leadership Council (CLC). 2008. *CLC quarterly report on HR news and trends*. [Online]. Available: http://www.clc.executiveboard.com. [Accessed 16 June 2008].

Costello, SJ. 1994. *Effective performance management* . The Business Skill Express Series. New York, NY: McGraw-Hill.

CTPartners. 2011. Dynamic markets trend talk. [Online]. Available: http://www.ctnet.com/uploadedFiles/The_Firm/Trend_Talks/Dynamic%20Markets%20TrendTalk_Global_2011.pdf. [Accessed 26 May 2014].

Dessler, G. 2009. *Fundamentals of human resource management*. London: Pearson Education.

Du, J & Nam Choi, J 2010. Pay for performance in dynamic markets: Insights from China. *Journal of International Business Studies*, 41:671–689.

Economic Research Institute (ERI). 2004. ERI White Paper. [Online]. Available: http://www.erieri.com/. [Accessed 16 December 2011].

Engle, AD & Dowling, P. 2007. State of origin: Research in global performance management – progress or a lost horizon? Conference proceedings of the VIIIth World Congress of the International Federation of Scholarly Associations of Management (IFSAM). Berlin: Germany.

Evans P, Pucik, V & Barsoux, JL. 2002. *The global challenge: Frameworks for international human resource management*. Boston, MA: McGraw-Hill.

Gilman, NP. 2009. *Methods of industrial remuneration*. Charleston, SC: BiblioLife LLC.

Grigoriades, CA & Bussin, M. 2007. Current practice with regard to short-term incentive schemes for middle managers. *South African Journal of Human Resource Management*, 5(1):45–53.

Gross, SE & Friedman, HE. 2007. Creating an effective total rewards strategy: Holistic approach better supports business success. *Mercer Human Resources Consulting CD – Your Guide to the Age of Talent*. United States: Mercer.

Grote, D. 2002. *The performance appraisal question and answer book: A survival guide for managers*. New York: American Management Association.

Guthrie, J. 2007. Remuneration pay effects and work. In P Boxall, J Purcell & P Wright (eds). 2007. *The Oxford handbook of human resource management*. Oxford, Oxon: Oxford University Press.

Harris, S & Clements, L. 2007. What's the perceived value of your incentives? *The Magazine of World at Work: Workspan*, 2:21–25. Scottsdale, United States: WorldatWork Press.

Hellqvist, N. 2011. Global performance management: A research agenda. *Management Research Review*, 34(8):927–946.

Kanin-Lovers, J & Cameron, M. 1994. Broad banding: A step forward or a step backward? *Journal of Compensation and Benefits*, 9:39–42.

Kaplan, RS & Norton, DP. 2004. *Strategy maps*. Boston, MA: Harvard Business School Press.

Latham, GP & Russo, SD. 2008. The influence of organisational politics on performance appraisal. In S Cartwright & CL Cooper (eds). 2008. *The Oxford handbook of personnel psychology*. Oxford, Oxon: Oxford University Press. [380–410]

Latham, GP, Almost, J, Mann, S & Moore, C. 2005. New developments in performance management. *Organisational Dynamics*, 34(1):77–87.

Lawler, EE. 2000. *Rewarding excellence: Pay strategies for the new economy*. San Francisco, CA: Jossey-Bass.

Leonard, B. 1994. New ways to pay employees. *Human Resource Magazine*, 39:61–62.

Luthans, F. 2005. *Organisational behaviour*. New York, NY: McGraw-Hill.

Marchington, M & Wilkinson, A. 2008. *Human resource management at work: People management and development*. London: CIPD.

Mathis, RL & Jackson, JH. 2004. *Human resources management*. 10th ed. Mason, OH: Thomson South-Western College Publishing.

Milkovich, G & Newman, J. 2009. *Compensation*. 9th ed. Boston, MA: Irwin McGraw-Hill.

Milliman J, Taylor, S & Czaplewski, AJ. 2002. Cross-cultural performance feedback in multinational enterprises: Opportunity for organisational learning. *Human Resource Planning*, 25.

Nelson, B & Sptizer, DR. 2003. *The 1001 Rewards & Recognition Fieldbook: the Complete Guide*. New York: Workman Publishing Company.

Neubauer, RJ. 1995. Broad banding: Management Fad or Saviour? *Compensation and Benefits Management* 11:50–54.

Nixon, A. 2011. Adapted from *A Handbook for Measuring Employee Performance*. Office of Personnel Management, US Government. [Online]. Available: Retrieved from: http://spectrain.wordpress.com/tag/cross-cultural/. [Accessed 11 February 2014].

Odendaal, A. 2009. Motivation: From concepts to applications. In SP Robbins, TA Judges, A Odendaal & G Roodt (eds). 2009. *Organisational behaviour: Global and South African perspectives*. Cape Town: Prentice-Hall. [168–191]

Peterson, S & Luthans, F. 2006. The impact of financial and nonfinancial incentives on business unit outcomes over time. *Journal of Applied Psychology*, 91(1):156–165.

Porter, C, Bingham, C & Simmonds, D. 2008. *Exploring human resource management*. New York, NY: McGraw-Hill.

Price, A. 2004. *Human resource management in a business context*. London: Thomson Learning.

Riggio, RE. 2009. *Introduction to industrial/organisational psychology*. London: Pearson Education.

Rubino, J. 2006. *Principles of powerful Living*. Mumbai: Jaico Book House.

Schneier, CD, Beatty, RW & Baird, LS. 1987. How to construct a successful performance appraisal system. In CD Schneier, RW Beatty & LS Baird (eds). 1987. *The performance management sourcebook*. Amherst, MA: Human Resources Development Press.

Schreuder, AMG & Coetzee, M. 2006. *Careers: An organisational perspective*. Cape Town: Juta & Co Ltd.

Schuler, RS & Huber, VL. 1993. *Personnel and human resource management*. 5th ed. St Paul: West.

Schultz, D & Schultz, SE. 2010. *Psychology and work today*. 10th ed. Cape Town: Pearson Education.

Sherman Garr, S. 2011. *Retaining talent in dynamic markets*. [Online]. Available: http://talentmgt. com/articles/view/retaining-talent-in-dynamic-markets. [Accessed 24 June 2014].

Shore, T & Strauss, J. 2008. The political context of employee appraisal: Effects of organisational goals on performance ratings. *International Journal of Management*, 25(3):599–612.

Torrington, D, Hall, L, Taylor, S & Atkinson, C. 2009. *Fundamentals of human resource management*. London: Pearson Education.

Vosloo, SE. 2005. Compensation. In PM Muchinsky, HJ Kriek & AMG Schreuder (eds). 2005. *Personnel Psychology*. Cape Town: Oxford University Press. [263–295]

Weiss, JW. 2001. *Organisational behaviour and change: Managing diversity, cross-cultural dynamics, and ethics*. Mason, OH: South-Western College Publishing.

WorldatWork. 2007. *The world at work handbook of compensation, benefits & total rewards*. Hoboken, NJ: John Wiley & Sons, Inc.

CHAPTER 13
COST-OF-LIVING DATA, EXPATULATOR AND CALCULATIONS
Steven McManus

13.1 INTRODUCTION

The cost of living is defined as "the monetary cost of maintaining a particular standard of living, usually measured by calculating the average cost of a number of specific goods and services required by a particular group. The goods and services used as indexes may be the minimum necessary to preserve health or may be what is considered average for a given income group, depending on the purposes of the index" (Encyclopaedia Britannica, 2014).

In the context of expatriate compensation, we are concerned with the monetary cost of maintaining an expatriate standard of living between two geographical locations, generally referred to as the home and host locations.

The minimum expectation of an expatriate compensation programme is to protect the purchasing power of an expatriate's salary, irrespective of global location. To do this, two key inputs are required. Firstly, consistent, up-to-date cost-of-living data for each geographical location are required. Secondly, a consistent approach to calculating expatriate compensation using the cost-of-living data is required.

13.2 COST-OF-LIVING DATA

Exchange rates are volatile as they are based on short-term factors and are subject to substantial distortions from speculative movements and government interventions. In the short term, exchange rates, even when averaged over a period of time such as a year, are not a good measure of the comparative value of a salary in relation to its comparative international purchasing power. In the short to medium term at least, apparent changes in the comparative level of remuneration between one country and another may be principally a function of changes in the exchange rate.

The cost of living for an expatriate is different from that for a local resident. It has an impact on not only their home spending but also their host country spending, and the exchange rate.

Personal spending obligations back home (for example, savings, mortgage, private/personal retirement/investment funding, private healthcare, and so on) together with home statutory obligations have an impact not only on the amount of host spending expatriates have at their disposal, but also what they need to spend it on.

Spending patterns have an impact on expatriate salary calculations as a result of cost-of-living differences and availability of goods and services, as well as the degree to which the expatriate (and his/her family) adapt to local culture and lifestyle. In most places, local goods and services are much cheaper than imported products.

13.2.1 Cost-of-Living Indexes

Cost-of-living differences are most often reported in the form of cost-of-living indexes. A cost-of-living index is an overall number which takes into account the prices for a defined set of different goods and services. When you travel to another country, you will notice that price differences are not the same for all goods and services. In Hong Kong, for example, groceries, particularly at the markets, are relatively cheap, but accommodation is relatively expensive because of limited space and high demand. An expatriate provided with accommodation in Hong Kong will experience an overall lower cost-of-living difference compared to an expatriate who must rent his/her own accommodation. The cost-of-living difference is therefore dependent on the expatriate's spending pattern.

A cost-of-living index (COLI) is a price index that measures the relative cost of living over time. It measures differences in the price of goods and services. COLI measures change over time in the amount that consumers need to spend to reach a certain level or standard of living. The COLI is typically a number, whereas the Base Index is 100.

A Consumer Price Index (CPI), on the other hand, is a measure of the average change over time in the prices paid by consumers. CPI is typically a percentage change compared to the previous period. An increase in CPI is called inflation, while a decrease is called deflation. Both the COLI and the CPI use a market "basket" of consumer goods and services.

A COLI is also used to measure the price of the same quantities and types of goods and services in different geographic locations. The COLI used in this way shows the difference in living costs between different locations. CPI, on the other hand, typically measures changes in the cost of living in one geographic location, over a defined period of time.

An international COLI measures the differences in the local currency price of the same quantities and types of goods and services in different countries converted to a single currency. This shows the difference in relative living costs between international cities. The cost-of-living difference between locations indicates the difference in the amount of money that consumers need to spend to maintain a certain level or standard of living.

A simple but popular COLI that illustrates this concept is the well-known "Big Mac Index", which comprises the local price of a Big Mac burger converted into US dollars, the assumption being that the higher the US dollar price, the higher the cost of living is, and vice versa. However, not all aspects of cost of living are factored into the price of a Big Mac. The cost of housing, education, and medical care, for example, are unrelated to the cost of a Big Mac.

Among other uses, COLIs are used by organisations and individuals in the calculation of expatriate salary and cost-of-living allowances in order to ensure consistent salary purchasing power between the home and host country.

Next we will discuss how to calculate a COLI between two locations applicable to expatriate employees.

13.2.2 Cost-of-living "baskets"

For consistency, hundreds of different goods and services are grouped into similar or related groups called "baskets".

For accuracy, the exact quantity and type of each of the goods and services within each basket are defined. Using these definitions, the prices of the same quantities and types of goods and services in each geographic location are obtained from at least three different suppliers representative of those that would typically be used by expatriates.

When calculating the cost of living between two locations, the difference in the aggregate cost of all the selected basket groups are examined in each location using the average reported price in each location for the same quantity of each item. The 13 basket groups do not count equally. They are weighted according to expatriate expenditure norms.

Each basket has a different weighting representing the portion of an expatriate's income spent on each basket. As an example, most people would spend more on household-related costs such as rent, water and electricity than they would on clothing each month. Basket weighting therefore represents the average percentage of income spent by a typical expatriate anywhere in the world. This may well differ from one individual to the next, from one income level to the next, and from one culture to the next. The weighted percentages represent a standardised global norm in order to be able to compare like for like around the world. The following basket weights are used for a typical full set of baskets (Xpatulator.com, 2014):

- Alcohol and tobacco 2.0%
- Clothing 2.5%
- Communication 2.0%
- Education 5.0%
- Furniture and appliances 5.0%
- Groceries 16.5%

- Healthcare 5.0%
- Household 30.0%
- Miscellaneous 3.0%
- Personal care 3.0%
- Recreation and culture 6.0%
- Restaurants, meals out, and hotels 2.0%
- Transport 18.0%

13.2.3 Cost-of-living data collection

Within each basket, the cost-of-living data are based on the cost of the same defined products and services for each geographical location. The raw price data can be gathered by expatriates based in each location, by locally employed agents, or by research analysts who survey comparable items that are available internationally. A minimum of three prices for the same brand/size/volume of product is usually used to determine the average price for each item in each location. The items are priced on a quarterly basis, as prices do not tend change monthly, and tend to rise and fall with inflation for local products and services and by the amount of change in the exchange rate for imported products.

As an example, the different basket groups may be comprised as follows (Xpatulator.com, 2014):

- Alcohol and tobacco: Alcoholic beverages and tobacco products
  - Alcohol at bar
  - Beer
  - Cigarettes
  - Locally-produced spirit
  - Whisky
  - Wine.

- Clothing: Clothing and footwear products
  - Business suits
  - Casual clothing
  - Children's clothing and footwear
  - Coats and hats
  - Evening wear
  - Shoe repairs
  - Underwear.

- Communication
  - Home telephone rental and call charges

- – Internet connection and service provider fees
- – Mobile/Cellular phone contract and calls.

- Education
  - – Crèche/Pre-school fees
  - – High school/College fees
  - – Primary school fees
  - – Tertiary study fees.

- Furniture and appliances: Furniture, household equipment and household appliances
  - – DVD player
  - – Fridge–freezer
  - – Iron
  - – Kettle, toaster, microwave
  - – Light bulbs
  - – Television
  - – Vacuum cleaner
  - – Washing machine.

- Groceries: Food, non-alcoholic beverages and cleaning material
  - – Baby consumables
  - – Baked goods
  - – Baking
  - – Canned foods
  - – Cheese
  - – Cleaning products
  - – Dairy
  - – Fresh fruits
  - – Fresh vegetables
  - – Fruit juices
  - – Frozen [foods]
  - – Meat
  - – Oil and vinegars
  - – Pet food
  - – Pre-prepared meals
  - – Sauces
  - – Seafood
  - – Snacks
  - – Soft drinks
  - – Spices and herbs.

- Healthcare: General healthcare, medical and medical insurance
  - General practitioner consultation rates
  - Hospital private ward daily rate
  - Non-prescription medicine
  - Private medical insurance/Medical aid contributions.

- Household: Housing, water, electricity, household gas, household fuels, local rates and residential taxes
  - House/Flat mortgage
  - House/Flat rental
  - Household electricity consumption
  - Household gas/Fuel consumption
  - Household water consumption
  - Local property rates/Taxes/Levies.

- Miscellaneous: Stationery, linen, and general goods and services
  - Domestic help
  - Dry cleaning
  - Linen
  - Office supplies
  - Newspapers and magazines
  - Postage stamps.

- Personal care: Personal care products and services
  - Cosmetics
  - Haircare
  - Moisturiser/Sun block
  - Nappies
  - Pain relief tablets
  - Toilet paper
  - Toothpaste
  - Soap/Shampoo/Conditioner.

- Recreation and culture
  - Books
  - Camera film
  - Cinema tickets
  - DVD and CDs
  - Sports goods
  - Theatre tickets.

- Restaurants, meals out and hotels
    - Business dinner
    - Dinner at restaurant (non-fast food)
    - Hotel rates
    - Take away drinks and snacks (fast food).

- Transport: Public transport, vehicle costs, vehicle fuel, vehicle insurance and vehicle maintenance
    - Hire purchase/Lease of vehicle
    - Petrol/Diesel
    - Public transport
    - Service maintenance
    - Tyres
    - Vehicle insurance
    - Vehicle purchase.

Given that it is costly and time consuming to create comprehensive baskets yourself and to price hundreds of goods and services accurately in each location on a regular basis, it is generally more cost effective to use a third-party service provider.

13.2.4 How to calculate a Cost-of-Living Index (COLI)

The prices for the defined quantities and types of goods and services in each location need to be updated on a regular basis, ideally on a quarterly basis, and the resulting indexes are updated for each of the baskets in each location. These indexes are then used to calculate the COLI between any two locations.

When calculating a COLI, the objective is to calculate the difference in the cost of living between any two geographic locations using one of the locations as the base. We typically refer to the home location as the base location. The COLI for the base location is always 100.

The **formula** for calculating:

> **Base location index of 100** is as follows:
>
> (Base Location Index/Base Location Index) × 100
>
> **Host location cost-of-living index** is as follows:
>
> (Host Location Index)/Base Location Index × 100

When moving to a host city with a higher cost-of-living, the COLI will be greater than 100. When moving to a host city with a lower cost-of-living, the COLI will be less than 100. Where the COLI is below 100, it means that in real terms the cost of living in the host city is lower than in the home city. This means that if a COLI of less than 100 were to be applied to an employee's salary, that person would actually be paid proportionately less spendable salary in the host city, as the cost of living is lower. It is important to note that the majority of organisations do not apply a COLI of less than 100 because it makes it difficult to persuade employees to take up an assignment as they tend to see it as a reduction in salary. Would you uproot yourself and move overseas in exchange for less money?

Example 1

An Australian employee is moving from Perth to London, where healthcare and communication will be provided by the employer.

More expensive in London:

- Alcohol and tobacco +4.77%
- Clothing +21.85%
- Education +31.53%
- Furniture and appliances +16.03%
- Groceries +16.35%
- Household +50.72%
- Miscellaneous +137.47%
- Personal care +11.18%
- Recreation and culture –6.82%
- Restaurants, meals out, and hotels +34.99%
- Transport +19.80%

The overall difference in cost of living when moving from Perth and London is +28.06%.

In this case the cost-of-living index is 128.06 and it would be applied as it is.

> ### Example 2
>
> A British employee is moving from London to Mumbai, where the employer will provide housing and education,
>
> More expensive in Mumbai:
>
> - Alcohol and tobacco –37.53%
> - Clothing –9.58%
> - Communication –44.92%
> - Furniture and appliances –19.31%
> - Groceries –24.03%
> - Healthcare –31.24%
> - Miscellaneous –72.43%
> - Personal care –24.94%
> - Recreation and culture –35.73%
> - Restaurants, meals out, and hotels –33.11%
> - Transport –27.99%
>
> The overall difference in cost of living when moving from London Mumbai is –30.53%
>
> In this case the cost-of-living index is 69.47 and it would not be applied as doing so would result in the employee taking a reduction in salary for uprooting and moving to Mumbai.

13.3 EXPATRIATE CALCULATIONS

Expatriate compensation calculations seek to ensure that purchasing power is equalised for different currencies, given the relative cost of the same basket of goods at the exchange rate versus the same currency. This means that a given home salary, when converted into a host salary, will buy the same basket of goods and services in both the home and host country. The amount by which we need to adjust an expatriate's salary is found in the cost-of-living index (COLI), discussed in the previous section.

13.3.1 Why the selection of cost-of-living baskets is important

The basket of goods and services used in expatriate compensation calculations should comprise only the baskets that expatriates will be expected to pay for using their host country salary. If, for example, the company provides the expatriate with accommodation, housing should be excluded from the expatriate cost-of-living calculation.

As an example, let us calculate an expatriate salary for an individual being transferred to the Hong Kong office by ABC International from the Dubai office, where he earns a salary of $5 000. In our example, it is assumed that a global compensation and benefit structure is in place (that is, that the practices in Dubai and Hong Kong are the same). Our objective is to calculate what salary to pay in Hong Kong in order to have the same purchasing/spending power as $5 000 in Dubai.

Scenario 1:

Only a cash salary is provided (no benefits).

The overall cost-of-living difference including all baskets is 45.09% (Xpatulator. com, 2014):

$5 000 × 1.4509 = $7 254.50

Scenario 2:

A cash salary is provided as well as company-paid accommodation.

The overall cost-of-living difference excluding the housing basket is 6.76% (Xpatulator.com, 2014):

$5 000 × 1.0676 = $5 338.00

Scenario 3:

A cash salary is provided as well as company-paid healthcare and education.

The overall cost-of-living difference, excluding the medical and education baskets (but including housing) is 45.73%:

$5000 × 1.4573 = $7 286.50

In each scenario the cost-of-living difference, taking into account the three spending patterns, resulted in different expatriate salary calculations.

By choosing baskets impacted on expatriate spending, a more accurate cost-of-living difference can be determined. The result is a more accurate expatriate salary calculation.

13.3.2 Application of cost of living to compensation

There are several ways in which a cost-of-living difference can be applied in an expatriate compensation calculation.

Home gross salary (that is, before home tax and statutory deductions) and the cost-of-living difference between the home and host country can be used to calculate the host gross salary. Tax and any other mandatory statutory deductions are deducted from the resulting host gross salary in order to calculate host net salary in a top-down approach. Although the gross salary in the host country is equal, in terms of spending power, to the gross salary in the home country, the expatriate will experience increased spending power in low-tax countries and decreased spending power in high-tax countries.

Home net salary (that is, after home tax and statutory deductions) and the cost-of-living difference between the home and host country can be used to calculate the host net salary. The resulting host net salary is then grossed up, in a build-up approach, by the amount of tax and any other mandatory statutory deductions, so that the net salary in the host country is equal in terms of spending power to the net salary in the home country.

Lastly, organisations can use either the above top-down (gross) or build-up (net) approach by deducting the home salary from the host salary and paying the differences as a cost-of-living allowance so that the salary plus the host country cost-of-living allowance are equal, in terms of spending power in the host country, to the spending power of the home salary in the home country.

We advise using net (after tax) salary. This has will result in a net salary result in the new location, which would then be grossed up for tax and any other statutory deductions in the new location. A cost-of-living allowance is best suited to short-term assignments. The allowance is usually paid in the host location, while the salary and benefits continue to be provided in the host location.

13.3.3 Salary purchasing power calculation

The salary purchasing power approach seeks to convert the entire salary using the difference in purchasing power. This would be used where the organisation wishes to ensure equal pay for the same job, but adjusted for purchasing power (that is, cost-of-living differences).

Formula:

Salary in new location = Salary + (Salary × Cost-of-living difference percentage)

Example:

Salary calculation = $100 000 + ($100 000 × 40.2%) = $140 200

This means that an employee earning a salary of $100 000 requires a salary of $140 200 in the new location to compensate for a 40.2% higher cost of living.

13.3.4 Calculation of cost-of-living allowance

The cost-of-living allowance (COLA) approach seeks to calculate a salary supplement to cover differences in the cost of living, particularly as a result of an international assignment.

The amount of COLA should enable an expatriate to be able to purchase the same basket of goods and services in the host location as they could in their home country. The basis for calculating a COLA is the cost-of-living index (COLI), which indexes the costs of the same basket of goods and services in different geographic locations. COLA is a simple, accurate method of measuring fluctuating salary purchasing power and ensuring parity.

Formula:

COLA in new location =

(Salary + (Salary × Cost-of-living difference percentage)) − Salary

Example:

Salary calculation =
($100 000 + ($100 000 × 40.2%)) − $100 000 = $40 200

This means that an employee earning a salary of $100 000 requires a COLA of $40 200 in the new location to compensate for a 40.2% higher cost of living.

13.3.5 International assignment calculation

A full international assignment calculation sets out detailed best practice guidelines for expatriate compensation. The objective is to make an expatriate's international mobility fair and financially viable, taking cognisance of the reward structure and market dynamics of the home and host country. The calculations use the build-up/home base approach and includes hypothetical tax, cost-of-living indexes, hardship premiums, exchange rates, expatriation premiums, benchmark housing allowances, and benchmark transport allowances. The objective is to ensure consistent, equitable treatment and benefits for all expatriate assignees and have a user-friendly reward structure to provide seamless coverage for different family scenarios.

The international assignment calculation is recommended for the calculation of the compensation and benefits for a typical expatriate assignment of six months' up to five years' duration in a large organisation with an established Expatriate Compensation Policy. For smaller organisations with fewer than ten expatriates, we recommend using the Salary Purchasing Power or Cost-of-living Allowance calculations, as these approaches are simpler and easier to implement.

To calculate an international assignment, follow these steps:

1. **Home base salary**: The international assignment calculation approach uses the home base salary as the starting point. This is the basic salary plus the cash value of all allowances and benefits. The base salary excludes all variable payments and payments related to performance. The home base salary is the fundamental building block of the home base build-up salary system. Purchasing power cannot be maintained if the home salary is not regularly reviewed. The home company is responsible for maintaining the home base salary in line with individual performance and home market movement.

2. **Hypothetical tax**: Using the home location tax table determine the tax that would be payable based on the home base salary above. This tax is referred to as "Hypothetical Tax" as it is not actually paid; it is used purely to calculate what the expatriate's home net salary is, in order to complete the calculations that follow. This is the typical/average (Hypothetical) Tax to be deducted from Home Base Salary, if applicable, in terms of home location prevailing tax rates.

3. **Home net salary**: Calculate the home net salary:

   > Home net salary = Home base salary less Hypothetical tax

4. **Percentage of host net spending**: Decide what percentage of the home net salary is to be used for spending in the host location. The international benchmark is 40 percent (Xpatulator.com, 2014). However, this can be increased or decreased in terms of company policy and the expatriate's circumstances.

5. **Host net essential spending salary**: Calculate the amount of essential spending – this is the amount of home net salary to be used in the host location:

   > Essential spending salary = Home net salary × Percentage Host net spending

6. **Home net balance**: Calculate the percentage of the home net salary to be kept in the home location. This is the balance of home net salary after having decided what percentage of home net salary is to be used in the host location. For example, if the host spending percentage is 40 percent, then the balance of 60 percent will be the home spending percentage.

7. **Expatriation premium**: Decide the percentage that will be added to the home net salary in order to encourage the expatriate to take up the assignment. This is compensation for the disruption of having to relocate (not to be confused with compensation for hardship). The international benchmark is 15 percent of the home net salary. However this can be increased or decreased.

8. **Cost-of-living Index**: Decide which cost-of-living baskets to include in the cost-of-living difference calculation. Only baskets on which the expatriate will spend his/her host salary should be included. Any baskets provided by either the employer or the state should be excluded, as the difference in the cost of living for these baskets will not have an impact on the expatriate.

9. **Hardship premium**: This is compensation for the change in the quality of living an assignee and his/her family (if applicable) are likely to experience, assessed in global terms, in a specific location. A hardship premium is a measure of the quality of living conditions in each location. The hardship premium is paid as a percentage of home base salary and is proportional to the degree of hardship. For example, minimal hardship 10 percent; some degree of hardship 20 percent; high degree of hardship 30 percent; extreme degree of hardship 40 percent (Xpatulator.com, 2014).

> Hardship Premium = Hardship percentage of host location less Hardship percentage of home location

Here is an example of an international assignment calculation for an expatriate being sent from South Africa to Qatar by a large multinational petroleum company:

Table 13.1: Example of international calculation

Home Base Salary: R600,000 Less Hypothetical Tax: R150,000 Home Net Salary: R450,000	
(R450,000 X 60% = R270,000)	(R450,000 X 40% = R180,000)
Home Net Balance of 60%: R270,000 Hardship Premium of 0%: R0 Expatriation Premium of 15%: R90,000 = Home Net Currency Balance*: R360,000 (R270,000 + R0 + R90,000 = R360,000)	Host Net Essential Spending of 40%: R180,000 Cost of Living Index: 139.25 (i.e. +39.25%) Exchange Rate: 0.3655 = Host Net Currency Spendable: QAR91,603 ((R180,000 + (R180,000 X 39.25%)) X 0.3655 = QAR91,603

13.4 CONCLUSION

Up-to-date cost-of-living data, segmented into basket categories for each geographical location, are essential inputs when calculating expatriate compensation.

The baskets of goods and services used in expatriate compensation calculations should comprise only those baskets that the expatriate will be expected to pay for using host country salary.

Cost-of-living indexes (COLIs) are calculated from the prices of the same quantities and types of goods and services in different geographic locations (base location = 100).

COLIs are used by organisations and individuals for expatriate salary purchasing power, cost-of-living allowance, and international assignment calculations.

13.5 REFERENCES

Encyclopaedia Britannica. *Cost of living*. [Online]. Available: http://global.britannica.com/EBchecked/topic/139483/cost-of-living. [Accessed 17 December 2014].

Xpatulator.com. 2014. [Online]. Available: http://www.xpatulator.com/. [Accessed 17 December 2014].

CHAPTER 14
TAXATION AND THE EXPATRIATE
Ray Harraway and Cinzia de Risi

14.1 INTRODUCTION

Tax is a significant cost and risk in any mobility programme that requires proactive planning and management. In the recently published 2013 **EY Global Mobility Effectiveness** survey, tax compliance is cited as the top challenge in all growth markets. This chapter outlines the basic tax principles to be aware of.

14.2 SOURCE AND RESIDENCY PRINCIPLES

The continent of Africa has 54 sovereign states, each with its own intricate tax regimen, in varying stages of development. All African countries levy tax, either on a source principle or based on the tax residency status of the person.

Table 14.1, below, summarises the basis of taxation of the major African countries.

Table 14.1: Basis of taxation of major African countries

Source Income	Worldwide income*	
Angola	Cameroon	Lesotho
Botswana	Congo	Mauritius
DRC	Côte d'Ivoire	Mozambique
Madagascar	Ethiopia	Nigeria
Malawi	Equatorial Guinea	Rwanda
Namibia	Guinea	Senegal
Swaziland	Gabon	South Africa
Zambia	Ghana	Tanzania
Zimbabwe	Kenya	Uganda

* In certain countries, "worldwide income" is interpreted as applying only to worldwide employment income.

14.2.1 Source principle

The source principle, sometimes called the "territoriality" principle, requires a determination of the origin of the employment income.

Under the source principle, as a rule-of-thumb, employment income will be taxed in the country where the services giving rise to that income are actually rendered. This is generally irrespective of the place where the employment contract is entered into, the place from where the remuneration is paid, and the residence status of the expatriate.

Most African countries do not specifically define "source" in their tax legislation. Only in the more advanced tax jurisdictions has the concept of source been "crystallised" by a number of tax cases.

In practice, there are departures from this rule-of-thumb and there are also norms and practices that may override it. For instance, some African countries will seek to tax employment income only if it is actually paid in-country or only if it is paid abroad but re-charged to an entity in the country. This uncertainty is best dealt with by obtaining advance rulings from the local revenue authority, where possible.

14.2.2 Residency principle

Under the residency principle, a tax liability is triggered in the country based on the expatriate's tax residency status, regardless of the source. The tax legislation of that country (so-called "domestic" legislation) would typically be used to determine the tax residency status.

Where the expatriate is regarded as a tax resident of both the home and the host country under their respective domestic regimes, the residence status must be decided under the provision of a double tax agreement (DTA) if one exists between the two countries.

An expatriate would typically be treated as a tax resident of the country by one or more of the following triggers:

- The number of days in a calendar or fiscal year physically present in the country, or

- By establishing some level of permanency in the foreign country, for example, a permanent home, or

- Nationality or citizenship.

As opposed to source principles, an expatriate who becomes resident in the foreign country would be liable to tax in that foreign country on their worldwide income and not only on their remuneration sourced in the foreign country.

In South Africa, tax residency is triggered only from a foreign national's sixth year of continuous presence in the country. One of the residency tests in South

Africa is a day test, based on a person's physical presence in the country. A person will be considered resident if that person spends or has spent the following periods of time in South Africa:

- More than 91 days in aggregate in the year of assessment under consideration, and

- More than 91 days in aggregate during each of the five years of assessment preceding the year of assessment under consideration, and

- More than 915 days in aggregate during the five preceding years of assessment.

In many other residence-based African countries, tax residency can be triggered sooner – after 183 days of physical presence in the country (that is, from a person's first year of presence in the country).

Some countries interpret "worldwide income" as a person's total income from all income streams, both passive (investment income) and active (employment income). However, in Kenya, for example, a Kenyan tax resident expatriate would be taxed only on his/her worldwide **employment income**, and not on worldwide passive income.

14.2.3 Hybrid application

Many African countries operate a hybrid of the two regimens above, where a resident is taxed on worldwide income and a non-resident on source principles. Having a sound knowledge of each location's tax legislation, interpretations and practices and, more importantly, how they interact with the expatriate's home country tax status, is critical.

In any event, an expatriate would, as a minimum, have a *prima facie* tax exposure on employment income earned from services rendered in a foreign country – from the first day of working in that country. Of greater concern is the possibility of double tax and how best to manage this (see section 14.6 – managing double tax).

14.3 TAX APPROACHES

Under many international assignment policies, the employer bears the burden of any additional tax and the related tax compliance obligations on behalf of its expatriate employees. This allows employees to focus on their assigned purpose instead of trying to come to grips with a complex and unfamiliar tax regimen.

This is achieved in a number of ways, but in principle, the employee is guaranteed a net tax package and the employer assumes the responsibility of paying the tax liabilities and addressing the tax compliance requirements in the host and the home countries.

There are three main approaches regarding host country taxes:

- *Laissez-faire*
- Tax equalisation, and
- Tax protection.

14.3.1 *Laissez-faire*

"*Laissez-faire*" refers to the situation where the expatriate is responsible for sorting out his/her own host country tax affairs with no involvement or assistance from the employer.

The advantages of this approach include the following:

- No additional costs or administration burden for the employer
- The expatriate can benefit from low tax host jurisdictions.

The main disadvantage of this approach is the risk of non-compliance and exposure to penalties, giving rise to reputational damage for the employer.

14.3.2 Tax equalisation

Tax equalisation and tax protection are similar in that the employer takes an active role in the expatriate's host country tax affairs.

The principle of tax equalisation is that the expatriate should be neither better nor worse off from a tax point of view by accepting an overseas assignment. The tax costs incurred by the expatriate will approximate what they would have been had the expatriate remained at home. The intent of tax equalisation is therefore that the expatriate neither suffers significant financial hardship nor realises a financial windfall from the tax consequences of the assignment.

The employer bears the responsibility for paying the expatriate's actual home and host country tax costs. In exchange, the expatriate "pays" to the employer a stay-at-home hypothetical tax as determined under the company's tax equalisation policy.

In determining the "hypo" tax deduction, the employer focuses on the remuneration that the expatriate would have earned if he had remained at home. Assignment-specific items paid, such as expatriate or assignment allowances, are ignored for purposes of this calculation. This hypo tax is used by the employer to settle the host and home country taxes. In addition, the employer will pay any taxes due over and above the hypo tax. If the home and host country taxes are less than the hypo tax, the employer enjoys the saving.

The advantages of tax equalisation include the following:

- Any tax savings are for the benefit of the employer and can be used to reduce the overall assignment costs. This occurs where the host country tax is lower than the home country tax. The employer can offset the cost of settling additional taxes, where the host country has higher taxes, against windfalls in cases where the host country has lower taxes, resulting in significant cost savings, especially with large outbound populations from high-tax countries;

- Corporate reputation is protected as tax equalisation facilitates expatriate tax compliance;

- Expatriates have no incentive to choose the country to which they would like to go based on tax differentials, improving geographic mobility.

A disadvantage is the administration burden of a tax equalisation policy, which tends to be time consuming and complex. Hypo tax is not easily understood, and can create endless negotiations with the employee.

14.3.3 Tax protection

Under a tax protection regimen, the employer ensures that taxation borne by the expatriate is no more than if he/she had remained at home. If the tax in the host country is higher, the excess is met by the employer. The employer reimburses the expatriate for excess taxes he/she incurs while on assignment.

Where the host country tax is lower than in the home country, the tax benefit would be enjoyed by the employee. If hypo tax is deducted, the difference between the (low) host country tax and the (higher) home country tax is refunded to the employee.

The advantages of tax protection include:

- The expatriate is not worse off in terms of taxes.

- Where the expatriate is not worse off there is no need to calculate hypothetical taxes, thereby reducing administration.

- It can be used as an incentive for an employee to accept an overseas assignment in a lower tax jurisdiction.

The disadvantages include the following:

- Employees will be reluctant to move to a higher tax country, thus inadvertently encouraging "cherry picking", and

- It will be more costly for the employer as the tax savings of sending an expatriate to a lower tax jurisdiction is to the expatriate's benefit and not the employer's.

14.3.4 Example

The example below demonstrates the cost impact for the employer of the two main approaches.

A South African national is assigned to Nigeria, a lower tax regime, with a total annual expatriate remuneration package of 720 000. All net allowances and benefits have been excluded for the purposes of this example.

Table 14.2: Illustration of example

	Equalisation		Protection	
Total remuneration	720 000	A	720 000	A
Hypothetical tax * (on 720 000)	205 685	B	205 685	B
Net home pay	514 315		514 315	
Nigerian tax payable	109 250	C	109 250	C
Cost to employer	623 565	A – B + C	720 000	A
Employee net salary on assignment	514 315	A – B	610 750	A – C

* Hypothetical tax (or hypo tax) is the home country taxes the expatriate would have paid had he/she not accepted the assignment.

In this example, the tax protection method results in the expatriate receiving the benefit of being sent from a higher to a lower tax jurisdiction. Under tax equalisation, the tax saving is for the benefit of the employer.

Variations from these main approaches exist, but the principles generally remain the same. For example, it is not uncommon to merely gross up the home net income of the employee for host country taxes and add a cost-of-living adjustment to arrive at a new gross package to be delivered in the host location.

14.4 DIFFERENT ASSIGNMENT CATEGORIES

Mobility programmes typically provide for assignments categories of different lengths and categories, each with differing tax implications.

The following categories are common:

- **Long-term assignment (LTA):** This is a formal assignment agreed to in writing, lasting more than one year, typically limited to a maximum of 5 years;

- **Short-term assignment (STA):** This has a duration of three to 12 months;

- **Business commuters (short-term business travellers):** This is an increasingly popular means of carrying out cross-border activities where employees undertake extended and/or regular business trips, but are not regulated by any formal assignment arrangement.

The tax implications and risk profiles differ according to each category.

14.4.1 Long-term assignment (LTA) expatriates

LTA expatriates will more readily break their tax residency status in their home location, resulting in a low- or no-tax liability back home. The primary tax exposure would be in the host location. These expatriates tend to be transferred to a local payroll in the host location to facilitate the employment tax remittances or withholdings. Alternatively, the employer would run a parallel, shadow, or "dummy" payroll in such a location to account for the obligatory personal tax exposure – see section 14.5 below.

14.4.2 Short-term assignment (STA) expatriates

The tax risk for STA expatriates is more problematic. These expatriates are likely to continue to be treated as tax residents in their home location and will also stay on the home base payroll. Expediting employer payroll remittances in the foreign country and managing the expatriate's personal tax compliance is therefore more challenging. These expatriates are more likely to face a tax exposure in both countries as the employment income from services rendered in the host location will be taxed on the source basis but also in the home location based on the residence basis of tax. Issues of double taxation and the managing of tax credits therefore arise.

14.4.3 Business commuters

This category includes:

- **Rotational assignment:** This generally relates to project-based assignments where the employee is on site for extended periods with regular intervals of home leave.

- **Commuter assignments:** This occurs where an employee works on site during the week and returns home over weekends.

This category of mobile employees carries the highest tax risk. The traveller tends to fall off the company's radar and create a myriad tax, immigration and other regulatory compliance risks, particularly where the stay in the host location is extended.

14.5 REMITTANCE OF EMPLOYEE INCOME TAXES

Once a tax exposure in the host country has been established, the next step is to decide how best to pay the taxes due to the relevant tax authorities.

The two main means to remit such taxes are either via a payroll or through a self-payment system, such as a provisional tax system.

14.5.1 Payroll-withholding requirements/obligations

Payroll-withholding requirements are not uncommon in Africa. These requirements to register as an employer to meet statutory withholding obligations also tend to be mutually exclusive from, and different to, the personal income tax filing requirements. In many cases, withholding and submitting tax through the payroll also acts as a final tax deduction system with no further compliance annual tax filing requirement on personal income tax.

A payroll withholding requirement can be met by either transferring the expatriate's pay to the actual host country payroll or by setting up a shadow payroll.

A host country payroll would assume responsibility for the payment of the net pay of the expatriate as well as the remittance of the necessary taxes.

The host country payroll would need to have the required sophistication to accurately determine the host country taxes under a tax equalisation or tax protection policy. The basis of tax equalisation and tax protection is that the expatriate is guaranteed a net salary, that is, the employer pays the taxes on behalf of the expatriate. The payment of this tax is typically regarded as a taxable benefit in the hands of the employee. The net package must therefore be converted to a grossed-up package to ensure that the employee is kept "whole" from a tax point of view. This calculation is often referred to as a "gross up".

14.5.2 Example

The simple example below demonstrates how a net salary is grossed up to arrive at gross salary.

A foreign national is placed on a South African payroll following his secondment from Nigeria.

His annual net of tax package for the year is R398 460.

	Gross up	
Net salary	178 460	
Cost-of-living adjustment	220 000	
Total net package	**398 460**	(A)
Step 1 – Calculate taxes on net package		
South African taxes on the net package	159 384	
Step 2 – Calculate gross-up taxes		
Gross-up taxes*	265 640	(B) **
Gross package in host country	**664 100**	(A + B)

* Assume a flat income tax rate of 40 percent for illustrative purposes.

** Best practice is to perform a full gross (that is, 159 384 / (1 – the tax rate) = 60 percent

Under a parallel or shadow payroll, the expatriate's pay remains on the home country payroll, or an international payroll through a global employment entity. The parallel payroll in the host country merely calculates the host country tax due on that pay for remittance purposes. The shadow payroll therefore facilitates the payment and monitoring of host country tax compliance.

14.5.3 Self-payment system

Where provided for in the host country, an alternative arrangement is where the host country taxes are paid by the expatriate, typically in instalments over the year to cover the full annual tax liability. This is unlike a payroll withholding, where the taxes are credited to the employer's payroll registration number. Under this arrangement, the tax payments are allocated to a particular expatriate and would typically also require the filing of a personal tax return to reconcile the taxes paid to the final income declaration.

Instalment payments inevitably lead to more administration as they need to be made per individual.

The way in which taxes should be paid over will be dictated by the applicable tax laws of the host location.

14.6 MANAGING DOUBLE TAX

Facing a double tax charge is not uncommon, and adds to the complexity and cost of running any international mobility programme. As mentioned earlier, this is particularly prevalent when dealing with short-term assignments and business commuters.

Double tax normally arises where:

- One country imposes tax on residency principles and the other on source.

- Both tax regimens are based on source principles, but they interpret the source concept differently.

- Both tax systems are based on residency, but they have different definitions of residence.

- Both countries impose tax on a person's residency status, but have a hybrid system for non-residents who are taxed on source.

Double tax can be reduced or eliminated where there is a double tax agreement (DTA) between the two countries. A DTA is the primary means with which to manage (and eliminate) double tax. A DTA is a bilateral agreement between two countries, the primary aims of which are to provide relief from double tax, and to provide for the sharing of information between the two countries. Unilateral tax relief from double tax may also be provided under the domestic tax legislation of the home country.

14.6.1 Double tax agreement (DTA) relief

DTA relief is provided either by exempting income from tax in one of the countries and granting full taxing rights to the other country, or by a credit system. The latter option allows both countries to tax the income but instructs the one country, generally the country of residence, to give a credit or rebate for the foreign taxes paid to the host country.

DTAs contain a number of articles, each of which deals with separate types of income streams. Employment income received by expatriates is normally dealt with by the Dependent Personal Services article. While this article is geared to provide relief in cases of double tax, it is more often relied on to exempt business commuters from tax in the host country. Many refer to this article as the 183-day rule.

Before this article can be invoked to exempt the income from taxes in the host country tax, there must be a valid DTA between the home and host country, and the expatriate or commuter must be classified as a tax resident of one of the countries, as defined in the DTA. In most cases this would require the person to be a tax resident in terms of the domestic legislation of one of the countries. In many instances, especially in the case of professional expatriates or long-term assignments, the expatriate may have inadvertently broken ties with his/her "home" country and therefore would not be regarded as a tax resident of that country. In this case, the DTA cannot be invoked.

Only once the above requirements have been met can one move to the technical analysis of whether the so-called 183-day rule applies. The 183-day rule carries three tests. Where all three tests have been passed, the person's country of residence would have sole taxation rights on the income earned from duties in the host country.

The three tests are commonly set out as on the following lines:

- The person is not present in the host country for a period exceeding 183 days in any 12-month period commencing or ending in the year of assessment of the host country, and

- The remuneration is paid by, or on behalf of, an employer that is not a resident of the host country, and

- The remuneration is not deductible in determining the taxable profits of a permanent establishment or a fixed base that the employer has in the host country.

These tests, particularly the third, have been debated extensively over the years. In principle, the aim is for one country to have "symmetry of treatment" between the ability to tax the employment income and allowing a corporate tax deduction for those costs. While simple in principle, in practice this raises a host of questions, including but not limited to, the question as to whether a recharge of the costs to the host entity would be seen as falling foul of this test.

The second test has also been under scrutiny, which has given rise to the concept of an "economic employer". Based on the principles and guidance from the OECD, if the "economic employer", regardless of the legal employment arrangement, is seen to be a resident of the host country, then this test will not be satisfied. A host entity can be deemed to be an economic employer where the services performed are integral to its business of the host entity. For example, the host entity can be deemed to be the economic employer if:

- It takes the responsibility for, and risk associated with, the services performed, or

- There is a recharge of the assignment cost to the host entity, or

- It has the authority to instruct, supervise and control the employee.

The economic employer concept is recognised and applied only in the more advanced tax jurisdictions.

In recent years, the number of DTAs with African countries (from countries both on and off the African continent) has accelerated significantly. For example, from July 2013 to July 2014, 16 new DTAs have been enforced, with a further 18 under negotiation.

Figure 14.1 below sets out the current position on treaty developments in Africa.

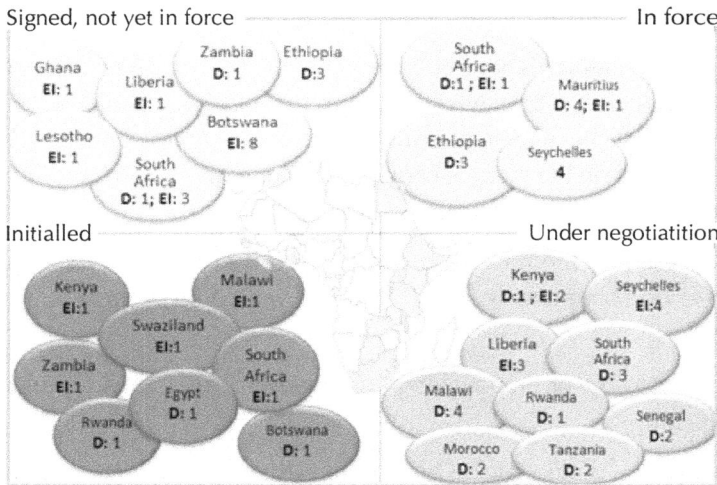

Signed, not yet in force ———————————————————— In force

Ghana EI: 1	South Africa D:1 ; EI: 1
Zambia D: 1	Mauritius D: 4; EI: 1
Liberia EI: 1	Ethiopia D:3
Lesotho EI: 1	Seychelles 4
Botswana EI: 8	
South Africa D: 1; EI: 3	

Initialled ———————————————————— Under negotiatition

Kenya EI:1	Kenya D:1 ; EI:2
Malawi EI:1	Seychelles EI:4
Swaziland EI:1	Liberia EI:3
Zambia EI:1	South Africa D: 3
Egypt D: 1	Malawi D: 4
South Africa EI:1	Rwanda D: 1
Rwanda D: 1	Senegal D:2
Botswana D: 1	Morocco D: 2
	Tanzania D: 2

D: Income/Capital double tax agreement
EI: Exchange of information agreement

(IBFD, 2013)

Figure 14.1: Treaty developments in Africa

14.6.2 Unilateral relief

Where no DTA is available to provide relief for double taxation, so-called unilateral tax relief in the home country may be available, depending on the country's domestic tax legislation. This relief takes the form of a rebate in the home country for the tax paid in the host country, and is often referred to as a foreign tax credit (FTC). Each country will have its own methods of how to calculate the credit and what limitations apply. Such relief provisions are more prevalent in advanced tax jurisdictions. While the domestic legislation of many African countries provides for this type of relief, realising this relief can be difficult. This is because FTC can be claimed only by filing a tax return and many African countries have no tax filing obligations.

14.7 TAX CHALLENGES IN AFRICA

Some of the challenges are outlined below:

- **Practice versus law:** Many tax authorities rely on practices which have evolved over time in spite of what is dictated by the tax legislation. While there are concerted efforts by many revenue authorities to address this challenge, the uncertainty still remains and will require upfront management to mitigate the risk of surprises.

- **Uncertainty in application of the legislation:** There is often inconsistency both in the understanding of the legislation and consequently in its application. Documented guidelines are lacking, particularly when tax law amendments are announced.

- **Retrospective application:** Law amendments can be implemented retrospectively, leaving no time for taxpayers to plan or provide for the additional tax costs.

- **Availability of published legislation and practice notes:** The tax legislation in some countries dates back to the mid-1900s, with no formal updates to a centralised tax code other than a series of *Government Gazettes* or other official State bulletins.

14.8 CONCLUSION

14.8.1 Tax developments in Africa

The growth prospects on the continent have led to many countries updating their tax laws and processes.

Some recent develpments in this area are:

- **Tax efficiencies:** Electronic filing of tax returns has been introduced to tax administration. In 2011 East African countries piloted online submission of tax returns and registration for tax numbers. Senegal, Botswana and Zambia are in different stages of implementing an electronic platform for filing.

- **Tax legislation:** There is a push to enhance the tax regimens to ensure that expatriates and commuters are in the tax net. Nigeria in particular has made significant changes to personal legislation, with a focus on expatriates. Ghana and Zambia have introduced social security legislation for expatriates.

- **Law enforcement:** There has been a noticeable increase in the number of payroll audits focusing on expatriates and tax compliance. There is also increased use of immigration records to identify tax exposures.

All of this information needs to be managed accurately and in real time. The next section sets out how a Reward Management System makes it possible to do so.

14.9 REFERENCES

International Bureau of Fiscal Documentation (IBFD). 2013. *Tax treaties database*. IBFD.

CHAPTER 15
CONTEXTUALISING A REWARD MANAGEMENT SYSTEM
Chris Blair

15.1 INTRODUCTION

A Reward Management System (RMS) goes a long way in assisting organisations to manage their Reward offering. This chapter describes the purpose and features of such a system.

15.2 PURPOSE OF A REWARD MANAGEMENT SYSTEM

The purpose of a Reward Management System is to manage your remuneration strategy and policy with minimal administration. The remuneration strategy's aim is to reward employees fairly, equitably and consistently in accordance with their value added to their organisation.

It allows you to get your pay and reward structure accurate through:

- Making better decisions
- Driving high employee performance
- Optimising financial performance
- Being fair, consistent and transparent
- Increasing efficiency
- Retaining talented people
- Attracting the best external talent
- Engaging and motivating staff at all levels, and
- Having happier, more motivated employees.

15.3 WHAT SHOULD A REWARD MANAGEMENT SYSTEM ACHIEVE?

The Reward Management System should be able to manage the organisation's remuneration strategy and policy (remuneration strategy) by implementing the reward policies, processes and practices required to support the achievement of the organisation's goals by helping to ensure that the organisation have the ability to attract and retain competent, well-motivated and committed people. *People should be rewarded for their performance and the value they add towards achieving the business objectives managed by the system.*

The reward management system therefore manages the Remuneration Strategy (Reward Strategy) to reward the right outcomes, and to convey the right message about what is important in terms of expected behaviours and outputs.

The reward management system reflects and captures the organisation's remuneration strategy and policy and should underpin the organisation's vision, mission and values. The old adage of "what gets measured, gets done" holds true, and also what gets done should be measured by the reward management system.

As such, remuneration will play a critical role in attracting and retaining high-performing individuals, thereby ensuring competitiveness in the market place. The reward management system will also reinforce, encourage and promote superior performance and achievement of the organisation's strategic goals. The system will not be a stand-alone process, but should be fully integrated into other management processes.

The basic purpose of our reward management system is to support the key strategy, purpose and criteria of the remuneration strategy and processes and align them to organisational needs. To achieve this purpose, the following criteria should be adhered to:

- Manage attraction, retention, measurement and motivation of competent, committed and superior performers.

- Reflect the dynamics of the market and the context in which the organisation operates.

- Ensure internal equity and consistency within the organisation.

- Take into account the availability of resources, with specific emphasis on specialised and critical skills categories.

- Align to, measure, and help to enact the organisation's mission, vision, goals, and values and strategic objectives.

- Guide the organisation in promotion and progression of staff.

- Manage each component of remuneration.

- Manage the reward of employees who consistently perform above expectations and are proficient in the role with a higher base pay and incentive payments.

- Utilise incentive or variable pay as a way to meet the strategic goals – incentive pay can be available to some employees with consideration of a number of factors and based on individual goals that relate to the organisation's objectives as well as overall performance of the organisation.

- Administer the remuneration strategy in a manner that is consistent and free of discrimination.

- Effectively communicate remuneration outcomes to support, reinforce, and align the organisation's values, business strategy, operational and financial needs with a goal of growth and sustainability.

15.4 SCOPE OF A REWARD MANAGEMENT SYSTEM

The reward management system can apply to all groups of employees including permanent and fixed-term contract employees (more than 12 months), independent contractors. and any group of employees identified by department, such as the Administrative/support staff, non-management, specialist/technical staff and management staff at all levels including executive staff; level, race, gender, skills category, scarce skills category, business-imperative skills, high-potential employees, or any other grouping of employees.

15.4.1 Responsibility for the reward management system

In accordance with the policy, it is the responsibility of line managers to:

- Review and plan the functions to be performed by each member of staff and prepare, maintain and submit up-to-date job profiles and duty lists.

- Review and manage the level of each job and request the re-evaluation of each job as and when necessary.

- Review and manage the performance of each member of their staff in accordance with the organisation's Performance Management Policy.

- Ensure the best interest of the organisation and its employees when making considerations regarding remuneration.

- Accurately communicate all elements of the remuneration structure to staff they are accountable for using the Reward Management System.

It is the responsibility of Human Resources staff using the reward management system to:

- Facilitate the implementation through line management of all aspects of the remuneration and related strategies/policies.

- Develop and maintain the strategies, information, database records and tools required to implement the remuneration and related policies such as pay scales, job profiles, position grades, performance ratings, and so on.

- Benchmark remuneration and practice on a regular basis, against the relevant market, and make recommendations where changes are required.

- Identify, review and take corrective action for all deviations highlighted by the reward management system from established remuneration and related strategies/policies.

15.4.2 Remuneration strategy for a Reward Management System

The remuneration strategy is designed to be aligned to the organisational strategy and the execution of that strategy through the reward management system. This in turn will maximise the performance and effectiveness of the organisation, thus increasing stakeholder returns.

The guiding principles for the remuneration of staff are to:

- Provide remuneration that attracts, retains, measures and motivates staff and helps to develop a high performance culture.

- Ensure that remuneration levels are competitive compared to the market.

- Provide a "total reward" approach which involves creating the right mix of non-financial as well as financial rewards.

- Encourage highly competent individuals to consistently and effectively apply their competencies to enhance business performance.

- Cap remuneration at a maximum monetary value, related to market remuneration, per job level, above which no individual may progress.

- Develop a remuneration process that provides for equitable pay and is fair, consistent and transparent but differentiates between non-performance, and average and excellent performers.

- Ensure alignment with business strategy.

- Be fit for the purpose, not one-size-fits-all.

- Be flexible and adaptable in response to the ever-changing environment.

- Be fair and equitable and supportive of diverse needs (remuneration does not discriminate based on criteria that are not work related or outside the employee's control such as race, gender, family responsibility, disability, age, and so on).

- Reinforce teamwork and a culture of belonging and high commitment.

- Comply with legislation.

- Stand up to scrutiny by stakeholders.

- Inculcate a culture of high performance and eradicate entitlement.

- Manage affordability in the implementation of the remuneration strategy.

15.5 DESIGN PRINCIPLES USED IN THE REWARD MANAGEMENT SYSTEM

The remuneration principles that are used in the Reward management System are usually as follows:

- **Competitive pay levels:** Paying remuneration packages that are competitive relative to the defined target labour market.

- **Pay for performance:** Remuneration practices that will remunerate high-performing employees for the performance, delivery and contribution that they make to the company.

- **Internal equity:** Remuneration differentiation between employees will be based on criteria that are fair, objective and transparent.

- **Cost management:** Manage the total cost of employment for all employees.

- **Total reward approach:** The remuneration strategy solution of the company should encompass a balanced design that includes all of the following components:

  - Guaranteed pay
  - Variable pay
  - Performance management
  - Employee growth and development
  - Non-financial remuneration and recognition
  - Work environment.

- **Regular revision:** The remuneration strategy as well as each component of the remuneration policy is dynamic and should be revisited regularly to ensure that its remuneration approach keeps pace with both the company's objectives and market practices.

- **Communication:** There should be commitment to ensuring that all employees are made aware of the defined remuneration strategy with clear statements of what remuneration is designed to achieve.

15.6 COMPONENTS OF THE REWARD MANAGEMENT SYSTEM

The reward management system is an accurate, flexible, easy-to-use tool for developing attractive, competitive and motivating reward structures at all levels –

based on both market comparisons and corporate objectives. It simplifies the process for everyone.

The reward management system allows your HR staff, line managers, and executives to work together to:

- **Get an instant overall view of your company's reward structure,** based on current and accurate value-added data and research.

- **Maintain your market competitiveness** by comparing your current reward structures against real market data from a combination of different surveys.

- **Compare reward** across jobs, industries and locations – salary benchmarking and job evaluation.

- **Balance your reward budget and meet your financial obligations**. Value-added data is used to plan salaries, control tight budgets, and award appropriate **market leading salaries, benefits** and merit increases.

- **Create consistent salary review processes** (across teams and skill areas) by using reward reviews. The **reward review** simplifies annual adjustments, creating configurable performance- and merit-based programmes for target groups and individuals.

- **Build** and **review** comprehensive **total reward profiles**.

- **Create a competitive and flexible reward strategy** that links performance to reward, covering:
  - Base salaries
  - Short-term incentive plans
  - Long-term incentive plans
  - Retirement plans
  - Medical aid plans
  - Bonuses
  - Share incentive plans, and more.

- **Create total reward packages** and **action plans** (based on analysis and reporting) for individuals or target groups.

- **Regularly monitor internal equity** and the overall effectiveness of your reward policies by using the **integrated reporting** function.

- **Reduce administration costs.** Workflows are automated and scenario planning is integrated to analyse and adjust all reward components, with data roll-up enabled throughout the organisation.

15.7 RULES AND CRITERIA FOR MOVEMENT WITHIN PAY SCALES

Only in exceptional circumstances should employees fall outside the scales. Movement within the scales is based on performance and the employee's current comparison to the pay scales.

15.7.1 Placement within the pay scales

Employees are placed, based on their performance, at the relevant salary scale level as follows:

- **Minimum:** Does not meet required performance levels also referred to as poor performers. The employee's performance is below the standard requirements set. Little or no evidence exists of the employee's competence.

- **Lower guide:** Partially meets required performance levels/delivery standards. The employee's performance partially meets all the threshold requirements set. Evidence exists of the employee's competence.

- **Midpoint** – Meets required performance levels. **The employee's performance exceeds the threshold requirements set for the job**. Tangible evidence shows that job outputs have been met. The National Market Median (P50) is used as an anchor here.

- **Upper guide:** Exceeds the required performance levels. The employee's performance meets the stretch requirements set. Tangible evidence exists of the employee's sustained exceptional and on-going achievements far beyond the requirements of the post

- **Maximum:** Outstanding performance. The employee's performance is visibly outstanding on a sustained basis and far exceeds the requirements set. Tangible evidence exists of the employee's *ongoing* achievements.

15.7.2 Typical rules and criteria for the Reward Management System

15.7.2.1 New appointments

When appointing an employee to a new position, the following criteria should be considered:

- **Minimum salary scale:** The newly appointed employee is below the job requirements (for example, a trainee). Little or no evidence exists of the newly appointed employee's ability to perform. The newly appointed employee needs to be trained and gain experience.

- **Lower guide of salary scale:** The newly appointed employee meets the threshold job requirements but requires further development. Some evidence exists of the newly appointed employee's performance from his/her CV and past references. Further training and experience is required to become fully competent.

- **Midpoint of salary scale:** The newly appointed employee fully meets the job requirements based on his/her CV and past references.

- **Upper guide of salary scale:** The newly appointed employee exceeds the job requirements. Evidence of the newly appointed employee's past performance/ experience/track record exceeds the requirements set. Tangible evidence exists of the employee's past achievements.

15.7.2.2 Appointments to higher positions applied for

When an employee is appointed to a higher position with a higher grade, they should be appointed as per the appointment guidelines above or receive a 10 percent increase, whichever is the greater.

15.7.2.3 Employees paid outside the pay range

In cases where the individual's current remuneration is already within the salary band of the next job grade, such a person should be paid a once-off cash payment based on performance at the midpoint of the pay scale and normalised within the next five years to fit within the salary band.

In such cases the once-off cash payment will be capped against the performance management score, with its commensurate increase multiple at the 50th percentile of the pay scale.

15.7.3 Relationship between pay scales and annual increases

The criterion for movement within the scales is both *pay scale-related* and *based on the performance* of the individual in the job. Underperformers who are overpaid gradually retard increases through the link between annual increases and performance.

As a guideline, the distribution as indicated in Table 15.1 will be applied for the entire organisation.

Table 15.1: Performance ratings

Performance Category	Increase Scale Description	Desired Distribution
Exceptional performance (E)	Evidence of performance against the standard indicates that this person in addition to achieving targets and standards for full performance in all five performance areas as well as all Behaviours/Values, **consistently exceeds challenging and stretch goals over the entire spectrum of dimensions and creates a new standard of performance for relevant peer group.**	Less than 5 percent of staff
Full performance plus (F+)	Evidence of performance against the standard indicates that this person in addition to achieving targets and standards for full performance in all five performance areas as well as all Behaviours/Values, is a complete, full performer who regularly exceeds challenging and stretch goals.	Around 20 percent of staff
Full performance (F)	Evidence of performance against the standard indicates that this person achieved targets and standards for full performance in all five performance areas as well as all Behaviours/Values.	Around 70 percent of staff
Not yet full (NYF1)	Evidence of performance against the standard indicates that this person is not yet a full performer. Improvement in one or more performance area is needed.	2.5 percent of staff
Not yet full minus (NYF–)	Evidence of performance against standards indicates that immediate and significant improvement is needed. This person has been in a not-yet-full performance mode for a relatively long period of time and despite all efforts is not showing signs of improvemen.t	2.5 percent of staff

The above desired distribution is demonstrated graphically in Figure 15.1.

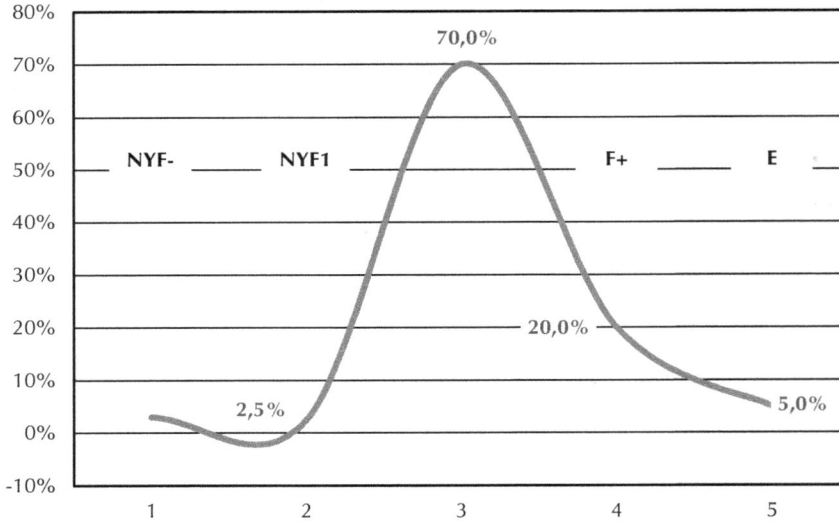

Figure 15.1: Performance rating distribution curve

15.8 LATERAL MOVEMENT IN THE ORGANISATION

An employee moves from one Business Unit/Division to another Business Unit/ Division to a position at the same job grade due to:

- Organisational restructuring, or
- Voluntary transfer request.

In such cases the individual will be moved to the other Business Unit/Department remaining at the same remuneration level with no increase, unless the current remuneration is below the minimum total guaranteed package (TGP) of the pay range applicable to the new position (for example Generic to Critical).

15.8.1 Annual salary reviews

In order to maintain an appropriate remuneration market comparison *vis-à-vis* the market, remuneration should be reviewed each year. Annual remuneration reviews should be informed by:

- Projected inflation, that is, CPI as indicated by the South African Reserve Bank
- Internal equity
- External market
- Performance/delivery
- Affordability

- Contextual variables related to the business.

Individual performance ratings are the driving factor in the annual remuneration review of each individual.

Individual increases are taken into account as follows:

- Consider the overall salary history of the individual i.e. their fit to the existing pay range.

- Consider the individual's unique market worth.

- Actively manage the salaries of good performers who are considerably underpaid.

- "Slow down" the pay of overpaid people (i.e. under-performers who are paid at the top of the pay range).

- Cap pay to the maximum of the pay scale, thereby ensuring that no one individual is paid above the maximum of the pay scale.

15.9 MIGRATION TOWARDS TOTAL PERFORMANCE-BASED SALARY INCREASES

This is applicable to all employees who still receive an inflation-linked increase. Total performance-based pay is determined utilising the results of the business unit performance integrated with the individual performance management result. The process of migration to Total Performance-Based Pay should be implemented over a five-year period, as is illustrated in Tables 15.2 and 15.3.

Note: A figure of 10 percent CPI increase is utilised as an illustrative value.

Table 15.2: Phased approach to performance-based pay

Year	Weighted Cost-of-living Increase Percentage (CPI Informed) (A)	Weighted Final Score on Key Performance Areas (B)	Weighted Performance Score (A + B) = (C)	Annual Increase
1	80%	20%	A + B	C
2	70%	30%	A + B	C
3	60%	40%	A + B	C
4	50%	50%	A + B	C
5	Movement to Total Performance-Based Pay, as illustrated below			

Total Performance-Based Pay inclusive of Business Unit Performance:

Table 15.3: Total performance-based pay

Year	Departmen-tal/Sectional BSC Score (A)	Weighted Final Score on Individual Key Perfor-mance Areas (B)	Weighted Final Score (A + B) C	Annual Increase
2021/2022	**10%**	**90%**	**(A + B)**	**C**

15.9.1 Management and executive reviews

It is recommended that the system is migrated to Total Performance-Based Pay.

Total performance-based pay is determined utilising the results of the divisional performance itegrated with the individual performance management result. The process of migration to Total Performance-Based Pay should be implemented over a five-year period, as is illustrated in the example of total performance-based pay for an increase of 10% pa in Table 15.4.

Table 15.4: Total performance-based pay

Year	Business Unit BSC %	Weighted Final Score on Individual Perfor-mance %	Business Unit BSC Score (A)	Weighted Final Score on Individ-ual Perfor-mance Score (B)	Weight-ed Final Score (A + B)	Annual Increase
1	80%	20%	4,5	4,0	4,4	8,80%
2	60%	40%	3,0	4,0	3,4	6,80%
3	40%	60%	3,5	3,0	3,2	6,40%
4	20%	80%	2,5	3,5	3,3	6,60%
5	0%	100%	3,0	4,5	4,5	9,00%

15.9.2 Performance-related pay approach

Table 15.5 demonstrates the salary increase model, assuming an example of an average increase of 6%:

Table 15.5: Salary increase model

Individual's current comparison to salary scale	Percentage Increase				
At pay scale maximum	0%	0%	4%	5%	6%
Between pay scale upper guide and maximum	0%	0%	5%	6%	7%
At pay scale midpoint (higher than lower guide and lower than upper guide)	0%	0%	**6%**	7%	8%
Between pay scale lower guide and minimum	0%	0%	7%	8%	9%
At pay scale minimum	0%	0%	8%	9%	10%
Individual's performance rating	Not yet full minus	Not yet full	Full Performance	Full performance plus	Exceptional performance
	(NYF-)	(NYF1)	(F)	(F+)	(E)

Using Table 15.5 with an average increase of 6 percent, an individual who is paid at the maximum of the salary scale but whose performance level is at an F (Full Performance) would get a 4 percent increase, while an individual who is paid at the minimum of the salary scale but whose performance level is at an E (Exceptional Performance) would get a 10 percent increase. An individual paid at the midpoint of the salary scale and whose performance level is at an F (Full Performance) would get the average increase of 6 percent.

15.9.3 Capping of remuneration

The reward management system manages the pay of employees who exceed the maximum of the market by:

- Adopting an approach where no individual may be paid above the maximum of the market unless such an individual is paid at a premium compared to the market.

- Normalising the exceptions in the shortest possible time period, giving no annual increase, but paying a once-off cash bonus calculated at the midpoint of the pay scale scaled against the individual performance management score.

15.9.4 Incentive schemes

It is important that alignment is ensured between the following elements of the Human Capital Management Strategy:

- Remuneration strategy
- Performance management
- Short-term incentive scheme
- Long-term incentive scheme.

15.9.4.1 Short-term incentive scheme

Market illustrative short-term incentives are calculated as indicated in Table 15.6:

Table 15.6: Market-illustrative short-term incentive increase quanta

| Strategic level | Typical title | Typical Paterson | Performance | Market STI Quanta – Annual – % of TGP | | | |
				Lower quartile	Median	Upper quartile	90th percentile
Top Management; Strategic Intent	Group CEO	F Upper	On-target	30%	60%	75%	200%
			Stretch	50%	78%	110%	500%
	CEO/MD; Subsidiary CEO/MD; Group Functional Director	F Lower	On-target	20%	33%	57%	75%
			Stretch	35%	56%	73%	180%

Strategic level	Typical title	Typical Paterson	Per-for-mance	Market STI Quanta – Annual – % of TGP			
				Lower quartile	Me-dian	Upper quartile	90th per-centile
General Management; Strategic Execution	CEO/MD; Subsidiary CEO/MD; Functional Director	E Upper	On-target	15%	25%	45%	65%
			Stretch	25%	52%	65%	110%
Senior Management; Strategic Execution	Functional Director	E Lower	On-target	12%	20%	35%	55%
			Stretch	20%	40%	55%	75%
Middle Management; Qualified Professionals; Experienced Professionals	Manager	D	On-target	10%	15%	20%	40%
			Stretch	14%	35%	45%	60%
Advanced Operational; Skilled Technical; Academically Qualified; Junior Management	Supervisor, Foreman, Superinten-dent	C	On-target	5%	8%	12%	20%
			Stretch	10%	12%	20%	30%
Operational and Primary; Semi-skilled		B	On-target	5%	7%	10%	17%
			Stretch	7%	9%	15%	22%
Operational and Primary; Unskilled		A	On-target	5%	7%	10%	17%
			Stretch	7%	9%	15%	22%

Short-term incentives will be determined through a Total Performance Base with the line-of-sight principle applicable (as shown in Table 15.7), that is, the final rating is determined by the direct impact on organisational and business unit/divisional strategy execution.

Table 15.7: Weighted distribution on line of sight

Job grade	Organisation	Division/Department	Employee
F	100%	0%	0%
E	70%	20%	10%
D	50%	30%	20%
C	40%	30%	30%
B	20%	40%	40%
A	0%	50%	50%

15.9.4.2 Long-term incentive scheme

The long-term incentive scheme is usually applicable only to the Upper Band employees of the organisation and only based on the discretion of the Board and the availability of funds. The multiples will be determined on an annual basis within the market to ensure annual and contextual alignment.

Market illustrative Quanta Multiples are illustrated in Tables 15.8, 15.9 and 15.10:

Table 15.8: Appreciation share multiples

Strategic level	Typical title	Paterson Grade	Appreciation share multiples				
			P10	P25	P50	P75	P90
Top Management; Strategic Intent	Group CEO	F Upper	0.92	2.69	8.12	17.90	30.86
	CEO/MD; Subsidiary CEO/MD; Group Functional Director	F Lower	0.55	2.37	5.76	12.60	21.40
General Management; Strategic Execution	CEO/MD; Subsidiary CEO/MD; Functional Director	E Upper	0.42	1.78	4.36	9.92	18.61

Strategic level	Typical title	Paterson Grade	Appreciation share multiples				
			P10	P25	P50	P75	P90
Senior Management; Strategic Execution	Functional Director	E Lower	0.33	1.43	3.49	7.69	15.77
Middle Management; Qualified Professionals; Experienced Professionals	Supervisor, Foreman, Superinten-dent	D	0.28	1.19	2.63	4.40	11.43
Advanced Operational; Skilled Technical; Academically Qualified; Junior Management		C	0.14	0.59	1.40	2.63	5.71
Operational & Primary; Semi and Unskilled		B, A	0.14	0.59	1.22	2.19	4.84

Table 15.9: Full share multiples

Strategic level	Typical title	Paterson Grade	Full share multiples				
			P10	P25	P50	P75	P90
Top Management; Strategic Intent	Group CEO	F Upper	0.28	0.81	2.45	5.41	9.32
	CEO/MD; Subsidiary CEO/MD; Group Functional Director	F Lower	0.17	0.71	1.74	3.81	6.46

Strategic level	Typical title	Paterson Grade	Full share multiples				
			P10	P25	P50	P75	P90
General Management; Strategic Execution	CEO/MD; Subsidiary CEO/MD; Functional Director	E Upper	0.13	0.54	1.32	3.00	5.62
Senior Management; Strategic Execution	Functional Director	E Lower	0.10	0.43	1.05	2.32	4.76
Middle Management; Qualified Professionals; Experienced Professionals	Super-visor, Foreman, Superin-tendent	D	0.08	0.36	0.79	1.33	3.45
Advanced Operational; Skilled Technical; Academically Qualified; Junior Management		C	0.04	0.18	0.42	0.79	1.73
Operational & Primary; Semi and Unskilled		B, A	0.04	0.18	0.37	0.66	1.46

Table 15.10: Annual multiples

Strategic level	Typical title	Paterson Grade	Annual multiples				
			P10	P25	P50	P75	P90
Top Management; Strategic Intent	Group CEO	F Upper	0.06	0.16	0.49	1.08	1.86
	CEO/MD; Subsidiary CEO/MD; Group Functional Director	F Lower	0.03	0.14	0.35	0.76	1.29

Strategic level	Typical title	Paterson Grade	Annual multiples				
			P10	P25	P50	P75	P90
General Management; Strategic Execution	CEO/MD; Subsidiary CEO/MD; Functional Director	E Upper	0.03	0.11	0.26	0.60	1.12
Senior Management; Strategic Execution	Functional Director	E Lower	0.02	0.09	0.21	0.46	0.95
Middle Management; Qualified Professionals; Experienced Professionals	Supervisor, Foreman, Superinten-dent	D	0.02	0.07	0.16	0.27	0.69
Advanced Operational; Skilled Technical; Academically Qualified; Junior Management		C	0.01	0.04	0.08	0.16	0.35
Operational & Primary; Semi and Unskilled		B, A	0.01	0.04	0.07	0.13	0.29

15.9.5 Sales commission scheme

A sales commission scheme applicable to employees will be implemented to ensure that the earnings potential is increased by driving the correct behaviour amongst sales staff. The commission scheme principles are usually as follows:

• The earnings potential of the individual is directly linked to the sales that they generate (infinitely variable).

• Commission quanta.

Commission earning potential is governed by two related factors:

- The ease of making the sale, which in turn influences
- The remuneration mix – guaranteed pay versus variable pay (commission).

Table 15.11 serves as a calculation guide.

Table 15.11 Commission calculation guide

"Ease of Sale"	Easy	Medium	Difficult
Guaranteed Pay	Market related	Market related	Low
Variable Pay	Low	Medium	High
Ratio (GP:VP)	High	Balanced	Low

15.10   KEY SKILLS DEFINITIONS

Cognisance should be taken of these prevailing categories and skill levels. Attraction and retention options are suggested for each category.

15.10.1 Critical skills

These are the skills categorised as essential for the sustainability and effective service delivery of business and they are based on core business requirements. Should these skilled positions leave the organisation, it would be significantly affected due to the considerable impact on the operations of the organisation should the position remain vacant for any period of time. Critical Skills are classified into Critical Specialists and Mission Critical Skills.

15.10.2 Scarce skills

These skills are based on market demand and supply factors. In most instances scarce skills may also be critical as well and may receive the remuneration treatment for both categories. This is particularly apparent in highly technical areas in Southern Africa. It is therefore important to determine whether the scarce skills as determined by the market are also critical enough within the organisation to warrant special remuneration treatment.

Scarce skills reflect the demand and supply of a particular skill at a particular time. The skill requirement may not necessarily mean it is complex, but could imply that, owing to circumstances, only a few people in the market have these specific skills. The situation changes over time when skill-pipelining facilitates more people acquiring this level of skills, negating their "hot skill" status.

15.10.3 High fliers

These skills reflect a very high level of consistent competence and performance over *a long period* of time and tend to attract the attention of an organisation's executive management. Their market value increases over time and they may command relatively higher pay.

15.11 SKILLS PREMIUMS AND SPECIFIC REMUNERATION TREATMENT

15.11.1 Critical skills

15.11.1.1 Base pay (guaranteed pay)

In order to stay competitive, making decisions with regard to payment of critically-skilled employees will usually focus on the upper guide of the pay scale. This will enable managers of these staff to ensure that the guaranteed portion of their packages is compatible, to both attract and motivate skills identified as critical. To this end it is crucial that the organisation subscribes to a robust remuneration survey so that accurate market quartiles can be determined.

15.11.1.2 Variable pay

This part of the employee's total remuneration includes variable pay components such as a performance incentive scheme or a reward and recognition scheme. Measurable targets are in place and the pay-outs of these schemes will be targeted at a competitive market quartile. The organisation may wish to target a higher "on-target" percentage for critical skills.

15.11.1.3 Market premiums/allowances

As per the base pay description above, critical skills are catered for within the pay scales and don't attract premiums or allowances based on external market comparisons. This is explained diagrammatically in Annexure A.

15.11.2 Scarce skills

15.11.2.1 Base pay (guaranteed pay)

In order not to distort the salary scales within an organisation, these employees would be paid within the applicable grade range. It should be ensured that the guaranteed portion is in line with the appropriate levels of employees within the same grade.

15.11.2.2 Variable pay

This part of the employee's total remuneration includes variable pay components such as a performance incentive scheme or a reward and recognition scheme. Measurable targets are in place and the pay-outs of these schemes will be in line with the rest of the organisations remuneration policy.

15.11.2.3 Market premiums/allowances

Where appropriate, a *scarce* skills premium will be placed over and above guaranteed pay (GP). By keeping GP constant, the incumbent can be brought back to the appropriate base pay should demand and supply factors change. The scarce skills premium is a market premium over and above the base pay. The premium will be on top of guaranteed pay as a "bonus premium" and can be removed once the demand and supply situation has changed.

This premium is not guaranteed and the quantum should be in line with the market rate to complement a guaranteed basic pay. This premium is not regarded as part of the employees' guaranteed portion of pay, but should be taken into account when comparisons are done on clean wage per employee. It is important to note that not all scarce skills are equal and therefore suggesting a standard market premium would be the wrong approach. Each position should be interrogated and the size of the premium determined by the level of scarcity. The premium is usually expressed as a percentage of the midpoint of the organisation's pay scale and the same level of premium is paid to individuals irrespective of their position within that scale. This concept is illustrated in Annexure A below.

15.11.3 High fliers

Employees in this category consistently display improvement in performance and skills level over a long period in accordance with the performance management system. They may be innovative, have wisdom, and command sapiential authority over their areas of influence. They also command respect among peers in the field. Their market value increases over time and they will command relatively higher pay.

15.11.3.1 Base pay (guaranteed pay)

Pay should be gradually moved towards the upper guide of the pay scale. Pay scales will adjust according to the market and consequently, employees can be maintained on upper guide level depending on the consistency and level of outperformance.

15.11.3.2 Variable pay

These employees would generally earn larger performance incentives than their peers based on the attainment of robust performance measures.

15.11.3.3 Premiums/Allowances

No premiums will be considered for this category. Any variable pay is usually catered for in the bonus scheme where the employee, due to them being a top performer, usually achieves their stretch targets and resultant relatively high level of bonus.

Annexure A: Skills premiums

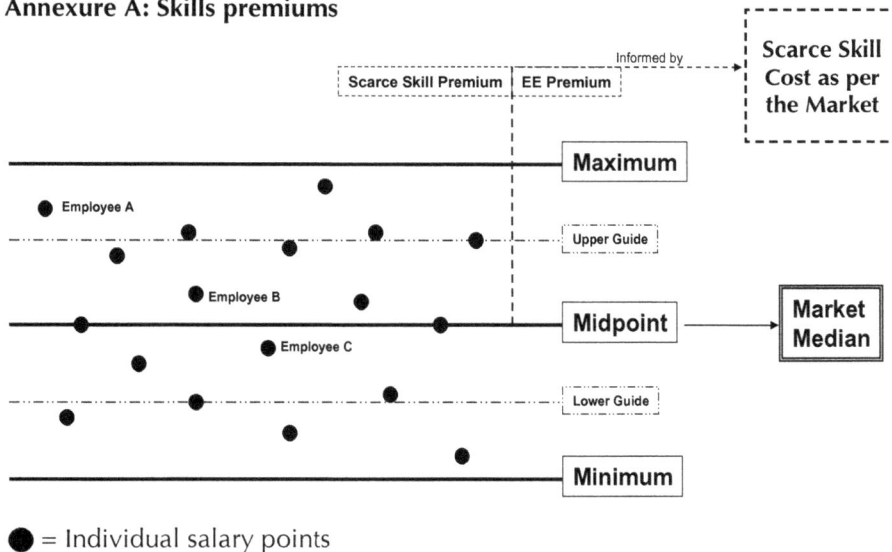

● = Individual salary points

Figure 15.2: "Hot skills" remuneration treatments

15.12 PAY-SCALE DESIGN

In the above example, the organisation's pay scales have been aligned to the market median and the midpoint of the above scale has been anchored at this market quartile. A spread has then been applied to either side of this midpoint to create the minimum and maximum salary levels for the scale. This would be done for every grade level within the organisation and employees paid within this range.

15.13 REMUNERATION OPTIONS

Employee A could be a critical skill or a high-flier. This is evident by the employee's position in the pay scale in relation to his/her peers. By paying Employee A above the upper guide of the pay scale, they are effectively being paid at a higher market point than Employee C. As salary scales move in line with the market, the only way that an employee should be able to get to that point would be through consistently good performance where they would move through the scales faster than their peers (high-flier) due to higher increases or if the skill was deemed critical and paid around the upper guide or maximum of the pay scale to reflect a different market quartile (upper quartile if the pay scale is wide enough).

Let us assume that Employee B and Employee C are both scarce skills. Their scarce skill premium would be determined by the cost of that scarce skill in the market or an agreed premium would be applied (as per Table 15.12 below).

In the first scenario, the difference between the midpoint of their salary scale and the "market cost" of the scarce skill is what would determine the level of premium payable. This premium would then apply to both Employee B and Employee C even though their salary levels are different. In other words, it applies to the skills category and not the employee.

It is typical to apply an agreed premium to certain *levels* of skill. An example of how this may work can be seen in Table 15.12 below.

Table 15.12: Example of application of premiums to skills levels

Description	Percentage Premium
Mission Critical. At least 25% or more of these posts have been vacant in the past year, where offers have been made but the pay scales alone cannot attract the required skills to join the organisation due to scarcity premiums or evidence exists of high turnover in the order of 25% or more.	10% of the applicable pay scale midpoint
Critical Specialists. At least 10–25% of these posts have been vacant in the past year, where offers have been made but the pay scales alone cannot attract the required skills to join the organisation due to scarcity premiums or evidence exists of high turnover in the order of 10–25%.	7.5% of the applicable pay scale midpoint

Description	Percentage Premium
Specialist. At least 5–10% of these posts have been vacant in the past year, where offers have been made but the pay scales alone cannot attract the required skills to join the organisation due to scarcity premiums or evidence exists of high turnover in the order of 5–10%.	5% of the applicable pay scale midpoint

15.14 21ST CENTURY REWARD MANAGEMENT SYSTEM – POWERED BY LUMESSE

Using the right Reward Management System such as the 21st Century Reward Management system powered by Lumesse will help you to get your pay and reward structure right.

21st Century Reward Management System is an accurate, flexible, easy-to-use tool for developing attractive, competitive and motivating reward structures at all levels – based on both market comparisons and corporate objectives. It simplifies the process for everyone.

21st Century Reward Management System allows your HR staff, line managers, and executives to work together to:

- Get an instant overall view of your company's reward structure, based on current and accurate value-added data and research.

- Maintain your market competitiveness by comparing your current reward structures against real market data from a combination of different surveys.

- Compare reward across jobs, industries and locations.

- Balance your reward budget and meet your financial obligations.

- Value-added data is used to plan salaries, control tight budgets, and award appropriate market leading salaries, benefits and merit increases.

- Create consistent salary review processes (across teams and skill areas) by using reward reviews. The reward review simplifies annual adjustments, creating configurable performance- and merit-based programmes for target groups and individuals.

- Build and review comprehensive total reward profiles.

- Create a competitive and flexible reward strategy that links performance to reward, covering:

- – Base salaries
- – Short-term incentive plans
- – Long-term incentive plans
- – Retirement plans
- – Medical aid plans
- – Bonuses
- – Share incentive plans, and more.

- Create total reward packages and action plans (based on analysis and reporting) for individuals or target groups.

Performance management and performance related pay remain a top priority for all international organisations. The next chapter covers this important trend in more detail.

CHAPTER 16
PERFORMANCE MANAGEMENT
Dr Mark Bussin

16.1 INTRODUCTION

A particularly crucial part of successful talent management in emerging markets involves setting up appropriate performance management (PM), remuneration and benefit structures. Employees are hired by organisations for the purpose of performance. The nature of the performance varies, but the expectation of compensation in exchange for performance does not. Just as employees have a right to expect to be paid for the work they perform, organisations have a right to measure performance and reward employees commensurately with this measurement.

The apparent simplicity of this *quid pro quo* relationship is dispelled when one delves a little deeper and starts to question how performance is measured and what qualifies as fair/appropriate remuneration. The complexities become even more pronounced when considering the differing local versus expatriate pay universes and cross-cultural differences in understanding what constitutes both performance and value for organisations and employees. This chapter examines the importance of performance management and describes how to set up a balanced, equitable yet competitive reward and remuneration system in an emerging market context.

16.2 GLOBAL PRACTICES, OR THE NEED TO CONTEXTUALISE/LOCALISE

Some experts argue that globalisation has been a contributor to convergence of managerial mind-set and practice. Others suggest that there is a need to contextualise human resource management practices for the country and company. In this case, the following factors need to be considered:

- National culture across countries and differences in values across societies. This has a bearing on whether to lean towards, for example, 360-degree feedback or traditional performance feedback by manager, or whether to focus on individual or team incentives.

- Employee attitude towards performance management and collective versus individual outlook.

- Industry type and job family category have a bearing because certain processes lend themselves better to certain industries and job families. For example, consulting companies are more likely to measure contribution, outputs and billing.

- The extent to which the CEO owns the performance management process. In high-performing organisations CEOs own the performance management system and use it to drive organisation strategy.

The suggested approach, especially for multinational companies (MNCs), is to use a hybrid approach of providing the international or corporate framework, but guide organisations on how to adapt them for local circumstances. In my experience of having worked in 23 countries across all continents, there is one golden rule – keep the performance management and reward system simple and easy to explain and understand. Do not over-complicate the process or the system.

The text that follows is intended to provide practical building blocks, much like Lego, where you can build your own system, based on good practice and best fit.

In emerging markets there is the opportunity to take the best practices and lessons learnt from developed economies and improve on them. Similarly, one has the opportunity to not to adopt the strategies and systems that did not work. Set out below is a description of some of the global practices that have been adopted in many emerging markets because they work there, plus strategies and practices that may be unique to emerging markets. There are many emerging market practices that could be exported to developed economies, but that is a subject for another place. Recommendations are made along the way.

16.3 PERFORMANCE MANAGEMENT

Organisations have traditionally focused on the process of *performance evaluation* which is effectively the measurement or appraisal of performance. In the last two decades the concept of *performance management* has emerged which adopts a future-orientated strategic focus aimed at maximising current performance and future potential. Performance management extends beyond the concept of performance appraisal and refers to the system or framework through which organisations set work goals, determine performance standards, assign and evaluate work, provide performance feedback by means of performance appraisals or formal reviews, determine training and development needs and distribute rewards (Briscoe & Claus, 2008).

The conceptual foundation of performance management relies on a view that performance is more than ability and motivation. Clarity of goals is seen as key in motivating and helping employees understand what is expected of them. The objectives of performance management often include: motivating performance, helping individuals develop their skills, building a performance culture, determining who should be promoted, exiting individuals who are poor performers, and helping implement business strategies (Lawler III, 2003). Performance management supports the overall business goals by linking the work of every individual employee and the manager to the overall mission of his or her work unit. When employees are clear about what is expected of them and have the necessary support, their sense of purpose, self-worth and motivation increases (Costello, 1994).

Performance management establishes an organisational culture in which all employees take responsibility for the continuous improvement of their performance. The main purpose of appraising and coaching employees is therefore to instil in them the desire for continuous improvement (Latham, Almost, Mann & Moore, 2005).

16.3.1 Performance appraisal

Performance appraisal and measurement should form an integral part of the overall performance management system of the company in order to be effective. Organisations use performance appraisals to assess and evaluate employees' job performance formally. They provide the opportunity for employees and managers to sit down and have a dialogue about performance and development at least twice a year. Appraisals look back over the past year to review performance and objectives, then look forward to set objectives and targets for the next year and to identify learning and development needs to improve performance (Porter, Bingham & Simmonds, 2008).

Within a performance appraisal, performance should be assessed on the basis of predetermined organisational standards. This allows for a comparative and normative assessment of individuals and productivity. The assessment in turn functions as the foundation for pay increases and promotions, provides feedback to help improve performance and recognise weaknesses, and offers information about the attainment of work goals.

The nature of performance appraisal causes it to be a management activity fraught with difficulties. There is a personal nature to assessing or rating the work efforts of another human being that is difficult to overcome, and in a sense, performance appraisal should be a personal as opposed to an impersonal experience for employees. Most employees want to feel that their efforts are noticed and appreciated by their organisations. The manager must therefore maintain a fine balance between being a counsellor or coach and being a fair judge of employee performance.

16.3.2 Performance management challenges in emerging markets

Multinational enterprises in emerging markets are increasingly using cross-cultural virtual and situational teams to increase speed in launching products to market and in bringing together employees from different locations, functional areas, and cultural perspectives. While the diversity of this type of workforce is a significant source of competitive advantage, the impact of geographic spread and cultural diversity also presents many challenges to conventional management practices.

For example, there can be significant differences in how individuals in different cultures provide and seek performance feedback (Milliman, Taylor & Czaplewski, 2002). The definition of what constitutes performance and the consequences of poor performance are also varied (Evans et al, 2002).

The Western concept of performance management may not always suit other cultures. The manager–subordinate relationship is often a point of contention as a result of power distance or discomfort with critical feedback. For example, Chinese culture sometimes shows a preference for group-orientated appraisals rather than individual assessment; and in India, it may be inappropriate and disrespectful to disagree with one's supervisor (Evans, Pucik & Barsoux, 2002; Cascio, 2006).

One of the purposes of global performance management is to build and maintain a strong, overarching integrative corporate culture (Hellqvist, 2011). To achieve this corporate culture a thorough acknowledgement and understanding of the diversity of local cultures is essential. Training for managers about how to conduct global performance management systems including diversity and cultural competency is vital; otherwise implementation could well be a waste of time and money (Cascio, 2006). Adequate training must be provided to both the appraiser and the appraise in order to avoid the many rating errors that are common in performance appraisal. Training should include cultural, legal and customer differences by country providing managers with the tools to improve on the process. Managers must also be given the opportunity to build the required relationship with their employees (Appelbaum, Roy & Gilliland, 2011:570).

16.3.3 Characteristics of performance management

Performance management is not an appraisal event, but an on-going process involving performance planning, feedback, evaluation and development. The emphasis is on providing employees with feedback on their success in achieving specific performance goals and expectations, as well as on their ability to develop core competencies and skills (Chingos & Marwick, 1997). The three core phases of the performance management cycle are illustrated in Figure 16.1.

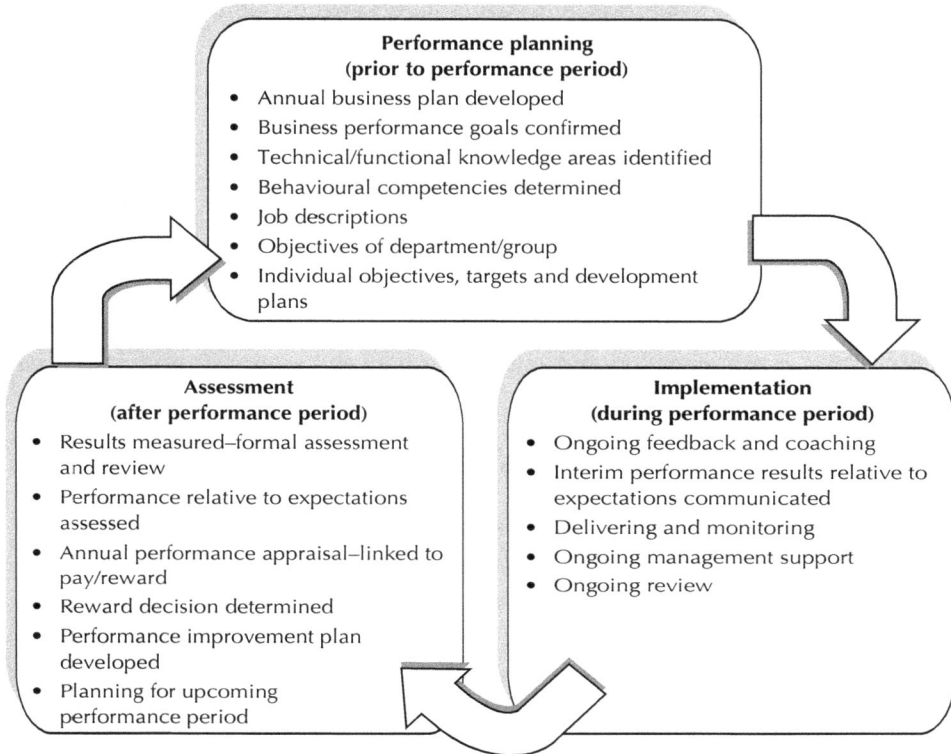

Figure 16.1: The performance management cycle (Costello, 1994)

16.3.3.1 Performance planning phase

The performance planning phase refers to the confirmation of business performance goals, technical/functional knowledge areas and behavioural competencies used to measure job performance. The planning phase starts before the period over which performance is measured. It involves identifying applicable performance criteria that link to the organisation's business plan and defining success at varying levels of the organisation. This process of performance planning is most effective when there is broad employee participation. It requires the manager and the employee to get together for a performance planning meeting where they discuss what the person will achieve over the next twelve months (the key responsibilities of the person's job and the goals and projects the person will work on) and how the person will do the job (the behaviours and competencies the organisation expects of its members (Chingos & Marwick, 1997; Grote, 2002).

Translating organisational objectives into individual performance targets and responsibilities begins with accountability. In the context of performance management, a key accountability is simply an area of responsibility for which the employee is expected to produce results. Each job holder, regardless of current levels of performance, can achieve better results if behavioural objectives based on personal development are built into the planning process.

16.3.3.2 Implementation phase

The implementation phase is ongoing throughout the performance period. It emphasises opportunities for informal feedback and coaching by managers to improve and develop employees' job performance. In this regard, feedback is important because employees want to know how they are doing relative to performance expectations. The most significant aspect of this phase is the opportunity for enhancing communication and interaction between managers and employees throughout the performance period.

16.3.3.3 Results assessment phase

The results assessment phase typically occurs at the end of the performance period. At this time, results on all dimensions are evaluated relative to expectations, and a performance improvement plan is developed. This phase serves two main purposes. The first is to determine the appropriate employee reward system linkages such as annual cash incentive pay-outs, base salary increases, and general development and training needs. Secondly, it contributes to planning for the upcoming performance period by highlighting necessary adjustments to business performance goals, functional knowledge areas and behavioural competencies that may be necessary in response to changing job and organisational requirements (Chingos & Marwick, 1997).

16.3.4 Developing a performance appraisal system

The performance appraisal system forms an integral part of the overall performance management framework of the organisation. The development of a formal performance appraisal system can be divided into ten interrelated phases. In a similar way to the performance management process, the development of a performance appraisal process is an **ongoing process**. Every time there are changes in the organisation's focus that influence personnel practices, the performance appraisal process should be reviewed and the necessary changes should be implemented.

Phase 1: Determine the purpose of the performance appraisal system	Phase 2: Determine the performance criteria and dimensions	Phase 3: Determine who will be involved in performance ratings
Phase 10: Evaluate and adapt	**Fair employment legislation** **Code of good practice**	Phase 4: Select the most appropriate appraisal method(s)
Phase 9: Implement system/ conduct appraisals		Phase 5: Get senior management buy-in
Phase 8: Train raters	Phase 7: Design appraisal system	Phase 6: Involve employees

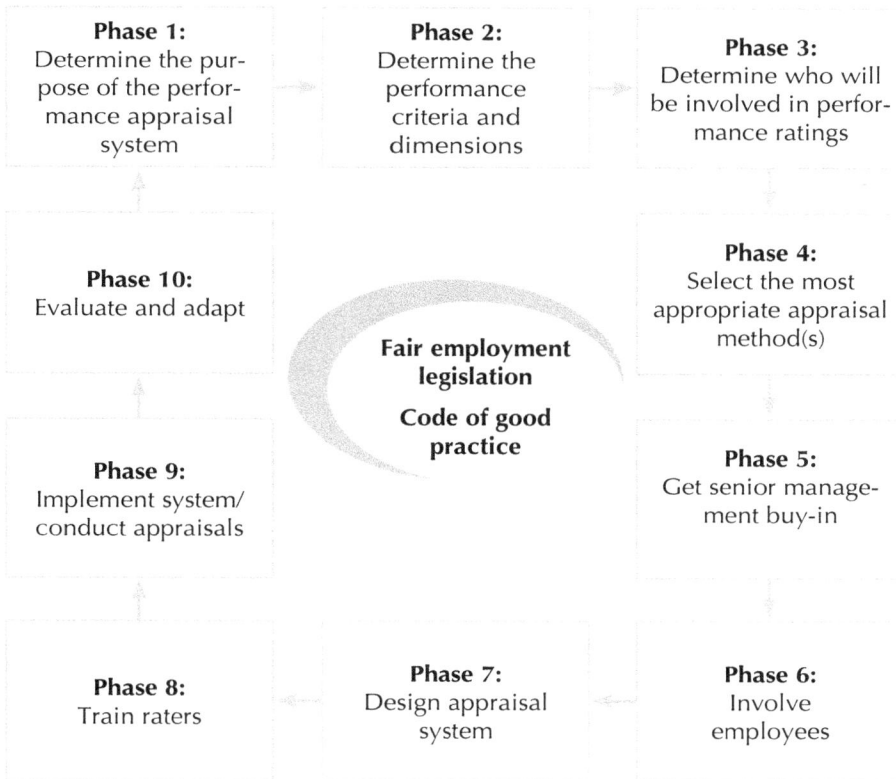

Figure 16.2: Phases in developing a performance appraisal system (Bussin & Botha, 2010)

Performance appraisal information can be used for **three broad purposes** in the organisation (Bussin & Botha, 2010). **Firstly**, it can be used to make personnel decisions such as salary increases, incentive payments, promotion and demotion decisions, and even dismissal. When performance appraisal information is used to make personnel decisions, employees are often compared with each other. Someone may be promoted to the managerial position because that person had a higher performance rating.

Secondly, performance appraisal information can be used to identify employee strengths and weaknesses. This can assist the manager or employee in identifying performance problems and producing personal development plans to address these performance problems. The purpose is to change or reinforce behaviour, not to compare employees' work behaviour with each other (Mathis & Jackson, 2004). Information on an employee's job-related strengths and weaknesses can be utilised in the **third** broad category of performance appraisal information uses, which is employee career planning and development, including further training and development. If managers/supervisors know what their employees' strengths and weaknesses are, and employees know how they want their careers to progress,

213

the performance appraisal information can provide valuable information on what employees need to do in terms of further training and development to move on to the next step in the career plan.

16.4 PERFORMANCE APPRAISAL METHODS

There are many different performance appraisal methods in use today. As shown in Table 16.1, the different methods can be grouped into six broad categories: performance can be assessed by using objective methods, subjective methods, comparative methods, rating methods, goal-based methods, and methods of computerised performance monitoring. Each set of methods uses different performance dimensions and/or different ways to collect and interpret the performance information in order to produce a performance rating for every employee. It is essential to ensure that employee job performance is measured using valid and culturally relevant performance criteria and standards for each performance dimension.

Table 16.1: Categories of performance appraisal methods (Bussin & Botha, 2010)

Common categories	Typical methods
Objective methods	• Quantity of work • Quality of work • Attendance • Safety • Critical incidents
Subjective (judgemental) methods	• Essays • Narratives
Comparative methods	• Ranking • Paired comparisons • Forced-distribution
Rating methods	• Graphic rating scales • Behavioural checklists • Frequency of desired behaviours • Behaviourally anchored rating scales (BARS) • Behavioural observation scales (BOS)
Goal-based methods	• Management by objectives (MBO) • Balanced scorecard • Outputs

Common categories	Typical methods
Computerised performance monitoring	• Electronic performance monitoring and evaluation

It is important to note that no single performance appraisal method is suitable for all jobs and situations. Therefore it may be more appropriate to use a combination of methods. The most successful implementations have involved the concept of setting objectives or preferably outputs, within key result areas (KRAs) and key result indicators (KRIs). A five-point rating scale is most commonly used with the following descriptors, with approximate desired distribution of scores in brackets:

1. Far exceeds expectations (15%)
2. Exceeds expectations (25%)
3. Meets expectations (45%)
4. Meets some expectations (10%)
5. Does not meet expectations (5%).

16.5 RATERS OF PERFORMANCE

The most common method of rating performance is still the manager rating the subordinate.

The use of **multi-source (360-degree)** feedback is becoming more popular. With this approach, performance information is collected from managers, supervisors, peers, customers and subordinates. The information from all these sources is collated, provided to the employee, and discussed with the manager. The employee and manager collaborate to compile a personal development plan to address any weaknesses that are identified. Multi-source feedback is more effective when all the participants know that the information will be used for development purposes and not for making promotion or salary increase decisions. In some organisations it may be essential to guarantee that raters will remain anonymous, although this may have a negative influence on the ability of multi-source feedback to improve organisational communication.

Not only can the appraisal instrument assess the wrong performance dimensions, it can also unintentionally drive the wrong behaviours. A good example of this is the parable of the beekeepers, described below.

Show me the Honey!

Once upon a time in Yemen, there were two beekeepers, each of whom had a beehive. The beekeepers worked for a company called YemBees Ltd. The company's customers loved its honey and the business aimed to produce more honey than it had the previous year. As a result, each beekeeper was told to produce more honey at the same quality. With different ideas about how to do this, the beekeepers designed different approaches to improve the performance of their hives.

YemBees Beekeeper One

The first beekeeper established a bee performance management approach that measured how many flowers each bee visited. At considerable cost to the beekeeper, an extensive measurement system was created to count the flowers each bee visited. The beekeeper provided feedback to each bee at midseason on his individual performance, but the bees were never told about the hive's goal to produce more honey so that YemBees Ltd could increase honey sales. The beekeeper created incentives, special awards for the bees which visited the most flowers.

YemBees Beekeeper Two

The second beekeeper also established a bee performance management system, but this approach communicated to each bee the goals of the hive – to produce more honey. This beekeeper and his bees measured two aspects of their performance: the amount of nectar each bee brought back to the hive and the amount of honey the hive produced. The performance of each bee and the hive's overall performance were charted and posted on the hive's bulletin board for all bees to see. The beekeeper created a few awards for the bees that gathered the most nectar, but he also established a hive incentive programme that rewarded each bee in the hive based on the hive's production of honey—the more honey produced, the more recognition each bee would receive.

YemBees: Performance prediction

What do you think might have happened to each hive at the end of the season when the Queen Bee would report back to each beekeeper?

YemBees Beekeeper One at the end of the season

The first beekeeper found that his hive had indeed increased the number of flowers visited, but the amount of honey produced by the hive had dropped. The Queen Bee reported that because the bees had -filled fields they'd spotted on the way back to the hive that could have helped improve the performance of all the bees. After all was said and done, one of the high-performing bees told the beekeeper that if he'd been told that the real goal was to make more honey rather than to visit more flowers, he would have done his work completely differently.

As the beekeeper handed out been so busy trying to visit as many flowers as possible, they had limited the amount of nectar they would carry so that they could fly faster. Also, because the bees had felt that they were competing against each other for awards (because only the top performers were recognised), they would not share valuable information with each other, such as the location of the flowerthe awards to individual bees, unhappy buzzing was heard in the background.

YemBees Beekeeper Two at the end of the season

The second beekeeper, however, had very different results. Because each bee in his hive had focused on the hive's goal of producing more honey, the bees had concentrated their efforts on gathering more nectar to produce more honey than ever before. The bees had worked together to determine the highest nectar-yielding flowers and to create quicker processes for depositing the nectar they'd gathered. They had also worked together to help increase the amount of nectar gathered by the poor performers. The Queen Bee of this hive reported that the poor performers had either improved their performance or had transferred to another hive.

Because the hive had reached its goal, the beekeeper awarded each bee his portion of the hive incentive payment. The beekeeper was also surprised to hear a loud, happy buzz and a jubilant flapping of wings as he rewarded the individual high-performing bees with special recognition.

The moral of the story is:

Design your systems carefully because they will affect the behaviour of your staff. Measuring and recognising accomplishments rather than activities – and providing feedback to your "worker bees" – can often improve the results of the hive (Nixon, 2011).

16.6 PERFORMANCE APPRAISAL INTERVIEWS

The performance appraisal interview is essentially an interactive conversation between a manager and his or her employee. At this interview the manager communicates his or her perception of the level of job performance to the employee – whether the job performance exceeds expectations, or not, and to produce action plans that will lead to improved job performance, where necessary. A proposed structure for a performance interview is included in Table 16.2.

Table 16.2: A proposed structure for a performance appraisal interview (Bussin & Botha, 2010)

Purpose	Discuss the purpose of the performance appraisal system and the interview with the employee. Provide the employee with the opportunity to indicate what he or she wants to achieve in the interview.
Employee's views on performance for the past review period	Employee is requested to provide his or her own interpretation of his or her work performance of the past review period. Allow enough time to provide the necessary detail required to assess performance fairly.
Manager's views on employee job performance	The manager indicates how he or she perceives employee's job performance, substantiating perceptions with appropriate examples where possible. Indicates where he or she agrees and disagrees with employee's perceptions, and discusses issues where improvements are required.
Discussion of performance rating, using the performance appraisal instrument	Explain rating for each performance dimension and reason for providing said rating, allow employee opportunity to agree or disagree and finally agree on a rating. Agree on an overall rating if one is required.
Discussion of action plans to improve job performance	Solicit suggestions from employee on job performance areas that need improvement, make own suggestions and agree with employee on which suggestions to implement.

Discussion of action plans for employee development	Afford employee opportunity to state career goals and how he or she thinks these goals can be met. Agree on action plans for career development and suggest ways in which they can be implemented.
Discussion of performance objectives/goals for the next review period (if required by the system)	Agree performance goals for the next review period with employee if required by the appraisal system. Goals must be realistic, challenging, measureable and relevant.

Tips for conducting an effective performance appraisal interview include the following:

- Use the "sandwich" technique. Mention areas in need of improvement in the employee's work between positive aspects.

- Emphasise the reason for the appraisal.

- Give the employee enough opportunity to voice his/her opinion about the appraisal; it might explain the reason for performance that does not meet the requirements.

- Never get aggressive during an interview, irrespective of what an employee says. **STAY CALM.**

- Provide enough time for the employee to accept the appraisal – acceptance of criticism does not always come immediately.

- Do not try to convince the employee of anything while he/she is aggressive.

- If remarks in respect of personality are made, they should never be vague – say exactly what is meant and motivate with examples.

- Show interest in employee's work-related problems.

- Provide positive criticism. If an area for improvement is discussed, offer a possible solution or an improvement of the method.

- Ensure that the employee understands that the appraisal of their performance can change the next time around, but that the onus to improve is upon him or her.

- Be willing to listen and discuss, but be very firm.

- Ensure that the employee understands what is expected of him or her.

- Do not be afraid to praise good performance, as it can improve the employee's work satisfaction and positively influence attitudes.

- End the interview with a summary of strengths and areas for improvement, and summarise the plan of action.

In emerging markets, it is the performance conversation that is important. The forms and pieces of paper that need to be completed should never hijack the conversation. Sometimes the forms are so long and cumbersome that they do hijack the conversation and then it becomes a one-way talking "at" the employee. Keep the form succinct.

16.7 USING PERFORMANCE MANAGEMENT TO RETAIN TALENT IN EMERGING MARKETS

Increased demand for the limited supply of talent in emerging markets has driven employee turnover rates into the double digits. By actively and consistently focusing on personal and professional development, performance management supports employees' efforts to improve themselves. Development is an extremely effective retention strategy – it can be more valuable to employees than higher compensation because it keeps their skills competitive. It also shows employees the organisation is willing to invest in them, which can influence their loyalty (Sherman Garr, 2011).

Historically, organisations in emerging markets have focused development primarily on improving technical skills. In order to encourage a broader approach, organisations are now putting processes and structures in place that support development planning, and they are seeing positive results. For example, Accenture have created a development planning tool that recommends specific development activities for employees based on their performance appraisals. Development activities vary based on an employee's job family and level within the organisation. Focused development support is helping the organisation to more effectively retain the 6 000-plus new employees it hires annually in emerging markets (Sherman Garr, 2011).

The trend is to strengthen the link between performance and reward. Whether it is done individually or as a team, division or organisation needs to be considered in the context of the country, culture and industry. The next section sets out retention practices appropriate for emerging markets. Emerging markets have adopted a hybrid approach to reward – some parts are best practice from developed economies, and some have been "home-grown".

16.8 REFERENCES

Appelbaum, SH, Roy, M & Gilliland, T. 2011. Globalization of performance appraisals: Theory and applications. *Management Decision*, 49(4):570–585.

Briscoe, DR & Claus, M. 2008. Employee performance management: Policies and practices in multinational enterprises. In A Varma, PS Budhwar & A DeNisi (eds). 2008. *Performance management systems: Global perspective*. London: Routledge. [15–39]

Bussin, M & Botha, J. 2010. Performance evaluation. In M Coetzee & D Schreuder (eds). 2010. *Personnel Psychology*. Cape Town: Oxford University Press. [328–367]

Cascio, WF. 2006. Global performance management system. In GK Stahl & I Bjorkman (eds). 2006. *Handbook of research in international human resource management*. Cheltenham: Edward Elgar.

Chingos, PT & Marwick, KP. 1997. *Paying for performance – a guide to compensation management*. New York, NY: John Wiley & Sons, Inc.

Costello, SJ. 1994. *Effective performance management*. The Business Skill Express Series. New York, NY: McGraw-Hill.

Evans P, Pucik, V & Barsoux, JL. 2002. *The global challenge: Frameworks for international human resource management*. Boston, MA: McGraw-Hill.

Hellqvist, N. 2011. Global performance management: A research agenda. *Management Research Review*, 34(8):927–946.

Latham, GP & Russo, SD. 2008. The influence of organisational politics on performance appraisal. In S Cartwright & CL Cooper (eds). 2008. *The Oxford handbook of personnel psychology*. Oxford, Oxon: Oxford University Press. [380–410]

Latham, GP, Almost, J, Mann, S & Moore, C. 2005. New developments in performance management. *Organisational Dynamics*, 34(1):77–87.

Lawler, EE. 2000. *Rewarding excellence: Pay strategies for the new economy*. San Francisco, CA: Jossey-Bass.

Mathis, RL & Jackson, JH. 2004. *Human resources management*. 10th ed. Mason, OH: Thomson South-Western College Publishing.

Milliman J, Taylor, S & Czaplewski, AJ. 2002. Cross-cultural performance feedback in multinational enterprises: Opportunity for organisational learning. *Human Resource Planning*, 25.

Nixon, A. 2011. Adapted from *A handbook for measuring employee performance*. Office of Personnel Management, US Government. [Online]. Available: http://spectrain.wordpress.com/tag/cross-cultural/. [Accessed 19 July 2014].

Odendaal, A. 2009. Motivation: From concepts to applications. In SP Robbins, TA Judges, A Odendaal & G Roodt (eds). 2009. *Organisational behaviour: Global and South African perspectives*. Cape Town: Prentice-Hall. [168–191]

Porter, C, Bingham, C & Simmonds, D. 2008. *Exploring human resource management*. New York, NY: McGraw-Hill.

Sherman Garr, S. 2011. *Retaining talent in dynamic markets*. [Online]. Available: http://talentmgt.com/articles/view/retaining-talent-in-dynamic-markets. [Accessed 30 April 2014].

CHAPTER 17
HOW TO RETAIN YOUR EXPATRIATES
Craig Raath and Elmien Smit

17.1 INTRODUCTION

The fast-paced change in the global economy has become a norm. Environmental, social and technological change in the international markets of the business and the increased scarcity and cost of expatriates is an indication that long-term planning is risky but absolutely essential. Because of the changes that are occurring, it has become a challenge for organisations to make decisions about expatriate talent management in this complex, rapidly changing world.

The growing globalisation of industries forces organisations to employ a mobile population for the purpose of competing in overseas markets and to maintain multinational knowledge and expertise. Companies invest great amounts of money in sending their employees on assignment to foreign locations. However, the high turnover of expatriates and repatriates creates large losses.

Taking an international assignment is undoubtedly a challenge. An expatriate is a person working in a foreign country. It could be a permanent transfer or an assignment typically ranging from 30 days to three years, depending on the assignment. But an expatriate is always a citizen from another country. Each organisation may have a different purpose in deciding to go global. The establishment of the specific purpose for the global assignment is the first step in strategic international human resource management. Once this is determined, the rationale for the remuneration strategy evolves.

17.2 ORGANISATIONAL AND INDIVIDUAL PURPOSES FOR EXPATRIATION

According to Mello (2011), there are various reasons why an organisation might take the decision to become a global player. The first reason is that the market opportunity in other countries may be better. A second reason is that organisations might result in economies of scale by the expansion of scope and volume of operations in order to support global initiatives. Thirdly, in order to maintain competitive advantage organisations enter global markets; and lastly, as a result of acquisitions, it is possible that an organisation can be owned or partially owned by a foreign-based organisation.

Other reasons include:

- Business or market development
- The set-up, transfer, or integration of IT
- Management of an autonomous subsidiary
- Co-ordination or integration of foreign with domestic operations
- A temporary assignment to a vacant position
- Development of local management talent.

It is important that in the same way as the organisation has a purpose for entering global markets, there is also an individual purpose for the global assignment. Some of the reasons include the development of the employee for a top management position, the possibility of developing interpersonal or technical skills, and possibly, if the spouse of an employee has received a global assignment, the opportunity for the person to follow their spouse or partner. Baruch, Steele and Quantrill (2002) take it a step further and explain that the reasons people are willing to relocate to different countries include being exposed to different career opportunities or a better life style, and the opportunity to gain global experience, which makes them more marketable.

The slow recovery in the global economy, shifting workforce demographics, and the organisational need to control costs are all creating an increasingly challenging environment in the expatriate talent market. As a result, multinational organisations need to be prepared with dynamic expatriate talent-management strategies that can quickly be adapted to meet changing conditions worldwide.

Organisations need to incorporate global assignments, as part of the strategic approach is that organisations no longer focus only on local markets but are affected by global economies. There is a lot of opportunity entering developing countries and more specifically in the marketing of goods and services. As a means of lowering costs, operations can be outsourced to other countries and participation in joint ventures in foreign countries. Another reason global assignments need to be incorporated into the strategy is the growing culturally diverse workforce within organisations. Failure rates for expatriation are high, not only because people leave earlier, but also as a result of poor performance, or leaving the organisation soon after repatriation (Baruch et al, 2002). This is why it is important that there should be a strategic approach. The HR department should perform a proactive role and have clear strategies and goals in place, not only for expatriation but also for repatriation.

After investigation of the reasons why organisations and individuals engage in expatriation, it is clear that the expansion of operations globally cannot be done without the intervention and involvement of the HR department.

In order to obtain maximum return on investment (to avoid failed assignments and replacements of the expatriate, or damaged relationships with customers and suppliers in the foreign country) the following best practices go a long way towards ensuring the best chances of retention.

17.2.1 Determine appropriate selection criteria for expatriates

This refers to the abilities of the candidates and their families to adjust and function effectively in a new cultural environment. Conflict resolution, leadership, communication and social skills, flexibility and stability, technical ability, cross-cultural suitability, family requirements, language, and gender-related factors should be taken into account. Most of these criteria can be divided into technical competence skills, interpersonal competence/skills, domestic circumstances, and cultural circumstances.

17.2.2 Pre-departure training

This is considered to be the next critical step in attempting to ensure the expatriate's effectiveness and success abroad, particularly where the destination country is considered culturally tough and very different from domestic culture. Language and communication skills are vital here.

17.2.3 Post-arrival assistance

General adjustments which have to be made after arrival in a foreign country may create the need for psychological, socio-cultural and work adjustment. It is vital to follow up with the candidate and supply or offer support where applicable.

The abovementioned paragraphs explained why individual and organisational purposes for expatriation need to be incorporated as part of a strategic approach to managing global assignments.

Assuming that these basic steps are done properly and are in place, only then should one consider remuneration as part of the retention strategy.

17.3 REMUNERATION COMPONENTS

The following figure illustrates the typical expatriate remuneration components:

Figure 17.1: Typical expatriate compensation components (Mathis & Jackson, 2003:597)

With this figure, one can form a holistic picture of where payment for hardship fits into the remuneration context. Typical factors that shape the hardship of a country can include:

- *Economic factors*, such as poverty levels and level of service provision
- *Political factors*, such as freedom/tolerance towards different points of view/ lifestyles
- *Religious factors*, such as freedom/tolerance towards different religions
- *Public service factors*, such as provision of water, electricity, sanitation, and work permits, among others
- *Environmental/climate factors*, such as extreme weather conditions
- *Personal safety factors*, such as personal safety/level of crime
- *Health factors*, such as prevalence of disease and health standards
- *Education factors*, such as education standards, prevalence of international and/ or private schools
- *Transportation factors*, such as prevalence of public transport, fuel and road safety.

Ensuring that these components are market related and correctly applied goes a long way towards ensuring internal and external remuneration equity.

17.4 DIFFERENCES BETWEEN EXPATRIATE AND LOCAL TURNOVER

Expatriate turnover is a broad term that has many definitions in current literature. It has been defined as return prematurely to home or failure in an overseas assignment before the assignment contract has expired (Naumann, 1992; Forster & Johnson, 1996). Among many noteworthy reasons for expatriate turnover are flaws in the expatriate workers' selection process, such as the mismanagement of the relocation process and the inability to adjust to a foreign country culture.

Past research on the subject of expatriate turnover has identified three categories of expatriate workers turnover tendencies (Tyagi & Wotruba, 1993). These tendencies include:

- Work-related attitudes (job satisfaction and organisational commitment)
- Personal characteristics (age, education, and experience)
- External environmental factors (organisational climate, management practices, and supervisory behaviours).

It is generally accepted that while the three identified categories have a bearing on expatriate turnover and retention, the management of the business establishment can control only the work-related variables. The personal characteristics can, to some extent, be controlled by the expatriate employees' selection process and can be enhanced by effective training programmes. The external environment is usually difficult to change in the short run, although this can be done in the long run (Tyagi & Wotruba, 1993).

Given that 85 percent of all expatriate workers are accompanied by their spouses, the case of spouses' inability to adapt is a strong one. It is recommended that to ensure retention of expatriate workers, practical and psychological support must be provided to their families (Wells, 2008). Many accompanying spouses leave their careers behind them and often discover that neither their professional qualifications nor experiences correlate to job opportunities in the countries in which they settle. They also lose their support networks, which include their family and established childcare arrangements, and quickly feel isolated, unhappy, and anxious in the country in which they settle.

The implications of expatriate retention are wide: the loss of the resources they have put into a particular assignment; the potential damage done to the business establishment's reputation and goodwill; the negative impact on a worker of having failed to measure up to expectations in the overseas assignment; possible factors influencing family relationships; and the loss of a valued worker's expertise and experience.

Previous studies suggest that numerous factors impact on expatriate turnover including such issues as provision of appropriate cross-cultural training, in-country support, spousal adjustment, cultural distance, and relationships with host nationals (Gudykunst, 2005). In an increasingly globalised world, business establishments find themselves in competition for a highly specialised workforce of skilled workers who can perform effectively across cultures and in a variety of environments. In recent years there has been a decrease in the number of suitable candidates willing to accept an expatriate posting.

A significant percentage of expatriate workers leave their company within one to two years of starting work where such was not the original intention of either the employer or the employee. This has significant negative consequences for both the business establishment and the expatriate. It is most commonly related to a lack of retention strategies in the relocation of expatriate workers and their dependants (MacDonald & Arthur, 2003; Shelton, 2008).

Heneman and Judge (2003) argue that, in order for an organisation to retain employees who perform optimally, organisations must match reward to employees' preferences. On a practical note it is impossible to compile unique reward profiles for large to medium-sized organisations as it would be difficult to manage and administer these profiles, as indicated by Nienaber, Bussin and Henn (2011). A resolution to this issue is to design reward packages for employees, groups or divisions as suggested by Snelgar, Renard and Venter (2013). In other words, several types of reward will be grouped together, depending on the requirements of a certain employee group or segment (the specific reward package pertains to each expatriate within the organisation). For instance`, diverse reward factors are proposed to different employee groups such as job level, business unit, product line or life cycle, geographic location, generation, age, family size, occupation, education level or religion (Du Toit, Erasmus & Strydom, 2007; Mercer, 2008; Snelgar et al, 2013).

It involves an array of considerations, such as the type of assignment and its remuneration; investment in staffing and places to work; and numerous professional, cultural and family pressures that can overwhelm the hardiest executives (Economist Intelligence Unit, 2010).

17.5 FALL IN DEMAND FOR EXPAT TALENT

As expected, organisations will spend less time on retaining expatriates because of the high costs involved. With only one third of participants expecting the demand for expatriates to remain the same in the next year, just over half experience a lower demand for such employees, with a move away from dependence on expatriate labour. This is illustrated in Figure 17.2 below.

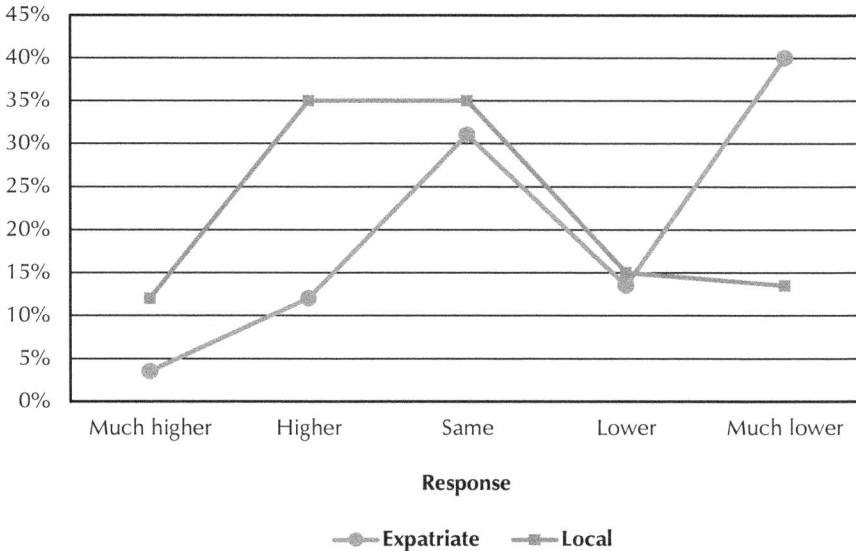

Figure 17.2: Expatriate versus local demand for the next 12 months (EY, 2013/2014)

There is a higher demand for local staff to occupy management, supervisory, technical/operational and professional skills, coupled with a much lower demand for expatriates.

Approximately one in three expatriates in executive positions, and one in five expatriates in other categories, can earn a premium three times that of their local counterparts. This is depicted in Figure 17.3 below.

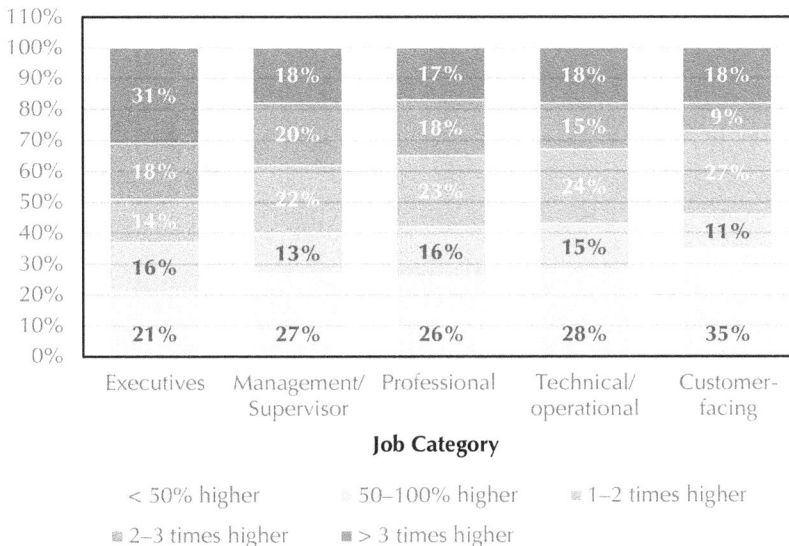

Figure 17.3: Expatriate premiums by category (EY, 2013/2014)

In a study to analyse trends among global expatriate workers, The Economist Intelligence Unit (2010:3) identified a number of key issues, which include the following concerns.

Cultural and family pressures present the greatest difficulties in facilitating expatriate workers retention. An inability to understand local culture and cultural conflicts is one of the greatest difficulties for expatriate workers. Cultural sensitivity is therefore regarded as the most important attribute by some margin for an individual seeking to work in a foreign country, and business establishments admit that it is not easy to find the right type of person in their ranks. More than half of expatriate workers do not relish the prospect of learning another language, suggesting a possible lack of commitment to their role.

The spouse's needs have become more important than ever in the acclimatisation of expatriate workers. Perhaps the greatest obstacle to the success of an expatriate placement lies with the expatriate's spouse and/or children, who may resent the sudden separation from their own career, social life, schooling and routine. The resulting strain on family relationships can often bring about a premature end to the work.

17.6 WHY CAN'T ORGANISATIONS RETAIN THEIR EXPATRIATE EMPLOYEES?

International assignment experience is valuable, and in the right context, it can create a competitive advantage, both for expatriates and the companies that employ them.

Returning expatriates (returnees) bring these things to the company:

- The ability to work and manage effectively in other countries.
- Information about specific local markets and customers.
- The ability to accelerate the transfer of knowledge between countries.

An inability to retain these returnees results in a highly unfavourable ROI for companies that have spent two to four times the returnee's pay during the assignment. Not only is it costly, but having returnees leave the company sends a warning signal to employees that taking an expatriate assignment may be "career threatening".

This is not just a problem for small to medium-sized companies that have little experience with expatriates. It includes large multinationals that have been sending expatriates overseas for years. Some of the problems include:

- **Unclear expectations:** During pre-assignment, top management may emphasise that international experience is critical for the company to survive in the new global business environment. During post-assignment, it is as though top management is suffering from amnesia. Management doesn't quite know how to utilise the experience.

- **Learning a "new" organisation:** Returnees see old co-workers who have been promoted while they have been gone. They wonder if the assignment has hurt their career. They must also get up to speed quickly with changes in organisation, strategy, management, culture, among others.

- **Under-utilisation of overseas experience:** Many expatriate jobs are highly challenging and very autonomous. Expatriates are chief spokespeople for the company with the host country government, professional business organisations, customers, legal entities, and the like.

17.7 HOW CAN EMPLOYERS BE MORE SUCCESSFUL WITH REGARD TO RETENTION OF EXPATRIATES?

Things have changed since the global recession, with international markets stabilising to differing extents. Asia, in particular, has enjoyed a robust recovery and continues to attract expatriates from all over. According to HSBC's *Expat Survey* for 2013, Thailand has become the most cost-effective place to live in the world, while Indonesia and Vietnam enjoyed high rankings for the career opportunities they present to expats.

According to Mello (2011), investing in repatriation has the greatest impact on the return on investment made in employees sent abroad. Issues to be addressed in a repatriation process can be seen in Table 17.1, below.

Table 17.1: Issues to be addressed in a repatriation process (Mello, 2011:619)

Career	Personal
Career anxiety – current place, future	Logistics
Organisation's reaction	Personal re-adjustments
Loss of autonomy	Family re-adjustments
Adaptation to change	

A specific repatriation process needs to address several critical career and personal issues outlined in Table 17.1. *Firstly*, with regard to career anxiety, the organisation should help the employee returning from overseas find an appropriate place that is connected with a career path for the future. *Secondly*, with regard to the reaction of the organisation, it should be suggested that the organisation makes the repatriate feel welcome and puts newly acquired skills to use. *Thirdly*, with regard to the loss of autonomy, in the planning process, some consideration must be given to the level of autonomy the repatriate enjoyed overseas and the appropriate corresponding types of responsibilities and work assignments when back in the home country. *Fourthly*, with regard to adaption, this refers to significant changes which have taken place at the home office. The repatriate needs to be provided with assistance in adapting to those changes in order to facilitate maximum performance in new assignments.

On the personal level, three major issues need to be addressed in repatriation:

1. Logistics, which includes savings needing to be transferred, currency to be converted, personal belongings packed and shipped, and much more.

2. Re-adjustment and reintegration into the community for the employee.

3. Re-adjustment and reintegration into the community for the employee's family.

Support for such facilitation for the employee and family can greatly assist the repatriation process.

Companies must be able to capitalise on their returnees' skills and knowledge. In order to do so, they need to cultivate a global vision and corporate culture. Companies that support repatriates value their international experience and utilise their global knowledge and contribution will realise true growth in the strategic development of the company.

17.8 THE FUTURE

In order to help HR professionals to manage an expanding globally mobile workforce more efficiently, Mercer (2014) suggests 10 resolutions:

1. **Step back and get some perspective**

   Knowing where your assignment policies stand versus those of your peers is an important first step in maintaining an effective global mobility programme. Some of your policies may vary significantly from those of your peer companies. That variation may be justified, but you should at least know its direction and extent.

2. **Get assignee feedback from the right source**

   Surprisingly, assignees rarely express dissatisfaction about their compensation and allowances in opinion surveys. But issues that typically bother them most – poor communications, lack of relocation support, ineffective service providers, and repatriation planning – cannot be fixed simply by spending more money. To get candid feedback that can result in meaningful policy improvements, consider using a third party that will keep assignees' responses confidential.

3. **Look at your map, then ask directions**

   Many employers are pushing beyond typical expatriate locations, such as Hong Kong, Shanghai, London, and Dubai to less typical ones (sub-Saharan Africa, smaller cities in China, Eastern Europe). Ensure that you have the proper incentives in place to support programmes in non-traditional host locations. And look carefully at expatriates' home countries; if they are leaving a relatively low-wage country such as India, the traditional "balance sheet" approach to compensation may not be appropriate.

4. **Check for the right mix of flexibility, complexity, and equity**
   Flexibility can be built in at the business level (so managers can decide on certain optional compensation elements for expatriates) or at the individual level (using lump sums that expatriates can spend as they choose). While managers may be pushing for more flexibility, it can lead to greater complexity in managing your programme and less equity among expatriates. Be prepared to give your leadership clear metrics so that they understand the balance of priorities.

5. **Scout host neighbourhoods for new expatriates**
   Housing costs are often the largest discretionary portion of total mobility costs (after salary and related taxes), and local housing markets can change significantly during the year. For expatriates heading out in future, be sure to use timely, accurate, neighbourhood-specific housing cost data for host cities. Set appropriate rental guidelines and communicate them clearly to expatriates and relocation firms before they search for housing. Consider moving your approval process further up the chain of command so that senior managers have to approve exceptions to stated policies.

6. **Match expatriate programmes to talent management strategies**
   Define specific competencies for global leaders and then ensure their global mobility programmes build bench strength to fill future leadership slots. As your company expands in other countries, it becomes increasingly important for senior executives to have hands-on experience outside their own home countries. For each assignment, consider whether it is growing the business, developing global leaders, or filling a critical skill gap, but do not leave talent mobility to chance.

7. **Track your business travellers and short-term assignees closely**
   As governments seek new areas of potential tax revenue, employers need to know precisely how many days per year their business travellers and short-term employees are situated in which locations, both domestically and internationally. It is critical to manage not only their presence, but their remuneration. Consider whether they should be on regular expense-reimbursement programmes or set up in serviced flats with cost-effective *per diem* expenses.

8. **Consider "local plus" as a compensation programme**
   Are some of your expatriates locally hired foreigners or directly hired on one-way or indefinite assignments? If so, a "local-plus" compensation package (adding a handful of allowances to local salaries) may be more appropriate

than a traditional home balance-sheet package premised on maintaining home country ties. Local-plus adjustments may be particularly appropriate in Asia, where this approach has gained traction in recent years.

9. **Localise when ties to a "home" country are loose**
    It may make sense to hire locally rather than to send an expatriate from a home country, depending on the country, the expatriate's role and purpose, and talent availability. Or you may be able to "localise" existing expatriated employees by aligning their compensation and benefits package with local market levels. Look critically at the duration of your longer-term expatriates' tenure in their host countries, if they have been in-country for five or more years, it may be time to consider localising them.

10. **Tweak index-based allowances**
    Re-examine assumptions made when computing cost-of-living allowances and hardship premiums based on differences between home and host locations. Most cost-of-living indexes embed assumptions about employees' familiarity with host location spending patterns. Changing those indices can be both cost-effective and realistic. In an increasingly global economy with younger workers, you may be able to reduce them over time.

17.9 CONCLUSION

International relocation can be a tumultuous experience. However, with the right mind-set and effective retention strategies, this can be a memorable journey for expatriates and the respective organisation.

In the end, it is important to consider the concept of "wholeness" with regard to the goals of compensation packages. The concept refers to the organisation's desire to ensure that the expatriate does not experience an overt gain or loss when all elements of the compensation package are combined. While finding a balance between the organisation's and expatriates' perceptions of "wholeness" can sometimes be difficult, the intentions of "keeping the employee as a whole" by not letting expatriates experience drastic lifestyle changes are paramount. All of this is in the interests of assisting and promoting the organisation in becoming the best organisation to work for in a competitive local and international market.

Some multinational companies are still willing to pay for the business acumen and experience that differentiate expatriates from local talent when they have identified a clear need. From this they recognise that expatriates have the desired set of skills and talent that local talent may not have. Nevertheless, these organisations should control costs and improve value. Having a well-planned expatriate workforce plan that is correlated to the organisation's strategic needs will help in understanding the implications of using expatriates, keeping abreast with changing needs, improving the organisation and the expatriate's ROI, and ultimately helping these companies to make the transition to local talent when the time is right.

We conclude with an inspiring quote that refers to the fact that HR practitioners and Industrial Psychologists must accurately anticipate the future and plan appropriately:

"We affect more than mere designs, machines, sales, and numbers – we touch people's lives. Almost never can we undo our mistakes." – Losey, Meisinger and Ulrich (2005).

17.10   REFERENCES

Baruch, Y, Steele, DJ & Quantrill, GA . 2002. Management of expatriation and repatriation for novice global player, *International Journal of Manpower*, 23(7):659–671.

Black, SJ, Gregersen, HB & Mendenhall, ME. 1992. *Global assignments: Successfully expatriating and repatriating international managers*. Jossey-Bass.

Du Toit, GE, Erasmus, BJ & Strydom, JW. 2007. Employee benefits as context for intergenerational conflict. *Human Resource Management Review*, 17(2):208–220. [Online]. Available: http://dx.doi.org/10.1016/j.hrmr.2007.04.002. [Accessed 12 July 2014].

Economist Intelligence Unit. 2010. *Up or out: Next moves for the modern expatriate*. A report from *The Economist* Intelligence Unit.

EY. 2013/2014. Sub-Saharan Africa talent trends and practices survey. [Online]. Available: emergingmarkets.ey.com/201314-sub-saharan-africa-talent-trends-survey/. [Accessed 4 August 2014].

Forster, N & Johnson, M. 1996. Expatriate management policies in UK companies new to the international scene. *The International Journal of Human Resource Management*, 7(1):177–205.

Gudykunst, WB. 2005. *Theorizing about intercultural communication*. Thousand Oaks, CA: Sage.

Heneman, HG & Judge, TA.. 2003. *Staffing organizations*. 4th ed. Boston, MA: McGraw-Hill.

HSBC. 2013. Expat Survey. [Online]. Available: *https://www.expatexplorer.hsbc.com/files/ pdfs/overall.../2013/report.pdf*. [Accessed 3 August 2014].

Losey, MR, Meisinger, S & Ulrich, D. 2005. *The future of human resource management*. Upper Saddle River, NJ: John Wiley & Sons.

MacDonald, S & Arthur, N. 2003 Employees' perceptions of repatriation. *Canadian Journal of Career Development*, 2:3–11.

Mathis, RL & Jackson, JH. 2004. *Human resources management*. 10th ed. Mason, OH: Thomson South-Western College Publishing.

Mello, JA. 2011. *Strategic management of human resources*. 3rd ed. Canada: South-Western Cengage Learning.

Mercer. 2008. *Total rewards*. Mercer snapshot survey: US reports. [Online]. Available: http://www. imercer.com/uploads/US/pdfs/mercer_us_total_rewards_survey_%20sept2008.pdf. [Accessed 25 June 2013].

Michaels, E, Handfield-Jones, H & Axelrod, E. 2001. *The war for talent*. Boston, MA: Harvard Business School Press.

Naumann, E. 1992. A conceptual model for expatriate turnover. *Journal of International Business Studies*, 22:499–531.

Nienaber, R, Bussin, MHR & Henn, C. 2011. The relationship between personality types and reward preferences. *Acta Commercii*, 11(2):56–79.

Shelton, T. 2008. Global compensation strategies: Managing and administering split pay for an expatriate workforce. *Compensation & Benefits Review*, 40(1):56–60.

Snelgar, RJ, Renard, M & Venter, D. 2013. An empirical study of the reward preferences of South African employees. *South African Journal of Human Resource Management*, 11(1):2–14. [Online]. Available: http://dx.doi.org/10.4102/sajhrm.v11i1.351. [Accessed 17 February 2014].

Tyagi, PK & Wotruba, TR. 1993. An exploratory study of reverse causality relationships among sales forces turnover variables. *Journal of the Academy of Marketing Science*, 21:143–153.

Wells, 2008. Expatriate turnover and retention management essay. [Online]. Available: http://www.ukessays.com/Essays/Management. [Accessed 24 July 2014].

CHAPTER 18
DISMISSAL OF EXPATRIATES: LEGAL GUIDELINES
Advocate Nasreen Dawood

18.1 INTRODUCTION

A poor or non-performing expatriate employee can become a major liability and an increasing source of frustration for any organisation. This is particularly so given the financial investment and concern for wellbeing that an organisation often expends on the expatriate employee. Globally, the United States of America has mastered dismissal of poor or non-performing individuals via the employment-at-will doctrine. In this instance, the employer has no obligation to articulate the reasons for termination carefully or to follow any specific pre-termination process. However, an American employer cannot use the employment-at-will doctrine in South Africa or the United Kingdom. If the expatriate employee is on assignment in South Africa or the United Kingdom, for example, the employer must carefully evaluate whether it has sufficient grounds to terminate the employee and must first follow specific pre-termination procedures.

This chapter aims to discuss the legal requirements to terminate an expatriate employee while on international assignment. Examples will be drawn from South Africa and the United Kingdom, which we believe form a good basis to "test" your thinking in other countries.

18.2 NO EMPLOYMENT-AT-WILL IN SOUTH AFRICA – CONTRACT GOVERNS EMPLOYMENT RELATIONSHIPS

A striking difference between employment law in South Africa and the United States of America is that in South Africa there is absolutely no concept of employment-at-will. In addition to this, the legal relationship between employer and employee is always contractual, whether or not there is a written contract (Lubbe, 2008; DeGiuseppe, 2010).

Another important distinction relates to the notice of termination of employment which must be given by both employers and employees. Under the American employment-at-will doctrine, the employment relationship may be terminated "with or without notice". In the United Kingdom, notice is always required. The notice period is usually agreed by the parties and set out expressly in a written contract of employment. If it is not, the South African labour courts will imply a period of *reasonable notice* which, in the case of notice given by employers, must be at least 30 days' notice. Consideration is also given to the length of time spent by the employee in a particular organisation (Lubbe, 2008; DeGiuseppe, 2010).

An unjustified dismissal without notice will be a breach of contract by the employer, which can give rise to a claim of damages. The longer the notice period, the bigger the claim will be. There are no jury trials, and punitive damages are never awarded in either South Africa or the United Kingdom. In South Africa in particular, given the history of poor labour laws, unjust, unfair discrimination and orientated dismissal under the apartheid regime, unfair dismissal in contemporary times is treated as a contentious issue. Often, the cases are given media coverage and treated in emotionally-charged tones. Organisations endeavour to guard against this situation (Lubbe, 2008; DeGiuseppe, 2010).

18.3 UNFAIR DISMISSAL PROTECTION IN SOUTH AFRICA AND THE UNITED KINGDOM

Employees who have accrued at least one year's continuous service acquire a statutory right not to be unfairly dismissed. It is not possible to "contract out" of this right. Furthermore, in South Africa, following the completion of one year's probation, it becomes very difficult to prove non-performance if all parties agree that a successful probationary period was completed (Lubbe, 2008).

There are, however, instances where the employer may well have serious grounds to defend a claim for unfair dismissal, but the burden is on the employer to prove that it had one of the following reasons for dismissing the employee:

1. Incapability (incapacity)
2. Lack of qualifications
3. Misconduct
4. Redundancy (or permanent lay-off)
5. Breach of statute/law, or
6. The catch-all of "some other substantive reason",

AND that it acted reasonably in treating that reason as sufficient to dismiss the employee.

A three-step process is generally followed in cases of potential dismissals which is premised on the notion of dialogue and investigation rather than autocracy.

Step 1: Write to the employee notifying him/her of the allegations against him/her and invite him/her to a meeting to discuss the matter.

Step 2: Hold a meeting to discuss the allegations – a meeting at which the employee has the right to be accompanied by a colleague or trade union representative – and notify him/her of the decision.

Step 3: If the employee wishes to appeal, hold an appeal meeting at which he/she has a right to be accompanied – and inform him/her of the final decision.

If an employee has been unfairly terminated in breach of the employee's statutory protections, the employee's remedy is financial. The amount of the compensation awarded will depend on the employee's financial loss, and this in turn depends on how quickly the employee has found, or is expected to find, an equally well-paid job (Lubbe, 2008; DeGiuseppe, 2010).

18.4 DISCRIMINATION CLAIMS UNDER UK AND SOUTH AFRICAN LAW

It is unlawful in the United Kingdom to discriminate directly or indirectly against employees (and other kinds of workers) on the following grounds (Lubbe, 2008; DeGiuseppe, 2010):

* Sex or marital status, or for any reason connected with pregnancy or maternity
* Race or national origin
* Religion or other belief
* Disability
* Sexual orientation
* Age.

However, in this instance, the employee would bring the matter to a United Kingdom court as one of discrimination and not unfair dismissal.

In South Africa, however, employees are protected from unfair dismissal based on unfair discrimination on one or more of the prohibited grounds as contained in the Constitution of the Republic of South Africa, 1996 and employment equity legislation and may bring a claim for unfair dismissal directly to the courts in cases of unfair discrimination. The prohibited grounds as contained in employment equity legislation are race, gender, sex, pregnancy, marital status, family responsibility, ethnic or social origin, colour, sexual orientation, age, disability, religion, HIV status, conscience, belief, political opinion, culture, language and birth, or any arbitrary ground. The burden of proof for an arbitrary ground would, however, lie with the employee, unlike the burden of proof lying with the employer for the other prohibited grounds.

18.5 DIFFERENCES BETWEEN INCAPACITY, PERFORMANCE, UNWILLING AND UNABLE

Many employers – if not most – confuse poor performance with negligence, incapacity, and even misconduct. This is because of a lack of understanding of the clear distinctions that separate the various conditions – in other words, the employer does not know what the charge should be. He knows only that what is happening is unacceptable to him, and the employee must be dismissed as quickly as possible.

The result of this uninformed action is that the employee is charged with negligence, poor performance, incapacity, and misconduct, and, as if that is not enough, the charge sheet also states that the trust relationship has irretrievably broken down and that the employment relationship has become intolerable (South African Labour Guide, 2010; Van Eck, 2002).

In establishing whether poor performance exists, one must ask the following questions in relation to the employee and the job:

1. Is the output sufficient?

2. Is the quality acceptable?

3. Have the many operating procedures being followed?

4. Are costs kept within budget or are they unacceptably high?

5. Is the effort put in by the employee sufficient?

6. Is it inability on the part of the employee to do the job at the required level – can the employee perform satisfactorily at a lower level?

7. Is it incompetence?

8. Is it carelessness – lack of attention to detail?

9. Is it a form of negligence but not misconduct? In other words, "I don't care"?

From the above, it now becomes clearer what the differences are between misconduct (behaviour) and poor performance (ability): misconduct deals with behaviour; performance deals with ability (South African Labour Guide, 2010; van Eck, 2002).

Being unable to engage in duties is often confused with being unwilling, and it is far more constructive to handle the matter given the rationale behind being "unable". In South Africa, this relates to skills transfer and is generally treated as historical trends of severely under-capacitating the majority of the population. This is due largely to the apartheid regime, dismantled for only twenty years at the time of writing. An employee unable to engage in certain duties or activities is generally amicable to dialogue in this respect, which is a first indication of space to improve and empower the person. A first, informal session with the employee is usually enough to determine this, but sometimes general HR processes where skills audits are done identify these shortfalls. Immediate enrolment in either requisite soft or hard skills training is the general trend, with clear guidelines for performance in this respect. Costs are attached to the organisation, but the employee may be bound to skills retention guidelines depending on internal organisational policies (South African Labour Guide, 2010; Van Eck, 2002).

In South Africa, it is unacceptable simply to decide that someone is unwilling to work without dialogue with the individual concerned. If, in this engagement, it is concluded that the employee is definitely unwilling to do a particular job or components thereof, immediate investigation into job description and performance agreements as well as previous performance agreements must be done. Sometimes a team is utilised for this purpose, but it is championed by the line manager. If it is deemed that the component of work is within the realm of job description of the employee, written and verbal communication must be sent in this respect. If there is still resistance, the matter is to be referred to labour units of the organisation to investigate the matter and possibly enter into disciplinary engagement (South African Labour Guide, 2010; Van Eck, 2002).

18.5.1 Incapacity

Incapacity is largely orientated around issues pertaining to the health of the employee. Generally, sick and annual leave must be exhausted before discussions on incapacity commence. For an expatriate, this has particular concerns given the change in medical service providers, alterations in quality, and financial strain, but fundamentally, incapacity constraints continue to be regulated by South African labour laws. The previous Labour Appeal Court held that the substantive fairness of a dismissal based on incapacity due to ill-health depends on the question whether the employee can fairly be expected to continue in the employment relationship, bearing in mind the interests of the employee and the employer and the equities of the case (Lubbe, 2008; DeGiuseppe, 2010).

Other factors to be considered would include the nature of the incapacity, the cause of the incapacity, the likelihood of recovery, and the likelihood of improvement or, indeed, recurrence. The period of absence and its effect on the employer's operations must also be considered, as well as the effect of the employee's disability on other employees. What kind of message would be sent out to the other employees if the employer consistently condoned an unhealthy employee's absences? The employee's work record and length of service must also be considered (Griffith, 1997).

The test is whether, because of the employee's absences and incapacity, and considering the frequency and duration of such absences, and the effect that it has on the morale of the employee's co-workers, the question to be asked is: Can the employer, in all fairness, be expected to wait any longer before considering dismissal? This approach has been held to apply both in cases of lengthy absence, and in cases of intermittent absences from the workplace. There are, however, certain rules to be followed in determining fairness (Lubbe, 2008; DeGiuseppe, 2010).

The employer must ascertain whether the employee is capable of performing the work that he was employed to do, and if not, the extent to which he is unable to perform those duties. The employee is entitled to participate in this investigation, which may require further medical investigation, and the employee can also be asked to demonstrate his ability.

If the employee's duties cannot be adapted in such a way that the employee is able to fulfil those duties, and no alternative position is available, then dismissal may be justified, noting that often dismissal is applied as a last resort. If the employees are offered a lower position and a lower salary is attached to that position, then the lower salary will apply. It is therefore obvious that the principles of procedural fairness and substantive fairness are applied to such dismissals, as it applies also to all types of dismissals, which include the case of expatriates (South African Labour Guide, 2010).

18.6 DISMISSAL, AND BUSINESS ETHICS PLAYING A ROLE IN DISMISSAL

Dismissals are the results of human action and not merely natural events such as hurricanes and earthquakes; dismissals are the objects of moral judgements. Business ethics have a serious role to contribute in dismissals. Wherever the situation arises, in the first place, business ethics as a kind of philosophical reflection on moral problems of the economy in general and of business in particular should try to make clear the following conditions: Moral judgements relate to actions by asking for the performance of the respective action. If someone says that it is condemnable to dismiss a father of four children, he also expresses that actors should forbear this action. If someone says that it is praiseworthy to give up a part of a possible profit in order to avoid dismissals, he also expresses that actors should perform this action (Hahn, 2009). One characteristic of moral judgements consists in the attitude with which they are brought forward: the author of a moral judgement presents it not as a matter of taste, but expecting general approval. The other characteristic is that a moral judgement refers to a general moral norm that implies the judgement (Hahn, 2009).

Besides explaining these more general aspects of ethical reasoning, the theorist should – in the second place – clarify the manner and the scope of business ethical reflection: First, one must not expect the business ethicist – doing his business seriously – to give a non-hypothetical and concrete order: "Do that!" Second, one should not presuppose that there is one single "right" ethical theory, which just has to be applied to business ethical problems in order to deliver the "right" solutions. The function of business ethics is not to relieve the actors of their decisions. Taking into account these limits of business ethics, what is left?

One should concede that there is a kind of middle position between recommending concrete actions and refraining completely from recommending anything (Hahn, 2009).

The object of business ethical reflection should consist in supporting actors who are responsible for morally relevant decisions in making these decisions in an enlightened manner. To say it again: Morality pays (Hahn, 2009).

18.7 LAWS, AND STEP-BY-STEP GUIDE TO DISMISSING EXPATRIATES

Terminating an expatriate contract can be as complicated as creating it. A key inclusion in the expat contract concerns the grounds for termination and it is crucial that a section that defines the notice and termination terms is included in order to prevent any issues. If this is not included in the contract, the laws of the host country may be applied, and this may have an impact on the notice period and the amount of severance pay that an expatriate is entitled to as an employee. Things that must be included in the contract are as follows:

- **Notice period:** How long after terminating an expatriate contract will the employee be expected to work? The notice period together with the employee's obligations and requirements during this period should be defined.

- **Severance:** If the contract is ended early on request of the employer and not "for cause", for example, gross misconduct or embezzlement, the employee may be entitled to severance pay.

- **Repatriation package:** The contract should contain clear details of the employer's post-agreement obligations. All of the factors that were considered when the employee formulated the contract to move abroad should once again come into play, and you may wish to ensure that the equalisation approach is once again applied. In addition to this, all repatriation costs should be included in the contract.

- **Other factors:** If the employee has children who will be attending school in the host country, the employer may wish to ensure that the contract contains provision for their educational expenses until the end of the school year or term. Repatriation training could be offered after terminating an expatriate contract.

This can help an expatriate to readjust to living back in the home country if the expatriate has spent a lengthy period of time overseas.

There are three key types of dismissal, according to Berry, 1999), namely:

The *first* type is generally understood as incompetency or poor performance dismissals. This comprises two potential situations, namely, during the probationary period, and during normal employment.

The *second* type translates as disciplinary dismissals and is effected after proved misconduct on the part of the expatriate. This is often done in a labour court.

The *third* type is economic dismissal. There are four legal prerequisites for this:

- Financial need (two years of distress)
- Exhaustive efforts to avoid dismissal
- Application of objective and fair standards in selection process
- Procedural due process.

For individual dismissals, the simplest and generally least traumatic way of obtaining a dismissal is by way of solicitation of resignation. Once an employee understands that this is a measure to be released from a work place without further actions, the process becomes smooth for both parties.

Additional means of dismissal include:

- Conciliation procedure
- Labour trial system (new as of 2006) (Berry, 1999).

18.8 CONCLUSION

Expatriate dismissals, like other employee dismissals, require substantive and procedural fairness. The expatriate contract sets the pace for how the dismissal will be managed and whether dismissal laws of the host or home country will succeed. Almost inevitably South African laws have been successfully applied, whether South Africa has been the host or home country.

18.9 REFERENCES

Berry, R. 1999. *The art of terminating an expat in Latin America*. [Online]. Available: http://www.wcl.american.edu/blr/01/3berry.pdf. [Accessed 1 August 2014].

Griffith, J. 1997. *The politics of the judiciary*. London, Fontana Press

Hahn, S. 2009. Dismissals: A case for business ethics! In M Baurmann & B Lahno (eds). 2009. *Perspectives in moral science*. [465–477]. [Online]. Available: http://www.rmm-journal.de/. [Accessed 5 August 2014].

Lubbe, J & Freer, G. 2008. Terminating employees in the UK for poor performance. [Online]. Available: http://www.globalbusinessnews.net/story.asp?sid=1021. [Accessed 3 August 2014].

Mendenhall, M & Oddou, G. 1985. The dimensions of expatriate acculturation: A review. *The Academy of Management Review*, 10(1):39–47.

Online Resource. 2014. *Human resources in the workplace*. [Online]. Available: http://www.workinfo.co.za/Articles/conduct_performance.htm. [Accessed 27 May 2014].

Online Resource. 2010. *South African labour guide*. [Online]. Available: http://www.labourguide.co.za/health-and-safety/368-the-south-african-labour-guide-labour-law-employment-and-health-and-safety-manual-2010. [Accessed 31 January 2014].

Van Eck, S. 2002. Latest developments regarding disciplinary enquiries. *South African Journal of Labour Relations*, 26(3):24–41.

CHAPTER 19
TRENDSETTING SOLUTIONS IN AN INCREASINGLY MOBILE WORLD
Simon Davies

19.1 INTRODUCTION

The world we live in is shrinking. We now refer to our planet as the global village, and globalisation is the buzz word.

With the advent of the Internet, connecting us all together and acting as a central nervous system, we can access people globally via Skype calls, social media and WebEx conferences without leaving the comfort of our homes. Despite this, the need for companies to transfer talent to overseas locations is as strong as ever.

Although assignment types and associated policy directives have changed over the years, the fact remains that companies need internationally mobile talent to grow their businesses. Three percent of the global population now work outside their country of birth and this trend is continuing, with Generation Y expecting to live and work in global locations as part and parcel of their career and development.

As technology continues its march forward, dictating the world we live and work in, one standard needs to remain at the very heart of the international mobility process and that standard is service: an intangible aspect within the mobility function. We will look at why it is such a significant key factor, why it is the spine of any successful expatriate programme, and why it forms the bridge that links policy to best practice.

A multinational business environment has multiple complexities with variables, and as a result will be more challenging to manage. A multicultural employment policy leads to an organisation having to deal with employees of many different nationalities, languages, religions and cultures in different offices across the globe. These employees react in very different ways to the various motivations and incentive schemes that companies provide. It is near impossible to find managers who are fully sensitive to all these different factors. As a result of this, it is very easy inadvertently to give offence and demotivate employees. This is also impacted on as country borders are becoming less restricted. Different markets stretch across borders and MNCs are perfectly placed to take advantage of this. Similar issues of language and cultural differences are also on the rise in the international workplace.

Recruiting for positions which have a global role is extremely difficult. In the current context, when there is a slowdown in the US and European markets, the impact is felt across the global community. International roles demand a very different set of skills: they require one to deal with economics, cultural diversities and dynamics in business. There is therefore a dearth of seasoned professionals who come with all-round exposure and experience in dealing with the range of complexities required for global positions.

What are some of the key challenges faced while hiring talent for global positions?

- There are not enough specialist recruitment agencies to cater for the growing demand of talent in this area.

- Various degrees of contractual, restrictive governance clauses can create a barrier.

- International business travellers have a heavy travel schedule and therefore it is difficult to set out the two- and three-tier interview schedules that normally apply.

What are the ways and means to tackle these challenges?

The approach has to be manifold. In recent years we have seen a focus on developing these professionals in-house. Nurturing talent and creating schools of knowledge within an organisation can lead to developing existing employees to take on global roles.

Direct campus and university hiring is also a way to mitigate the talent gap at the entry level. Another example is to hire international talent that is already in a country and settled. The issue is that the candidate is likely with a competitor and therefore the previously mentioned restrictions will apply.

With the War on Talent being one of the focuses for global organisations, attracting the right people into the right sectors and countries is critical to the development of any business and with a dearth of talent across many industries, having a well-established and beneficial assignment programme has never been more important. It should be widely accepted that this comes at a cost to the business. It is here that service is so important, and ranking high on the list of must-haves is the competitiveness of the proposed mobility package.

The old adage "you get what you pay for" is certainly true in many instances – and a subconscious expectation between what we see as value and what we see as service forms this expectation. One example of this is the popularity in recent years of travelling on one of the numerous low-cost airlines as opposed to the bigger, more established flag carriers. They serve a purpose and have a place in the market, but at a cost, with service being the trade-off.

Seldom do we accept poor service, and the more we are asked to pay, the greater are our expectations. We all form a mental picture of what is or is not acceptable, and nowhere is this more evident than when we are requested to move our personal effects and lifetime belongings. Moving home is said to be one of the most stressful events we undertake in life, and most of us will do it several times. Add to this the challenges of a new role in a new country for the assignee, and you have created a perfect scenario for those responsible, be it in HR or as a supplier, for ensuring that everything will run seamlessly, without a hitch, within budget and on time. This presents a number of obvious challenges on a number of levels, and selecting the correct moving and relocation company is a critical choice to be made.

This selection generally falls within the remit of the Human Resources director for those companies with international locations. Getting consistent levels of service from mobility providers is certainly a must-have for their business. Building partnerships and trust are key ingredients. Managing such an important department when faced with poor service provision will undoubtedly cost the business time and money as well as having a detrimental effect on the international assignee population in terms of morale. Bad news travels very fast in the expatriate community.

19.2 CORPORATE MOBILITY: THE SERVICE-FOCUSED GLOBAL SOLUTION

Change in the mobility sector has been rapid and constant. The majority of International Human Resources (IHR) departments have had to become more accountable for their decision-making processes around vendor selection. Traditional and historical supplier relationships have had to give way to a new set of qualifying criteria, compliance, governance and pricing forming the key areas.

Selection of all relocation services has become the joint responsibility of procurement and HR. Any company that has a need to send its staff overseas or domestically on an assignment will now go through an often lengthy procedure of assessment. Today, issuing a request for proposals (RFP) is now common practice for almost any organisation moving ten or more employees per annum, and especially when the nature of the business itself is highly controlled. One survey states that 63 percent of all companies that went to market via RFP stayed with the current incumbent rather than changing suppliers, thereby negating the risk for the need to build new relationships and undergo lengthy implementation processes.

Over the past decade we have entered a new chapter on how expatriates are managed and reported on. This new era has seen an increased focus on benefits paid to expatriates, audits, co-operation between countries and tax authorities, environmental policy, and the need for compliance. The shift from a highly administrative to a more strategic approach is well and truly under way, and all of this relies on flawless service delivery.

One supplier organisation that is constantly developing a different solution is K2 Corporate Mobility. Owner and founder Nick Plummer realised that as a direct result of the Sarbanes-Oxley Act of 2002, also known as the SOX Act, the mobility landscape would change beyond all recognition. These changes would exert an additional dimension of pressure on the various HR departments managing mobility, and the need for trusted partnerships would become integral to the operation.

K2 set a goal to align the mobility challenge of relocating people with the overall HR and business strategy working towards becoming true business partners. The company would effectively become an extension of the HR department without being a true outsource. All of this could be achieved only if impeccable service were in place.

As the need to become more strategically integrated with suppliers grew within IHR, it was recognised that a key factor to grow emerging market economies and create a presence in new locations is to move key people who can facilitate global leadership, provide training and grow the organisation's culture. K2 proposed to cut out layers of unnecessary and increased administration as well as manage the various vendors required to facilitate a global relocation logistically. As global organisations increasingly focused on the link between global mobility and talent management, the opportunity to save time was an added appeal. So a blend of fast responses and a make-it-happen approach would rival what was in many cases a rather tired process that was being offered by the various moving companies.

19.3 THE TRADITIONAL METHODOLOGY FOR MOVING STAFF INTERNATIONALLY

In the latter part of the 20th century, most moving companies were not in a position to manage the relocation and destination service provision, such as home search, school search, settling-in services, and tenancy management, as a total package. Destination services would invariably be initiated and managed locally by the host country and in many instances still are today.

With increasing pressure being brought on reducing costs in their core services of shipping provision, and identifying designated service provider (DSP) services as an avenue to expand both their revenue and market share, during the ten-year period from 2000 to 2010, the "tier 1" international removal companies responded by adding this service within their remit. Where it was widely accepted that shipping is a product of the total relocation provision, to this day not one former removals/shipping supplier can truly say it has mastered the provision of moving and relocation services as a joined-up global solution.

In fact, most moving companies simply substituted the word "relocation" within their existing name and proceeded to manage the services in partnership with one or more third-party providers. Only more recently have they started to develop this service in-house. Even then, it is difficult to replicate this in-house provision satisfactorily on a world stage, as third-party support will always be required.

Looking back to the last century, there were predominantly two ways in which shipping providers were selected.

A small number of organisations with high levels of assignees adopted a policy of selecting just one shipping company on the basis of set "matrix rates", either following a selection process or as a result of historical practice. While this might have reduced the time spent by the IHR department in making decisions as to whom to appoint for any given relocation, this practice would lead either to prices not being benchmarked and therefore being open to "abuse" and high cost to the business; or, in those instances where the provider was often held to low rates set to win the business, this resulted in service failures which were swept under the carpet as part of the large scale of the relocation programme.

The vast majority of companies, however, that needed to relocate staff overseas would typically welcome two or three (in some cases four) moving companies to quote on a forthcoming relocation/move for one of their relocating employees. This practice was commonplace worldwide. A panel of specialist international moving companies was normally selected on its ability to perform the highest standards worldwide either within its own network of offices or with affiliated ones through partner programmes. Such suppliers were linked because of the scale of the undertaking and the logistical need to partner with each other. Nevertheless, in many instances, bitter rivalries would develop. Price wars were common, and undercutting one's competitors would prove to be the Achilles heel for the industry. Undercutting costs to such a degree as to win the move would become the norm. Expectations were set extremely high, with moves often being booked just at cost. This resulted in one key element that would suffer most of all: service.

In both scenarios, IHR were now increasingly dealing with more and more service failures, which were often time consuming and ultimately damaging to the business. During this time, procurement also started to get more and more involved with the selection of service providers. The use of multiple providers can become disjointed and too time consuming, and can create a degree of confusion and uncertainty in the mind of the relocating party. The process may involve all of the below stages and possibly more before a supplier is appointed:

1. Setup an appointment to visit the home of origin for a pre-move survey, to ascertain the estimated volume of the items to be shipped.

2. During the survey, each company will talk through the various pieces of documentation required, explain the process, timelines, customs processes, and delivery.

3. The survey can take from 30 minutes to two hours, depending on the size of the amount to be shipped and the attention to detail required. It can take a whole day for three companies to visit, and invariably they will not be able to attend on the same day.

4. Different quotations are submitted by each company and they will almost invariably have different volume estimation, different parameters, and therefore

a different cost. For IHR, this proved to be extremely frustrating, as it is difficult to make an informed decision that is right in every instance. Many questions arise: Which estimation is correct? If the lower cost is selected, will I see additional costs added? Are there any exclusions? And so on.

5. The influence in the home may persuade the relocating party that they prefer company B over company A or C. While IHR will take the individuals' preference into account, if company B should be more expensive than the next quotation, this will need justification within the relocating budget and therefore becomes a difficult decision to be made by IHR.

6. Insurance cover inconsistencies: each company will offer a different and often complicated and time-consuming process for completing the forms and making claims, as well as variable percentages for insurance cover.

Clearly this was not ideal, and with multiple suppliers involved, it presented a compliance and process nightmare.

It was clear that a more practical solution to managing the international shipping of household goods and personal effects for a company's relocating employees could be found. During his research, Nick Plummer spoke to countless HR professionals and built a profile of their most common recurring dislikes. The results were staggering: over 80 percent of those asked presented the same frustrations:

- Unaccounted-for additional costs (often avoidable)
- Confusion over policy and allowances created by vendors
- Lack of response from co-ordinating staff
- Ineffective insurance process and claims procedure
- Multiple suppliers for one service
- Lack of HR stakeholder control as a result of local vendor control
- Time pressures resulting from this method.
- Having to wait for and chase up quotations
- Wide variation in costs
- General lack of control during the process
- Blame attributed to culture and lack of ownership of issues. Often a failed move would result in blame being placed on the partner or external supplier.

Given the above findings, it was clear that there was an obvious gap in what had previously been felt to have been a well-serviced market. Service failure, lack of ownership and lack of overall responsibility were the primary causes of these reoccurring frustrations for IHR.

What was required was a simple solution that addressed these main issues and points of anguish. A solution was needed for better management of the household goods provision which could be implemented with limited risk, and most importantly, a programme was required that would remain competitive and stand the test of time.

A different approach to supplier management would equally be required – one that focused on service delivery, and not, as was the case with the movers, one that was built on reciprocal tonnage or financial incentives.

19.4 WHAT DID THIS DIFFERENT APPROACH ACHIEVE?

The major difference was to offer the corporate client the option not only to initiate new relocations through a smart bespoke web-based intranet platform (K2 Ascent), but also for IHR to have access via this platform to transparent reporting at all stages of the relocation as well as year-to-date (YTD) reporting on demographics, budgetary costs and spend overviews, achieving better compliance, process and best practice.

Move expectations would be set out clearly with the assignee and in line with any policy and allowances. With just one single survey at the home of the assignee, producing a detailed analysis of all shipping requirements, valuable time would be saved. The detail of information gathered at survey would be managed with a panel of preferred accredited vendors allowing best value for origin and destination rates, based on stringent service parameters. Shipping and air freight services could also be directly sourced from approved vendors.

Once the costs were obtained from the three most cost-effective suppliers, a bid summary could be submitted to HR. Selection of the chosen supplier was simplified, as all vendors had been pre-approved and the lowest price option would still guarantee top-level service. The volume could be guaranteed and no additional costs would be applied (except for incidentals such as customs duties, demurrage changes, and the like).

The introduction of a clear Insurance policy that simplified the process for the assignee would make the whole moving experience simpler. K2 would manage all administration related to the move in-house including customs formalities at export and import, bills of lading and airway bills, and insurance paperwork. They would also provide dedicated client managers to build the relationship with the relocating family at every level, ensuring that expectations would be met and exceeded.

19.5 OPTIMISING INTERNATIONAL ASSIGNMENTS

As the world of mobility continues to evolve we should consider how, in a cost-conscious environment, we can best leverage international assignments.

Even in this age of increasingly effective virtual meeting technologies, there is no substitute for working and living abroad. It's very hard to understand another culture unless you've lived there, and that understanding is crucial to business success in a global society. And if an organisation is going to move employees outside its home region, it is important to get it right. This means formalising the process and measuring the results.

The investment required to send employees on international assignment can be substantial, yet many organisations remain unclear about the benefits. Existing research indicates that there is limited measurement to determine how the benefits and costs compare, and therefore to establish what the return on investment (ROI) is for organisations. Without a clear understanding of the return, it is difficult for an organisation to determine how effective its expatriate programme is as part of its overall talent management strategy.

International assignments, like any business initiatives, are about achieving goals and delivering results. If these goals include learning and development, then these skills should be used for the benefit of the organisation. It is not unusual for assignees to go on assignment without clear business and development objectives, resulting in their spending too long working out what to do, and worrying about what will happen to them at the end of the assignment. Only a portion of time is actually spent doing the job. The aim of career management in the first instance should be to ensure that the assignee hits the ground running.

International assignments are invaluable in grooming future leaders; in some organisations working outside the home country is a pre-requisite for senior level appointments. Too often top performers with leadership potential have gained experience on assignment, but the company does not benefit from the investment as the repatriation fails. Not having a plan for repatriated employees wastes this long-term investment. Although research shows that there is no model system in place for ensuring optimum ROI, organisations are making positive steps towards achieving this.

Quite simply: sound processes, good ownership and thorough planning should result in better development, more successful assignments and successful repatriations. By offering the appropriate overseas opportunity to the right individual, organisations can maximise the return on their international assignee population while providing excellent career opportunities to their employees.

19.6 TWO STRATEGIES, ONE GOAL

It is important for international assignment objectives and philosophy to be aligned to business and HR objectives. Having access to the best talent continues to be a challenge for business leaders. We see global organisations increasingly focus on the linkage between global mobility and talent management. Their collective goal is to become more strategically integrated HR partners.

One of the main ways in which to grow emerging market economies and create a presence in new locations is to move key people who can facilitate global leadership, provide training, and grow the organisation culture. There are three questions that should be considered:

1. **How does mobility align to global talent management?**

We have increasingly learnt from moving people into the BRIC locations that we cannot just focus on the practicalities of getting an assignee from A to B and back again. Although it is essential that we get the move right, too often assignee feedback tells us that "out of sight [is] out of mind". It is critical that an assignment is managed within the greater talent framework. This means selecting the right candidate, actively managing performance, evaluating ongoing potential, and planning for the next role.

2. **Why is the governance process critical in securing the right people?**

It's all about return on investment (ROI). An upfront, transparent authorisation process with a well-documented business case, a cost estimate, and a thorough selection process signed by the business are critical to ensure that line managers own and are accountable for assignees and their performance. There is not always enough infrastructure, goal setting, assessing and reviewing of performance.

3. **How do organisations ensure maximum benefit from the investment in assignees?**

By providing opportunities to develop leadership competencies, a global mind-set and cultural adaptability, organisations develop leaders and benefit from the investment in their assignee population. Sound processes, good ownership and thorough planning facilitate ROI, and an effectively managed repatriation plan is key to a successful assignment. Companies often don't change until they reach crisis point or something happens. This is evident with the high failure rate of repatriations. Focus therefore needs to be on assignee retention.

19.7 THE CHANGING LANDSCAPE OF MOBILITY

The task of assigning people to live and work abroad can be a complex one. Not only are organisations expanding into emerging market locations that generate a host of new challenges, the varied elements of managing a mobile workforce are not to be underestimated. Reward, payroll, tax, legal, benefits, policy, and expenses require careful and thoughtful planning and execution. The days of traditional moves between New York/London/Hong Kong have been replaced with navigating the challenges of the less developed markets and an increased focus on compliance requirements.

The task of moving people to some of the remote locations where we are now doing business can be challenging. The challenge is not to mandate consistency and try to fit Africa into precise global policies and processes, but to recognise and manage some of the key differences and challenges within an overall global talent and mobility management framework.

"If you look at the likely potential of the 11 largest African economies over the next 40 years, their combined GDP by 2050 could realistically reach more than 13 trillion dollars, making them bigger than either Brazil or Russia." – Jim O'Neill, Goldman Sachs

Africa has six of the fastest growing economies in the world and is now more firmly established on the business agenda. There has been an upswing of moves into and within Africa as a result of the need for talent/specialised skills in markets where business is expanding and focusing on growth. More companies are deploying talent or trying to return talent to the continent.

As a result of globalisation, the mobility landscape is changing. There is a trend towards increased focus on benefits paid to expatriates, more audits, co-operation between countries and tax authorities, and the need for compliance in this heightened regulatory environment.

There has been a shift from a highly administrative to a more strategic approach. The goal is to align mobility with the overall HR and business strategy, working towards becoming true business partners. Organisations need to continue to review their model carefully, considering what to retain in-house versus what work can be moved elsewhere, for example, internal shared service centres versus outsourcing to external vendors.

Global mobility touches on so many areas and as such, collaboration and ensuring connections with benefits, reward, resourcing, payroll, corporate tax, legal, talent management are important.

Although a "one-size-fits-all" approach to mobility no longer applies, it is important to work from a consistent framework, recognising that there are global-, regional- and country-specific needs and differences.

19.7.1 Mobility framework

A mobility framework should include **the elements shown in Table 19.1.**

Table 19.1: Mobility framework

Philosophy	• "Moving the right person, to the right place, on the right package, at the right time"
Needs identification	• Identify core business drivers, assignee rationale and business case. • Mobility specialists are key to helping and challenging the business to identify need, through a documented business case.

Selection	• Candidate evaluation and selection based on role requirements, location specifics, personal circumstances and leadership potential • Intertwining talent/resourcing/HR is beneficial in helping to identify who from the candidate pool (local/new hire/assignee) best matches the role requirements.
Goal definition	• Based on anticipated business and talent outcomes • Essential assignment purpose and objectives, as well as personal development goals are defined, documented, and owned through the governance process and linked to ongoing performance management.
Move drivers	• Determine the value proposition. • Align the business priority with developmental priority and business value. • Determine the appropriate assignment policy.
Policy	• Support HR strategy requirements and regional needs. • No matter the number of policies, they should fall within a global framework with consistent data methodology and application.
Planning	• Due diligence and assignment structure analysis • Upfront planning.
Governance	• Rigour in justifying the assignment rationale and cost.
Return on investment (ROI)	• Manage the performance appraisal process by keeping focus on the assignment objectives. • Critically assess whether the assignment should continue once the objectives have been met. • Focus on next role and use of international assignment experience in career development.

Once the assignment is complete, repatriation and reintegration are required. These are two of the least successful phases of the cycle. The next chapter covers some aspects of best practice in this area.

CHAPTER 20
REPATRIATION AND REINTEGRATION
Dr Mark Bussin and Peter Karlak

20.1 INTRODUCTION

A great deal of effort and attention is paid to employees who are selected for international assignments. The selection process is often in and of itself an explicit indication that the employee is considered talented and worthy of extra responsibility and reward. Employees are sent on "expat" (expatriate) preparation courses; specialised HR departments are tasked with helping them make logistical arrangements; employees in their host countries often go out of their way to welcome the expats and ensure they have everything they need to settle in. Coming back home, on the other hand, is mostly treated as business as usual.

Returning international assignees often face an organisation where no-one really knows what they have done over the last few years, and no-one really cares. In some cases, there are no jobs waiting for the returning assignee, and even when an attempt is made to find/create a new position, the newly acquired skills and knowledge of the assignee are not leveraged for business benefit.

On a personal level, little or no effort is made to help returning assignees reintegrate socially. The assumption is made that they are "coming home" and that they will adapt and fit right back in, as though they had never left. The reality is often very different.

Repatriation involves a number of complex issues that extend beyond merely "coming home". This chapter examines the organisational and personal challenges of returning assignees and provides practical coping strategies to ensure a smooth transition where both the organisation and the individual reap the benefit of the international assignment.

20.2 BACKGROUND

Repatriation is the transition from a foreign country back to one's own, after working overseas for a significant period of time. International assignments attract significant costs for organisations, and although there is an understanding that all assignees will return to their country of origin at some point, the existence of policies and procedures that guide this return are not common (Yeaton & Hall, 2008). The result is a repatriation process that does not adequately prepare expatriates for reintegration into the workplace or their former personal and social circles.

The high post-assignment attrition statistics bear testimony to the fact that the repatriation process needs concerted attention if organisations are to retain their returning talent:

- Approximately 20 percent of repatriated managers leave their company in the first year (Martson, 2012).

- Sixty-nine percent experience significant "reverse culture shock" (Bureau of National Affairs, in Dougherty-Shepell, 2009).

It can take up to 18 months to adjust and reintegrate after an international assignment. How the repatriation is planned and the level of support provided to the repatriate during this period can make all the difference to retention and return on investment. A formal repatriation strategy that is clearly linked to career management and focuses on both the personal and professional growth of employees leads to the greatest returns.

20.3 ORGANISATIONAL OBJECTIVES POST-INTERNATIONAL ASSIGNMENT

The primary objective that an organisation hopes to achieve post international assignment is that of knowledge sharing and application. This is comprised of two facets:

- **Explicit knowledge:** Technical knowledge and skills

- **Tacit knowledge:** More complex and more deeply-embedded knowledge (Nery-Kjerfve & McLean, 2012).

Most expatriates will have gained international knowledge about global operations, characteristics of national markets, business climate and nuanced cultural patterns between the host and parent organisation. Upon return, the expectation is that repatriates will share and use this knowledge to improve performance (Arman, 2009).

In most cases, the knowledge and learning acquired by repatriates goes largely under-utilised as there are no formal and informal mechanisms and processes to enable the sharing of knowledge (Nery-Kjerfve & McLean, 2012). In addition, knowledge sharing will occur only when expatriates feel valued by the organisation and are seen by others as valuable reservoirs of knowledge (Crowne, 2009).

Organisations can facilitate the sharing and application of knowledge by considering the following mechanisms/strategies:

- The promotion of **structured, formal, feedback sessions** where repatriates are invited to brief their wider teams and senior leadership on the state of the business in the host country, the acceptance and success of the product/brand/ service in the host country, and the working relationship between the host and parent company. A template can be prepared to help repatriates plan for these feedback sessions and ensure that the organisation elicits the feedback they most require.

- The requirement for each **repatriate to write a proposal** for ways in which the company can use his/her international skills and insights. This creates a culture of dual accountability where repatriates are expected to play an active role in their reintegration and not just wait for opportunities to be provided.

- The creation of **communities of practice/interest** in the parent organisation. These can take the form of social media networks or informal gatherings, and can be focused on country or function. These communities become the first port of call when someone is looking for a contact in a host country, looking for insight into the local market, competitor analyses, and so on. These communities create networks where the knowledge and competencies of repatriates are leveraged and the repatriates themselves feel a sense of recognition and contribution.

- The use of **coaching and mentoring relationships**. Repatriates should be assigned/ asked to identify mentors to help transfer knowledge back into the parent organisation. This relationship will also help them navigate the changes in the organisation and adjust to coming home. Similarly the repatriate could be asked to mentor and coach new international assignees.

- The **debriefing of repatriates by HR/Global Mobility departments** will ensure that lessons learned in the international assignment space are used to improve the processes of expatriation and reintegration.

> **Monsanto Case Study**
>
> Monsanto is a global provider of agricultural products. At any one time, the company will have 100 mid- and higher-level managers on extended postings abroad. At Monsanto, managing expatriates and their repatriation begins with a rigorous selection process and intensive cross-cultural training, both for the managers and for their families. One of the strongest features of this programme is that employees and their sending and receiving managers, or sponsors, develop an agreement about how this assignment will fit into the firm's business objectives. *The focus is on why employees are going abroad to do the job, and what their contribution to Monsanto will be when they return. Sponsoring managers are expected to be explicit about the kind of job opportunities the expatriates will have once they return home.*
>
> Once they arrive back in their home country, expatriate managers meet with cross-cultural trainers during debriefing sessions. They are also given the opportunity to showcase their experiences to their peers, subordinates, and superiors in special information exchanges.
>
> (UK_Essays.com, n.d.)

- The hosting of **social network functions** to introduce the repatriate to new team members, reconnect with old team members and promote a feeling of team cohesion and inclusion.

In order to meet the organisational objectives of knowledge sharing and application, the repatriation and reintegration of international assignees should be included in the strategic planning conducted before employees are sent overseas.

20.4 INCLUSION OF REINTEGRATION IN STRATEGIC PLANNING

Most organisations start talking about reintegration a good six months prior to repatriation. Although this may seem like ample time, it is in fact far too late. Reintegration should form part of the strategic plan before an employee accepts the international assignment (Yeaton & Hall, 2008).

The approach to reintegration is heavily dependent on the organisation's approach to international assignments. Some organisations see international assignments as an integral part of leadership development and create programmes to facilitate the rotation of leadership talent as part of their career progression and personal and professional growth. In these organisations, global mobility is the norm and is accepted as part of business as usual. These organisations generally do a much better job of reintegration as their plans for international assignees are built into the organisational design and talent management processes.

Other organisations use international assignments to address capability gaps and fix problems. These organisations wait for a problem to present itself and then send senior leaders to fix the problem and build local capability. Since global mobility is not seen as a natural component of talent development, these organisations seldom have a plan for reintegration as they are focused on short-term problem resolution. It is ironic that the employees chosen for such assignments are generally considered top talent, yet very little is done to ensure that their talent is reintegrated and leveraged upon return.

Dowling, Schuler and Welch (1994) suggested that there are essentially four phases in the repatriation process:

1. Preparation
2. Physical relocation
3. Transition, and
4. Readjustment.

The first stage, **preparatin**, involves the development of plans for the future for both the company and the expatriate. This stage should begin when the offer of an international assignment is made. The potential expatriate can gather information about the new position and also investigate the potential career trajectory that will exist for him/her post-assignment. It is difficult, if not sometimes impossible, for an organisation to guarantee an assignee a specific role/job upon their return. There is no way to predict accurately the organisational changes that may occur while the employee is on assignment. It is therefore beneficial for the organisation to develop a process and methodology which will be used for the duration of the assignment to ensure that the assignee and his/her future reintegration are kept in mind in the home organisation.

Borchert & Wierschke (2000) suggest that the last nine months of an international assignment are used to complete the planning stage:

Nine to six months before returning home: The international assignee, the HR manager in the home-country and the assignee's line manager discuss the availability of positions which best fit the assignee's capabilities and the organisation's needs. It is the responsibility of the organisation to provide assignees with accurate and realistic information about job demands and definitions, and changes that have occurred in the organisation prior to return. This enables assignees to have more accurate expectations. During these discussions it is essential to reinforce the organisation's policy/strategy about the career progression of repatriates. Some repatriates may assume that their assignments entitle them to promotion. There may also be assumptions about pay that need to be addressed – assignees are often used to receiving allowances that cover living expenses and hardship while abroad. When these allowances are removed and salaries localised, repatriates may be unhappy with the perceived decrease in earnings.

If possible, it is good to arrange a home visit for assignees during this time. This visit allows the assignee to start making plans for coming home and can be used for interviews with other managers who have open positions.

Six to three months before returning home: The assignee needs to start preparing for physical relocation. This preparation can be managed by HR, internal global mobility departments, or dedicated outsourced relocation service providers. It is important to start addressing the social and emotional needs of repatriates at this time. The professional re-entry of the spouse also has to be considered at this point in time. From a logistics perspective, the company's moving policies and repatriation programmes should be provided. By three months before departure, the assignee should know the position/job he/she will be returning to.

The last three months: This period of time should be reserved for organisational purposes, finishing current projects and saying "goodbye" to all the people the family has met during their time in the host country (Borchert & Wierschke, 2000).

Preparation is followed by **physical relocation** of the expatriate. This stage refers to removing personal effects and travelling to the country where the home organisation is located. In this stage, the company can offer comprehensive and personalised relocation assistance to reduce the amount of anxiety the repatriate may feel.

Transition: This is the third step in the repatriation process, and includes the settling into temporary accommodation as well as making arrangements for administrative tasks. This makes the process of re-entry to the home organisation smoother.

Readjustment, the last step, involves coping with reverse culture shock and career demands that are followed by the re-entry (Dowling et al, 1994).

20.5 TRANSITION AND READJUSTMENT

The success of the transition and readjustment phases of repatriation is influenced by both personal characteristics and organisational strategies.

20.5.1 Personal characteristics and coping strategies

A significant amount of research has been conducted into how to identify the best candidates for international assignments. A major influence on this is the ability of the assignee to successfully manage transition and readjustment and continue their career development as productive assets in the home organisation. It has been found that people with higher levels of self-efficacy are more successful at adjustment (Andreason & Kinneer, 2005). In addition, younger or single people, women and high-level educated expatriates experience more distress (Andreason & Kinneer, 2005; Cox, 2004; Gregersen & Stroh, 1997; Hammer, Hart & Rogan, 1998).

Linehan and Scullion (2002) investigated the impact of gender on repatriate reintegration. While women generally reported that they encountered problems and strategies similar to those encountered by men, the main problem of female repatriates originates from the fact that women are less likely to be assigned for expatriation. The result is that their needs and expectations are not accurately captured by organisations. There is a lack of role models, and as a result, women tend to feel isolated. Women often suffer major personal and professional stresses during the re-entry phase because of having to assume the primary responsibility of assisting with the reintegration of the family into the home culture (Linehan & Scullion, 2002).

International assignments are often a period of profound personal and professional growth for expatriates. There is potential for assignees to experience change in their sense of self and personal identity, in particular among individuals who experience high levels of professional responsibility and independence (Nery-Kjerfve & McLean, 2012). When coming home, assignees have to adjust personally in terms of:

- *Socio-cultural adjustment:* adjustment to life style, social activities, relationships, financial conditions and to the culture of the home country

- *Psychological adjustment:* includes expectations, experienced stress and perception of loss of previously held conditions and relationships.

There is a host of personal symptoms and situations caused by reverse culture shock that repatriates and their families often encounter. Some of these include:

- Irritability/resentment

- Sense of difference and disconnect

- Disappointment

- Inability to concentrate

- Low morale

- Change in values/attitudes

- Marital conflict

- Fatigue

- Parent/child conflict

- Educational/adjustment problems for children

- Depression

- Feeling unappreciated personally/professionally

- Decreased productivity

- Loneliness (Dougherty-Shepell, 2009).

Although the personal characteristics previously mentioned, such as gender, age, and level of self-efficacy, may act as mediators and predictors of successful readjustment, there is still a lot that can be done to prepare and assist repatriates with reintegration in order to enhance the success of adjustment. It would be short sighted for organisations to expect repatriates to manage the personal issues related to reintegration on their own as these issues have such a profound influence on work.

20.5.2 Organisational strategies

During the period of "transition" there are a number of useful practices that can be implemented to assist repatriates. Some of these include:

- Preparing a repatriation directory (a list of contact names and numbers for the services the repatriate is likely to need)

- Organising reorientation programmes in the workplace (to inform the repatriate of changes that have occurred in the head office during his/her absence

- Organising technology and production training (to update employees on advances and changes that have taken place in the head office)

- Clarifying tasks and job placement

- Providing access to personal and career counselling

- Providing training for repatriates and families to ease reverse cultural shock

- Assigning a mentor to assist repatriates after the international assignment. (Nery-Kjerfve & Mclean, 2012).

The perception of organisational support is very important. Assignees recognise the opportunities that are inherent in international assignments, but also expect the organisation to recognise the associated personal sacrifices of social and personal upheaval. Repatriates do not want to feel irrelevant or unappreciated. Processes and procedures that show an interest in holistic reintegration can go a long way to making repatriates feel valued and nurtured.

Despite the obvious benefits of having policies and procedures to ease the transition and readjustment

> **Reverse Culture Shock**
>
> *"Re-entry shock is when you feel like you are wearing contact lenses in the wrong eyes. Everything looks almost right"*
>
> (Robin Pascoe, author of *Homeward Bound*).
>
> Reverse culture shock occurs when repatriates return home after an extended international assignment and realise that both they and their home culture have changed. When they first return they experience a sense of excitement and euphoria, seeing friends and family members, eating at their favourite restaurants, and so on. Once the initial euphoria wears off, they find themselves feeling out of place in their own culture. This is the experience of reverse culture shock; it's the bottom of the curve and often the roughest part of repatriation (Sykes, 2011).

phases of repatriation, there is a surprising lack of such organisational practices. This is mainly because there is a lack of expertise in this process. There are also costs attached to these processes which organisations would prefer to avoid. And finally, there are widely accepted false assumptions which ignore the problems assignees may experience during repatriation (Nery-Kjerfve & McLean, 2012).

20.6 TURNOVER OF REPATRIATES

The poor retention of repatriates has many root causes. First and foremost are unmet expectations. Repatriates think that when they return home they will be offered many job opportunities with increased levels of authority, responsibility and autonomy. They believe that their organisation will consider them as valuable and as special employees and treat them with due respect. This culminates in the expectation of a good position consistent with their desired career trajectory. There is also an expectation that co-workers will value their overseas experience and treat them with deference. As for non-work issues, the expectation is that interaction with other people, including their friends and families, will be easy. (Andreason & Kinneer, 2005; Suutari & Valimaa, 2002, in Arman, 2009).

These expectations are very seldom met. The gap between expectations and reality is a bitter pill to swallow. There is inevitable disappointment in the workplace as in general, repatriates are provided with limited job opportunities, unappreciative of the value of their overseas work experience. Task challenge, task diversity, and career prospects are not as good as expected. Loss of status and role conflict arising from structural changes or changes in the organisational culture of the parent company is also possible. In addition, contrary to their expectations, their co-workers may not welcome them back as heroes and they soon realise that in their absence, life has carried on pretty well without them (Arman, 2009).

These expectations can be managed, but this requires a structured and well-managed expatriation and repatriation process. Organisations that do not embed global mobility in their talent management and development programmes often struggle with this.

> **The Personal Touch**
>
> Policies and procedures can take you only so far in providing a good reintegration experience. It's the little things, the personal touch that can make all the difference. A senior banking repatriate relates her critical success factors after spending two years abroad on international assignment:
>
> "A key differentiator for me was my line manager. She made a personal effort to make my re-entry special. I remember when I arrived back in London, she sent me flowers to welcome me back. I hadn't seen flowers in two years. No-one had been kind to me in a work environment for two years. I always had my guard up. It made such a difference ... A critical success factor for me was understanding and accepting the uncertainty and risks of going on assignment. You leave home not knowing what's next. You have to accept the uncertainty. You can't expect a guaranteed position when you get back. That's not how things work. It's good to maintain key contacts at head office, but they also move ... The expat community are the greatest help with reintegration. You should definitely get involved in these types of communities."
>
> (London, June, 2014)

Another reason for poor retention of repatriates is that they often develop a greater commitment to their subjective career rather than to their organisational career. Repatriates believe in a "boundary-less career", namely "they think their assignment has helped them for their personal development and growth, but not necessarily for career advancement within their company" (Bossard & Peterson, 2005:26). They therefore seek challenging professional opportunities in other organisations when they return home (Nery-Kjerfve & McLean, 2012; Arman, 2009).

Adjustment difficulties also contribute to repatriate turnover. Employees often develop negative attitudes towards their organisations when they perceive a lack of support and appreciation for their dedication, hard work, knowledge, and skills (Nery-Kjerfve & McLean, 2012). This perception, although mostly subjective, is influenced by the perceived amount of effort the organisation makes in assisting with repatriation and reintegration.

There are many other factors which can affect the repatriation experience and subsequent turn-over intention. Family accompaniment, number of overseas assignments, time spent overseas, number of home country visits during expatriation, length of last assignment, and level of personal communication with friends, co-workers, superiors and family during expatriation, level of up-to-datedness with daily life events of home country are listed as some of these factors (Cox, 2004; Gregersen & Stroh, 1997; Liu, 2005; Morgan, Nie & Young, 2004).

20.7 RE-ENTRY TRAINING

Organisations cannot completely outsource the repatriation and reintegration of their returning international assignees. There are definitely components of the reintegration process for which the organisation has to take accountability and responsibility. There is, however, a place for re-entry training, which can be outsourced to professional facilitators or service providers. This training can form a vital part of managing the expectations of repatriates and can help them to plan all areas necessary for their return home. The training should include the returnee as well as their spouse/partner and children. Typically, re-entry training is one or two days in duration. The objectives of this training are to help the returnees get some closure on their experiences abroad, as well as explaining and planning for reverse culture shock. During the training, participants get the opportunity to talk about their experiences, and to be heard (Borchert & Wierschke, 2000).

The training process helps the participants to:

- Integrate some of their experiences.

- Understand that their feelings are part of an adaptation process (and not a personal deficit).

- Develop coping strategies.

- Overcome feelings of disorientation and loneliness (Borchert & Wierschke, 2000).

The nature of the training is personal and emotional, and organisations are advised to use external trainers who are skilled in facilitation and counselling. Even if an organisation believes they have these skills in-house, the use of an external facilitator promotes trust and open and honest conversations. The training can be conducted in groups of returnees across organisations, and this creates the added benefit of providing an opportunity for returnees to form a network to support each other when they arrive back home (Borchert & Wierschke, 2000).

Tips for Reintegration

1. Establish/continue a performance development plan with Head Office. Clearly define assignment objectives that tie specifically to the Business Unit's strategy. Identify ways to measure success.

2. Offer pre-assignment cultural training. Discuss ways in which the expatriate can articulate to the rest of the organisation what he/she has learnt about managing cultural difference.

3. Set and manage expectations during the assignment about reintegration into the home location.

4. Engage former expatriates with those currently on assignment.

5. Provide reintegration training. This identifies, clarifies, and addresses the issues expatriates may face upon their physical return.

6. Continue communication with the expatriate. Encourage connection with peers at home about the challenges encountered abroad.

7. Set up a mentor programme.

8. Find ways to utilise newly developed talents in the succeeding role.

9. Formalise the reintegration process in your International Assignment Policy.

10. Encourage expatriates to communicate regularly with all their home base support systems while abroad. Communication between the expatriate and the people in their office, with their partners and friends, and between their children and their friends is the best safety net they can establish before they leave.

11. Encourage expatriates to make an effort to maintain contact with their job-related networks, especially with possible future supervisors who may offer them good job opportunities. They should be proactive in career development and maintain visibility in business circles in order to avoid job-related disappointment.

12. Realise that the returning home will cause unexpected turmoil even in the best of times. The readjustment process will present challenges and difficulties. The reconnection process will take time. Don't minimise the effect this will have on the repatriates and their family.

13. Advise repatriates not to rely solely on the HR systems of their organisations; they should have dual accountability in managing the experience and solving possible problems.

14. Encourage line managers to take a personal interest in their repatriates. Educate them on what the repatriate may be experiencing so they are able to provide support and assistance.

(Arman, 2009; Paton, 2006; WVU: nd.)

20.8 CONCLUSION

In order to increase their return on investment for international assignments, organisations need to acknowledge the value and complexity of managing a slick and holistic repatriation process. Repatriation without a dedicated focus on reintegration will invariably lead to higher rates of repatriate turnover. HR departments need to play a critical role in the repatriation and reintegration processes as current trends such as globalisation and "boundary-less careers" increase the global mobility of top talent, and therefore their retention risk.

For expatriates, international assignments often represent a career development move that they expect will pay dividends upon their return home. They anticipate the adjustment and change inherent in moving abroad; but many underestimate the same adjustment and change in coming home. Both the expatriate and the organisation have to be proactive in managing the end-to-end reintegration process for it to be successful.

20.9 REFERENCES

Andreason, AW & Kinneer, KD. 2005. Repatriation adjustment problems and the successful reintegration of expatriates and their families. *Journal of Behavioral and Applied Management*, 6(2):109–126.

Arman, G. 2009. Repatriation adjustment: Literature review. *Journal of European Psychology Students*, 1:1–6.

Borchert, S & Wierschke, A. 2000. *Repatriating the expat – challenges and opportunities*. SIETAR EUROPA Conference: Brussels.

Bossard, AB & Peterson, RB. 2005. The repatriate experience as seen by American expatriates. *Journal of World Business*, 40(1):9–28.

Confidential conversation with bank employee, London, June, 2014.

Cox, JB. 2004. The role of communication, technology, and cultural identity in repatriation adjustment. *International Journal of Intercultural Relations*, 28(3):201–219.

Crowne, KA. 2009. Enhancing knowledge transfer during and after international assignments. *Journal of Knowledge Management*, 13:134–147.

Dougherty-Shepell, M. 2009. Reverse culture shock (or why do I hate being back home?). *International HR Forum*. [Online]. Available: http://internationalhrforum. com/2009/08/17/reverse-culture-shock-or-why-do-i-hate-being-back-home/. [Accessed 1 July 2014].

Dowling, PJ, Schuler, RS & Welch, DE. 1994. *International dimensions of human resource management*. 2nd ed. Belmont, CA: Wadsworth Publishing.

Gregersen, HB & Stroh, LK. 1997. Coming home to the arctic cold: Antecedents to Finnish expatriate and spouse repatriation adjustment. *Personnel Psychology*, 50(3):635–654.

Hammer, MR, Hart, W & Rogan, R. 1998. Can you go home again? An analysis of the repatriation of corporate managers and spouses. *Management International Review*, 38(1):67–86.

Linehan, M & Scullion, H. 2002. Repatriation of European female corporate executives: An empirical study. *International Journal of Human Resource Management*, 13:254–267.

Liu, CH. 2005. The effects of repatriates' overseas assignment experiences on turnover intentions. *Journal of American Academy of Business*, 7(1):124–130.

Martson, B. 2012. Home comforts can be hard to find for the expat. BBC. [Online]. Available: http://www.bbc.co.uk/news/business-16699617. [Accessed 4 July 2014].

Mirasol, K. 2012. Repatriation? Time to move toward reintegration. *Global Talent Management*. [Online]. Available: http://www.iorworld.com/blog/repatriation-time-move-reintegration. [Accessed 1 July 2014].

Morgan, LO, Nie, W & Young, ST. 2004. Operational factors as determinants of expatriate and repatriate success. *International Journal of Operations & Production Management*, 24(12):1247–1268.

Paton, N. 2006. *Expats often walk when they come home*. Management-Issues.com. [Online]. Available: http://www.management-issues.com/news/3756/expats-often-walk-when-they-come-home/. [Accessed 1 July 2014].

Nery-Kjerfve, T & McLean, GN. 2012. Repatriation of expatriate employees, knowledge transfer, and organizational learning: What do we know? *European Journal of Training and Development*, 36(6):614–629.

Sykes, A. (2011). Reverse culture shock: What, when, and how to cope. Expatica.com. [Online]. Available: http://www.expatica.com/nl/health_fitness/well_being/Reverse-culture-shock-101_16451.html. [Accessed 23 July 2014].

UK_Essays.com. nd. Case Study: Monsantos repatriation program management essay. [Online]. Available: http://www.ukessays.com/essays/management/case-study-monsantos-repatriation-program-management-essay.php. [Accessed 1 July 2014].

WVU. nd. US expatriate handbook. West Virginia University College of Business and Economics. [Online]. Available: http://www.us-expatriate-handbook.com/contents.htm. [Accessed 6 July 2014].

Yeaton, K & Hall, N. 2008. Expatriates: Reducing failure rates. *Journal of Corporate Accounting & Finance*, 75–78.

CHAPTER 21
EXPATRIATE MANAGEMENT SYSTEMS
Dr Marius van Aswegen

21.1 INTRODUCTION

Adopting and managing international assignments is essential for the growth and profitability of multinational companies and a key area of focus for organisations looking to expand into emerging markets. The mobility of expatriates is an area of investment for sustainable growth for companies through the development and establishment of new operations and transferring skills into a specific country of operation. Managing expatriate assignments does come with its fair share of administration and finding a way to streamline these administrative duties will enable companies to focus on the opportunities for investment and further growth.

Significant emphasis and focus is placed on expatriate remuneration. However, the pre-assignment and post-assignment conditions and processes are equally crucial to the success of an assignment. Coupled with the day-to-day management of the expatriate workforce there is a vast amount of documentation, administrative and operational processes that need to be in place in order to keep track of all expatriates on their various assignments, often spread over various locations in a number of countries, each with its own set of legislation and regulations.

Staying abreast of items associated with the international assignment such as legal entry-requirement documentation, length and type of assignment, and assignment location specifications can be administratively burdensome. Using Information Management System platforms can reduce the administrative portion of expatriate management by collecting and controlling assignment-specific information on one convenient platform where a reasonable measure of control can be exercised during the entire expatriate life cycle.

21.2 THE EXPATRIATE INFORMATION MANAGEMENT SYSTEM

An Expatriate Management System can be described as an Information Management System (IMS) which is custom designed for the purpose of assisting a company's International Mobility Team to manage their expatriates as well as the full expatriation process.

According to the Comptroller of the Currency of the US Treasury, the goals of any information management system are to enhance communication among employees, deliver complex material throughout the organisation, provide an objective system for recording and aggregating information, reduce expenses related to labour-intensive manual activities, and support the organisation's strategic goals and vision. Information management systems create the link between information-gathering and the ability to analyse collected information for the purposes of informed decision-making. Expatriate management systems are distinct from other information systems because they are used to analyse and facilitate strategic and operational activities related to the functions of a company's expatriates and the need to manage these individuals on their various assignments.

These systems consist of physical hardware and software which provide enormous data processing and reporting power required to manage the flow of information effectively. The information that the system generates will provide management with critical decision-making data and could offer more features and components than needed by the average International Mobility Team. It is therefore necessary to select the right system which will provide the necessary added value and fits the needs of the organisation.

Expatriate management systems are ideally web-based and used for managing the following primary components:

- Countries
- Projects and project conditions
- Assignments
- Expatriates
- Documentation
- Data
- Tasks.

The system should provide the required information to the International Mobility Team and various business units to enable them to manage the expatriate process more efficiently and effectively, and to provide them with the information they need to make decisions. A web-based system also allows access to several users, each user having a specific "authority level" where he/she can capture and update data for the specific assignments. Therefore, an expatriate management system allows for a collaborative effort from the international mobility team and the expatriate in order to manage information on assignments.

The following are some of the benefits attained from making use of an expatriate management system:

- Companies are able to highlight their strengths and weaknesses in the expatriate management process owing to the availability of customised reports. The identification of these aspects can help the company improve their expatriate management processes and operations.

- The system provides an overall picture of the expatriation programme, including all projects and expatriates, and acts as a communication and planning tool.

- The availability of the expatriate data can help the international mobility team to align their internal processes in accordance with a logical process flow.

- The system will ensure and allow the international mobility team to control and plan the renewal and tracking of critical documentation such as expiry of work permits and visas.

- The ability to upload and store documents ensures that they are easily accessible by all stakeholders of the assignment.

21.3 CORE ELEMENTS AND SYSTEM SOLUTIONS

An Expatriate Management System should offer specialised solutions that support the operational aspects of international mobility for a holistic and proactive expatriate management approach. The typical core elements of an expatriate management system should include the ones listed below.

21.3.1 Integrated system

With the use of an expatriate management system, the management and control of international mobilisation within a company is centralised. All information is available in one secure location, making the management process easier, faster and more efficient, with multi-user levels that can be accessed by authorised role players at any time, ensuring integrated management.

Decentralised control is also possible and would be typically implemented for companies that own more than one legal entity. These types of set-ups on an expatriate management system would have one main administrator for all subsidiaries and business units within the group, and several users for each entity.

A fully integrated management system will manage expatriate tasks and administrative responsibilities, offering the organisation a total solutions package.

21.3.2 Technology

An expatriate management system provides the user with a web-based process-driven system and solution that eases the expatriate management process by allowing the users to manage their expatriates throughout the various phases of the expatriate life cycle and the tasks that are associated with each phase.

The expatriate management system is a multi-user platform and serves to ease the administrative tasks related with managing expatriates. Therefore, the system should have an uncomplicated design, a logical navigation flow, and be user-friendly. Capturing data should be simple and concise and data should be easily accessible once captured.

The technology used by such a system will have the capability to notify and allow an organisation not to lose track of renewing work permits, visas and the necessary legal requirements for an expatriate to work in any host location. It also serves as a cache for documents to be stored per assignment location and the expatriates that are on assignment in the host locations.

From the information captured by the mobility team, the expatriate management system should also provide notice on when an assignment is due either for renewal or for the expatriate to be repatriated. This will give the international mobility team as well as the expatriate adequate time to prepare for repatriation. The life cycle of the expatriate assignment can therefore be easily monitored.

21.3.3 Reporting

An expatriate management system processes the raw data captured by the users of the system and produces the output, which is in the form of a report that presents aggregated data. The report then facilitates analysis of the data and decision making based on the analysis. The reporting solution gives the international mobility team instant access to any essential expatriate data that they require as well as the general status and operation of international mobility within the business.

The reporting function can be a very powerful tool for the mobility team and the business in general. Reporting can be done in various formats depending on the specific requirements of the business.

The system reports consolidate information in a format that makes it easy for managers to review and analyse. Customised dashboards with various charts and graphs are very popular as they visually illustrate the data from the system, providing a quick reference to the international mobility team and showing the status of the expatriate function at a single glance.

These reports can be very detailed, indicating the status of all active expatriates' information such as work permits, visas, passports, evacuation policies, and spouse and child documentation, among others, indicating whether they are up to date, expired, or expiring soon. This is an invaluable tool for the international mobility team, which facilitates analysis and decision making. These types of reports are often referred to as summary reports.

Effective Information Management System architecture allows a company to respond more quickly and efficiently to changes in the market. Slow, difficult-to-use systems do not allow users to create specialised reports and typically do not provide critical information in time to make the necessary operational and tactical decisions. Therefore, it is essential to have a system that is underpinned by a fast, efficient information management system architecture that runs in real time, and provides up-to-date, pertinent information, allowing a company to respond more quickly to critical events.

21.3.4 Security and access

Expatriate management systems allow worldwide access and visibility of all assignees, policies and suppliers in one global system.

Expatriate management systems that have a multi-user platform, with multi-user accessibility, need to have good governance in terms of which users have the authority to provide or change information relating to the assignment.

All expatriate management systems' security protocols must pass stringent testing. All sensitive information must be secured through integrated password management, encryption of sensitive data and Secure Socket Layer (SSL) transmission. Users can be created by higher level management users within the system.

Each user receives unique login details and access to specific areas/domains within the system. For example, an expatriate will have access only to his/her specific domain, where he/she can update any of his/herr personal details and information specific to the assignment,. On the other hand, mobility managers will have access to most or all domains where they will be able to capture information on all assignments and be able to generate reports for analysis and decision making. All system users are provided with specific, high security authorisation accessibility to ensure that information always remains confidential.

21.3.5 System notifications

A core element of an expatriate management system lies in the technology of setting timelines in the system with regard to reminders and notifications, where the system prompts the user to take action on specific areas of the assignment.

The user needs to be proactively able to manage everyday responsibilities related to the expatriate assignment. These types of systems have the ability to prompt the administrator on upcoming tasks and duties, such as upcoming international assignment events, tasks and critical dates, by sending e-mail notifications directly to their Outlook inbox.

Many expatriate management systems enable seamless communication through integrating the system notifications with Microsoft Outlook, as well as facilitating and updating of the process status of specific assignments on the system. In addition to system notification, an integrated calendar can be a useful tool, allowing the user to set reminders, record important dates and view or manage tasks in a calendar exclusively looking at tasks related to international assignments.

The main purpose around this design is to enable the user to pre-determine the assignments and upcoming tasks for the company's expatriate workforce and to enable management on a daily basis to track the expatriation process from pre-assignment to demobilisation and finally the post-assignment phase of each assignee, which ensures efficient process control.

21.3.6 Document library

A further core element of an effective expatriate management system is the ability to store all documentation associated with the expatriates' assignments. This significantly simplifies document administration, with an added benefit of having a library of documents stored online. Having such backup documentation available assists in document control and having a multi-user platform. Stakeholders with predefined access security (for example, the manager and expatriate) will be able to access and upload such documents.

A centralised and integrated database updates and stores all information critical in managing expatriates and their assignments. The web-based document uploader enables employees to upload related documentation easily for fast and efficient processing, easy access, and secure filing.

Online secure access to all essential assignment related documentation removes the need for searching through hard copy files and prevents misplaced or lost documents. This type of feature also provides company-specific assignment templates to ensure compliance with standardised processes and documentation.

21.3.7 Information accessibility

Critical or specific information can be accessed immediately through predefined or customised report generating functions. Project and assignment information can be reported on at any given time.

Information such as medical aid details, evacuation plans, and emergency contact details are critical. An expatriate management system allows for immediate access to such information.

21.3.8 Employee self-service and communication tracking

Expatriates are able to access their personal information at any time to make the necessary updates. This lightens the workload of the administrator and ensures that the information is always up to date.

The communication tracking feature allows for the assignment administrator and relevant stakeholders to track communication between one another. This communication process is therefore fully transparent and informative, making it more convenient. Communication tracking will also allow users to assign and trade tasks among one another, ensuring the completion of all critical tasks.

21.4 TURNKEY PROCESS APPROACH TO IMPLEMENTING AN EXPATRIATE MANAGEMENT SYSTEM

The illustration below depicts the typical turnkey process associated with an expatriate management system:

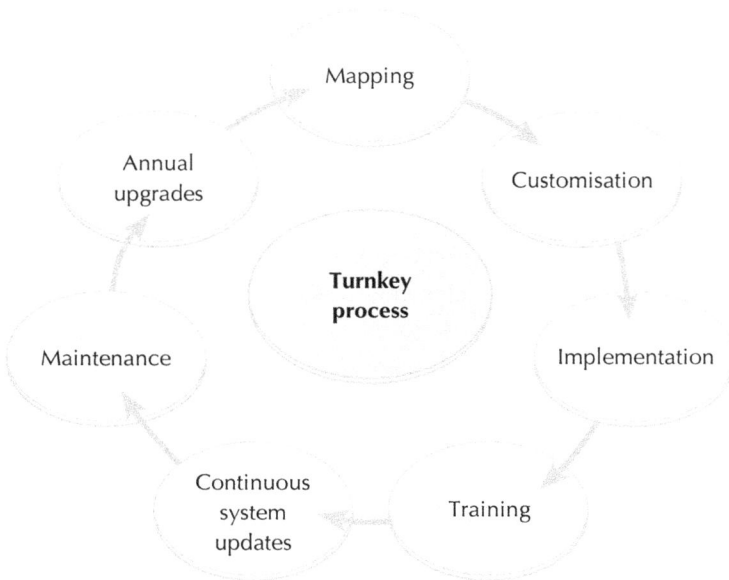

Figure 21.1: Turnkey process

A turnkey service solution is suggested when considering implementing an expatriate management system. This includes an initial analysis of the organisation requirements (mapping), customisation and implementation of the system within the company-specific environment in order to ensure the full integration of the system into the existing assignee management process of the company. Each step in the turnkey approach is addressed in more detail below.

21.5 MAPPING

The first stage of implementing an expatriate management system is the mapping process. This stage acts as the blueprint and set-up phase of the system. Existing assignee processes should be analysed within the company in order to develop the best business solution for the company according to their desired requirements.

The mappng process typically includes the following:

- Review of the company's global expatriate procedures and global expatriate policy

- Familiarisation with the company's approach to package determination, salary build-up and tax equalisation or tax protection

- Process mapping of existing assignee procedures and processes

- Analysis of critical assignee management documents

- Identification of different user levels and/or business units

- Customisation analysis and implementation solution to be provided and signed off

- Analysis of any possible IT and security policy limitations.

21.6 CUSTOMISABLE SETUP

After all system requirements have been analysed and an agreed approach/route has been decided, the system needs to be customised according to the company's mobility framework. A reliable system service provider will focus on the specific requirements and utility of the system so that it is aligned with company needs.

The below provides an idea to what the system provider will take into consideration.

21.6.1 Client-specific requirements

- All goals and objectives of the customised system are clearly noted.
- These requirements are prioritised according to the development cycle.
- Schedules are closely monitored to ensure a timeously system delivery.

21.6.2 Customised report

- A system report is customised according to the company specific needs.
- Required tasks are also drawn up to allow for easy expatriate management.

21.7 IMPLEMENTATION

At the stage of implementation, the service provider would implement the system on site to ensure that the system works properly and that the customised amendments to make the system company-specific works correctly and that the company users can work effectively with the system.

The provider must ensure that the system is implemented efficiently and in a timely manner. Client involvement allows for an understanding of the system elements and functions, which include:

- Configuration
- Operations
- Various functions.

21.8 TRAINING

As with any online tool or system, training needs to be provided by qualified and equipped experts and IT specialists. Group or single-user sessions should be available to the company, depending on the number of users. During this phase, the trainer will take the users (who will have access to and use the system) through the step-by-step process of using the system, from capturing data to generating reports based on the data input.

The typical training process should be as follows:

- **Training of System Administrators:** The System Administrators will be those members of the mobility team that have the highest level of access. Administrators normally set up assignments and related tasks on assignments and the specific locations to where the company wants to send assessed expatriates who are fit to work abroad.

- **Training of non-system Administrators:** Non-system Administrators will normally be comprised of lower level team members of the International Mobility Team of a company as well as the expatriates who will have access to the system.

- **Practical application in the workplace:** It is important to explain the dos and don'ts of the system and how to apply the system architecture to obtain the most effective practical use thereof.

- **Simulator training**.

21.9 CONTINUOUS SYSTEM UPDATES

Continuous improvements allow for a system that is up to date with the latest developments in the expatriate environment to enable functionality that helps the user to meet the day-to-day expatriate management needs. Automatic updates can be done in order to keep the company a step ahead of global and technical developments taking place around the world.

21.10 MAINTENANCE AND SUPPORT

Maintenance and support from the system provider are necessary to ensure the sustainability of the expatriate management process.

Support services can include:

- Telephonic support
- Monitored email support
- Remote assistance using a remote desktop and a virtual private network, where available
- Planned or emergency onsite assistance.

All upgrades need to be carried out during a scheduled maintenance service in order to minimise downtime, making it more convenient for a company.

21.11 SUMMARY

The above outlines the necessary information and insight into expatriate management systems in order to enable the international mobility decision makers to determine the strategic and operational need for such a system within the expatriate workforce environment and provide the company with the appropriate system based on internal and external requirements. The core elements and type of functionality as stipulated herein form the basis of the typical foundation for an expatriate management system to be an effective administrative and management tool.

Expatriate management systems can serve to alleviate manual administrative tasks and make them easier to manage. However, the strength and successful implementation of such a system lies within the various administrators who will be using such a system on a day-to-day basis. It is paramount that a thorough understanding of the system is embedded in the users of the system and that the necessary training be provided so that the users of the system can take ownership of the expatriate management system. This is a crucial element in the success of any information management system and the utilisation thereof.

Finally, a company's expatriate workforce is crucial to its development. The administration of the company's global or regional mobility workforce is a crucial part of the expatriate assignment process. An expatriate management system provides this platform.

CHAPTER 22
CRITICAL SUCCESS FACTORS AND EPILOGUE
Dr Mark Bussin

22.1 INTRODUCTION

As important as international assignment remuneration is to an organisation, management often continue to undervalue the impact it has on assignees' morale, motivation and financial performance. The critical success factors to good international assignment package design involve the following:

- Include current and former assignees in the design process.

- Make use of research information and current best practice.

- Make use of tax experts regarding tax in both host and home countries (reciprocal tax agreements make this essential).

- Research shows that three- to five-year assignments provide optimum ROI.

- Candidates' soft-skill abilities (EQ) should be assessed before the candidates are assigned.

- Typically utilise international assignments as developmental opportunities for high-potential employees.

- Companies should invest time and effort in managing employee and spouse expectations.

- Companies should track employee career development over 10- to 15-year horizons.

- Most international companies use home country base salary to calculate the international assignment package.

- Increasingly, companies try to outsource the international assignment administration function.

- Companies should double their repatriation efforts, as many assignees stay longer than required on high levels of assignment remuneration.

22.2 BENCHMARK FINDINGS, AND LESSONS LEARNT

When doing the research on best-of-breed schemes, one often comes across the following as typical benchmark findings. This could serve as a lessons-learnt checklist for your scheme design:

- Companies generally assist with tax compliance.

- Companies strive to put international assignee on equal footing with that at home.

- Most companies use external consultants for overall design, COL and parity.

- Half the companies allow international assignees to complete "location ranking questionnaires" (typically 16 to 20 factors).

- Conversion to local conditions ranges from immediate to three years.

- The parent organisation is still responsible for the international assignee's career.

- Equity is managed by home base and job.

Other important design considerations include:

- Soft issues such as the spouse's loss of employment, repatriation, and re-skilling

- Volatile currency such as the and against the major currencies in the past

- Selling houses in the home country at a loss

- Provision of a car benefit in the host country

- COL index, particularly in high inflation countries

We would like to hear your views on expatriate remuneration, especially success stories that we could include as a case study in future versions of this book. Please e-mail me on drbussin@mweb.co.za

I look forward to your contributions.

APPENDIX 1
AFRICA VISA APPLICATION GUIDELINES
Adrenè van der Merwe

CWT was kind enough to let us use their Visa application guidelines for Africa as an appendix in this book. Of course, this information needs to be checked at source and in no way constitutes advice.

1. AFRICA

When processing visas on behalf of travellers, CWT will under no circumstances assist in processing the incorrect visa for ease of application or to circumvent any laws. We will at all times adhere to our Anti-Bribery Policy and Global Procedures on Visas and Passports Processing when dealing with all third party visa providers and Embassies/Consulates. We will therefore not be able to expedite visa processing unless the Consulate/Embassy charges an official expediting fee.

Information provided is valid at the time of publication but may be changed by relevant Consulates without prior warning and should be checked prior to visa submission.

- Passport must be valid for at least six months after the scheduled return date of travel.

- Passport must have at least two blank pages.

- Only biometric portrait photographs are acceptable.

2. ANGOLA

SA passports: Visas are required
Temporary SA passports are NOT accepted

Foreign passport: Check for residency permit – Visa fee applies

All Applicants are required to apply in person. With effect from 22 April 2014, the Consulate will process applications only in the area in which you reside, that is, either Johannesburg or Pretoria.

A Meet & Greet service is available and can be arranged through CWT. The traveller will be met at the Embassy between 09h30–10h00 for fingerprinting.

Documents must be submitted the day before the interview if the Meet & Greet service is used.

30-Day Visa

Visas are issued for 30 days' single entry.

A visa takes a minimum of 15 working days to be processed as it must be authorised by DEVA in Angola.

7-Day Visa

Travellers who intend to do business in Angola for no longer than 7 days.

Visas are issued for 7 working days only.

The visa is issued in 3–5 working days and released the day prior to the client's departure. (The applicant has only 48 hours to validate this visa on entry into Angola.) For clients leaving on a Monday morning, their visa will be released on the Friday afternoon. Visa must be validated on the Monday. Should the client amend or change dates, they will have to re-apply and pay for a new visa.

Submit: Monday – Friday, 09h30 – 11h00
Collect: Monday – Friday, 11h00 – 14h00

Requirements

- 2 recent colour photos.

- Application form.

- Copy of Yellow Fever certificate.

- Employment letter in Portuguese addressed to the consulate (translation services available at an extra cost).

- Invitation letter in Portuguese addressed to the Consulate.

- Full name of passenger and their passport number and expiry date must be stated on both invite and SA employ letter. These letters are valid for 30 days only.

- Copy of the hosts passport and company *Gazette*.

- Itinerary and e-ticket.

- Utility bill.

- Permit for SA (foreign passport holders).

Cost

30-day visa ~ R950.00

7-day visa ~ R1 100.00

A Meet & Greet service is always recommended to facilitate visa processing.

3. BOTSWANA

SA passports: Visas are not required for stays up to 90 days.
                      Temporary SA passports are NOT accepted.

Foreign passport: Check for residency permit – visa fee applies

A Meet & Greet service is available and can be arranged through CWT.

Submit: Monday – Friday, 08h00 – 12h00
Collect: Monday – Friday, 08h00 – 12h00

Processing time is 7–14 working days. The Embassy waits for a response from Botswana before issuing the visa. This could take up to 2 months to authorise.

Requirements

- Two identical colour passport photographs with applicant's name on the back.

- Application form.

- Employment letter.

- A letter of invitation from the host/company in Botswana is required with a certified copy of hosts National Identity/Residence Permit/Exemption Certificate/ Naturalisation Certificate. Fax copies are accepted. E-Mails are not accepted.

- All business invitation letters need to be accompanied by The Trading Licence & Certificate of incorporation.

- All invitation letters or hotel confirmations must be faxed direct from Botswana to the Embassy of Botswana in Johannesburg on 011 403 1286. This has to be done prior to submitting documentation to the Embassy.

- Original Letter from South African company is required from the employer stating – position held, period of employment, exact dates of your leave & expected date of return.

- Itinerary.

- Permit for SA (foreign passport holders).

Cost

Foreign passport ~ R1 000.00 (Subject to change)

4. CAMEROON

SA passports: Visas are required

Foreign passport: Check for residency permit – visa fee applies

Submit: Monday – Friday, 09h00 – 12h30
Collect: Monday – Friday, 12h00 – 13h00

Processing time is 2 working days.

Requirements

- 2 recent colour photos (reverse side must bear applicant's full names).
- Application form.
- Employment letter.
- Invitation letter – must have 3 stamps from the Foreign office. Business invitation letter certified by the Mayor or the Cameroon Immigration.
- Proof of accommodation (hotel reservation or certificate of accommodation).
- Itinerary and e-ticket.
- Valid international certificates of vaccinations for Yellow Fever and any other communicable disease declared by health authorities.
- Proof of accommodation.
- Permit for SA (foreign passport holders).

Cost

Visa for 1 – 3 months ~ R670.00
Visa for 3 – 6 months ~ R1 340.00

5. DRC (DEMOCRATIC REPUBLIC OF CONGO)

SA passports: Visas are required
                      Temporary SA passports are accepted for single entry only

Foreign passport: Check for residency permit – visa fee applies

Submit: Monday – Friday, 09h00 – 12h30
Collect: Monday – Friday, 13h30 – 14h30

Processing time is 24 hours.

Requirements

- 2 recent colour photos.
- Application form.
- Employment letter.
- Invitation letter.
- Itinerary and e-ticket.
- Permit for SA (Foreign passport holders).

Cost

Single entry (15 days) ~ R750.00
Single entry (30 days) ~ R1 125.00
Multiple entry visa (30 days) ~ R1 500.00
Multiple entry visa (45 days) ~ R1 875.00
Multiple entry visa (60 days) ~ R2 250.00
Multiple entry visa (90 days) ~ R2 650.00
Multiple entry visa (6 months) ~ R5 280.00

6. ETHIOPIA

SA passports: Visas are required

Foreign passport: Check for residency permit – Visa fee applies

South Africa citizens can now receive tourist visas on arrival in Ethiopia at the regular charge for a stay of up to 30 days if arriving by air (USD20). If arriving in Ethiopia by car, a visa is required and must be obtained prior to arrival in Ethiopia.

Business travellers still require visa before travelling to Ethiopia.

Submit: Monday – Friday, 09h00 – 12h00
Collect: Monday – Friday, 09h00 – 12h00

Processing time is 24 hours.

Requirements

- 1 (one) recent colour photo (concealed in an envelope).
- Application form.
- Copy of the passport.
- Employment letter.
- Invitation letter (The letter must have a stamp from the Foreign office).
- Itinerary and e-ticket.
- Yellow Fever certificate.
- Proof of accommodation.
- Permit for SA (foreign passport holders).

Cost

Single entry ~ R140.00
Multiple entry ~ R340.00

7. GABON

SA passports: South African passport holders do not require visas for a stay up to 30 days.

Foreign passport: Check for residency permit – Visa fee applies

Submit: Tuesdays and Thursdays only
Collect: Embassy may request applicant to personally collect the visa.

Processing time is 5 working days for an ordinary visa.

Requirements

- Two application forms to be completed by each applicant. 4 recent colour photos per application
- Employment letter stating position held, period of employment, expected date of return and contact details.
- A letter of invitation from the company in Gabon to be visited is required – stating nature of business and contact details of people to be visited.
- Itinerary and e-ticket.

- Hotel booking must be stamped and not be part of the flight itinerary. Yellow Fever Certificate and Malaria precautions
- Permit for SA (foreign passport holders).

Cost

Single entry   ~   R850.00
Multiple entry   ~   R1 250.00

The Visa fees are non-refundable.

8. GHANA

SA passports: Visas are required

Foreign passport: Check for residency permit – visa fee applies

Applications are captured online.

Submit: Monday – Thursday, 09h00 – 12h00
Collect: Monday – Thursday, 13h00 – 14h00

Normal submission, 6–7 working days Express submission, 3–4 working days. This excludes the day of submission and the Embassy is closed every Friday.

Requirements

- 1 recent colour photo (ensure photograph has been uploaded before completing the main section of the online visa application form).
- Copy of the passport.
- Employment letter.
- Invitation letter.
- Copy of the host's passport.
- Itinerary and e-ticket.
- Copy of the Yellow Fever certificate.
- Payments by postal order or bank guaranteed cheque, made payable to the Ghana High Commission.
- Tourist visas must include 3 months, bank statements and proof of accommodation.
- Permit for SA (foreign passport holders).

Cost

3 months single entry visa ~ R450.00

6 months multiple entry visa ~ R950.00

1 year multiple entry visa ~ R1 850.00

Express 3 months single visa ~ R1 250.00

Express 6 months multiple visa ~ R1 550.00

Express 1 year multiple visa ~ R3 050.00

9. KENYA

SA passports: Visas are required with effect from 01 July 2014
                      Temporary SA passports are NOT accepted

Foreign passport: Check for residency permit – visa fee applies

Monday – Thursday: 09h00 – 12h30 and 14h00 – 15h00
Friday: 09h00 – 12h30

Processing time is 5 working days for South African passport holders. Time may differ for foreign passport holders.
   Applicants must appear in person for biometrics.

Requirements

- 2 passport photographs.

- Copy of return air ticket.

- Copy of itinerary.

- Copy of the passport.

- A letter from your employer stating the nature of the business and contacts in Kenya.

- A letter of invitation from the company in Kenya. Copy of the Yellow Fever certificate.

- Proof of funds (bank statement). Permit for SA (foreign passport holders).

Cost

Ordinary visa ~ R750.00 ($70)

10. LESOTHO

SA passports: Visas are not required for stays up to 30 days

Foreign passport: Check for residency permit – visa fee applies

Submit: Monday – Friday, 08h00 – 16h00
Collect: Monday – Friday, 08h00 – 12h00

Processing time is 3 working days.

Requirements

- 2 recent colour photos.
- Application form.
- Copy of passport.
- Proof of sufficient funds.
- Employment letter.
- Invitation letter.
- Proof of accommodation.
- Itinerary and e-ticket.
- Copy of Yellow Fever Certificate.
- Permit for SA (foreign passport holders)

Cost

Single entry ~ R500.00
Multiple entry visa ~ R700.00

11. LIBERIA

SA passports: Visas are required

Foreign passport: Check for residency permit – visa fee applies

Submit: Monday – Thursday, 10h00 – 13h00
            Friday, 10h00 – 12h00

Collect: Monday – Thursday, 10h00 – 13h00
             Friday, 10h00 – 12h00

Normal processing time is 5 working days.
Urgent processing time is 24 hours.

Requirements

- 2 recent passport size photos (full face view on white background).

- Application form.

- Employment letter.

- Invitation letter.

- Itinerary and e-ticket.

- Copy of Yellow Fever certificate.

- 3 months, original current bank statements.

- Permit for SA (foreign passport holders).

Cost

Single entry (10 – 30 days) ~ R600.00
Multiple entry visa (3 months) ~ R1 200.00
Multiple entry visa (3 – 6 months) ~ R2 400.00
Urgent Visa fees are double.

12. MALI

SA passports: Visas are required

Foreign passport: Check for residency permit – visa fee applies

Submit: Monday – Friday, 09h00 – 12h30
Collect: Monday – Friday, 09h00 – 12h30

Normal processing time is 5 – 7 working days.
Urgent processing time is 48 hours.

Requirements

- 2 recent colour passport size photo (no headgear and sunglasses) normal glasses allowed.

- Application form.

- Employment letter.

- Invitation letter.

- Itinerary and e-ticket.

- Copy of Yellow Fever Certificate. Permit for SA (foreign passport holders).

Cost

Single Entry ~ R510.00
Urgent visa ~ R810.00

13. MOZAMBIQUE

SA passports: Tourist visas are not required for a stay up to 30 days. Business visas, as well as multiple entry visas, are required for work/ business related purposes.

Foreign passport: Check for residency permit – visa fee applies

Submit: Monday – Friday, 08h00 – 12h00
Collect: Monday – Friday, 08h00 – 12h00

Normal processing time is 24 hours.

Requirements

- 2 recent colour photos.

- Application form.

- Employment letter.

- Invitation letter.

- Itinerary and e-ticket.

- Copy of Yellow Fever certificate.

- Permit for SA (foreign passport holders).

Cost

Single entry ~ R500.00
Multiple entry (valid for 3 months) ~ R765.00

14. NIGERIA

SA Passports: Visas are required

Temporary SA passports are NOT accepted

Foreign passport: Check for residency permit – visa fee applies

Submit: Tuesday & Thursday, 10h00 – 14h00
Collect: Monday & Friday, 10h00 – 14h00

Closed on Wednesdays

Processing time is 15 working days.

Requirements

*   The Nigerian High Commission requires all clients to appear and lodge visa forms in person.

*   1 colour photo. Application form.

*   Valid passport and any previous passports with Nigerian visas.

*   Copy of passport.

*   Original employment letter.

*   Invitation letter (bearing current dates – cannot use a letter which is older than a month).

*   Copy of host's passport. Itinerary and e-ticket.

*   Certificate of Incorporation.

*   CAC 2 form.

*   Permit for SA (foreign passport holders).

Cost

Single entry ~ R3 040.00

3 Month ~ R3 240.00

6 Month ~ R3 840.00

1st time application fee ~ R6 000.00 (Non-refundable)

Cheque charge ~ R120.00

The application form must be loaded and paid on-line, using the applicants' Visa verified credit card.

Visa cost is not refundable.

Recommended process

Clients are recommended to register with the South African-Nigerian Chamber of Commerce if frequent travel will be conducted to Nigeria. This will facilitate visa applications and will not require travellers to apply in person. CWT can facilitate an official application on behalf of the traveller with a 5 – 7 working days' delay.

CWT can provide the required membership application forms upon request.

15. TANZANIA

SA Passports: Visas are not required for stays up to 90 days

Foreign passport: Check for residency permit – visa fee applies

Submit: Monday – Friday, 09h30 – 12h30
Collect: Monday – Friday, 09h30 – 12h30

Processing time is 24 hours from the day of submission.

Requirements

- 1 recent passport size colour photo.

- Application form.

- Employment letter.

- Invitation letter.

- Itinerary and e-ticket.

- Copy of the Yellow Fever certificate.

- Permit for SA (foreign passport holders).

Cost

Single entry ~ USD50.00

Double entry ~ USD70.00

Multiple entry ~ USD100.00

16. UGANDA

SA Passports: Visas are required

Foreign passport: Check for residency permit – Visa fee applies

Submit: Monday – Friday, 09h30 – 12h30
Collect: Monday – Friday, 14h00 – 16h00

Processing time is 48 hours from the day of submission.

Requirements

- 2 recent colour passport size photographs.

- Application form.

- Employment letter (stating period in Uganda and exact nature of business).

- Invitation letter.

- Itinerary and e-ticket.

- Copy of Yellow Fever Certificate.

- Copy of confirmed hotel reservation.

- Additional information may be required by way of interview.

- Permit for SA (foreign passport holders).

Cost

Single entry	~	R500.00
Multiple entry	~	R1 000.00

APPENDIX 2
INTERNATIONAL VISA APPLICATION GUIDELINES
Mack Moey

Singapore Visa Requirements

Foreigners holding travel documents issued by the following countries/regions will require a visa to enter Singapore:

- Afghanistan

- Algeria

- Bangladesh (Except Diplomatic/Official/Service passport holders)

- Commonwealth of Independent States (Except Diplomatic/Official/Service passport holders for a stay of up to 30 days)
    - Armenia
    - Azerbaijan
    - Belarus
    - Kazakhstan
    - Kyrgyzstan
    - Moldova
    - Russia
    - Tajikistan
    - Uzbekistan

- Egypt

- Georgia (Except Diplomatic/Official/Service passport holders for a stay of up to 30 days)

- Ukraine (Except Diplomatic/Official/Service passport holders for a stay of up to 90 days)

- India (Except Diplomatic/Official/Service passport holders)

- Iran

- Iraq

- Jordan (Except Diplomatic/Official/Service passport holders)

- Lebanon

- Libya

- Morocco

- Myanmar (Except Diplomatic/Official/Service passport holders)

- Nigeria (Except Diplomatic/Official/Service passport holders)

- People's Republic of China (Except Diplomatic/Service/Public Affairs passport holders for a stay of up to 30 days)

- Pakistan

- Saudi Arabia (Except Diplomatic passport holders)

- Somalia

- Sudan

- Syria

- Tunisia (Except Diplomatic/Official/Service passport holders)

- Turkmenistan (Except Diplomatic/Official/Service passport holders for a stay of up to 30 days)

- Yemen

Visitors holding these travel documents also require a visa to enter Singapore:

- Hong Kong Document of Identity

- Macao Special Administrative Region (MSAR) Travel Permit

- Palestinian Authority Passport

- Temporary Passport issued by United Arab Emirates

- Refugee* Travel Document issued by the Middle-East countries

- * These travel documents are subject to assessment of recognition for entry into Singapore.)

For information on obtaining a visa, please go to the Visa Application page.

Nationals of the Commonwealth of Independent States, Georgia, Turkmenistan and Ukraine may be granted entry into Singapore without visas* for a stopover stay, if they are on transit to or from a third country (both forward and return leg applies).

However, they are required to fulfil the following conditions:

- They are in transit to or from a third country

- They hold –
  - A valid passport
  - A confirmed onward air-ticket
  - Entry facilities (including visa) to the third country
  - Sufficient funds for the period of stay in Singapore
- They continue their journey to the third country within the 96-hour visa free period granted
- They satisfy Singapore's entry requirements, as determined by the Immigration & Checkpoints Authority officers at the Singapore Checkpoints.

Note: The grant of the visa free entry will be upon the assessment and at the discretion of the Immigration and Checkpoints Authority officer at the Singapore Checkpoint. Last updated on 18 August 2014

Nationals of Assessment Level I Countries

Procedure

(a) For Application in Singapore

Submit your visa application online via Submission of Application for Visa Electronically (SAVE) through a local contact with a SingPass account or a strategic partner in Singapore.

(b) For Application at our Overseas Mission

Submit your visa application at the nearest Singapore Overseas Mission or through the authorised visa agents of the Overseas Missions. The full list of Overseas Missions can be found at the website address: http://www.mfa.gov.sg/content/mfa/missions/singapore_mission/mission_locator.html. Please visit the respective Mission's website for the visa application procedure.

Documents required

(a) For Business Visit (attending business negotiation/discussion)

1) Completed Form 14A (original).

2) One recent passport-sized colour photograph (to be pasted on the top right-hand corner of (Form 14A) which meets the following requirements:
   - Image must be taken within the last 3 months .
   - Photograph should be in colour, must be taken against a white background with a matt or semi-matt finish.

- Image must show the full face and without headgear (headgear worn in accordance with religious or racial customs is acceptable but must not hide the facial features) .

3) Photocopy of the applicant's passport biodata page. Please ensure that the passport is valid for at least 6 months from the date of entry.

4) Completed Form V39A (Letter of Introduction for Visa Application)[1].

5) Computer printout of the Singapore registered business entity's detailed business profile (showing the names of all the directors/shareholders) from the Instant Information Service, Accounting and Corporate Regulatory Authority (ACRA) and printed within the last 3 months .

[1] Letter of Introduction (LOI) may be issued by a local contact in Singapore. For visa applicants attending business negotiation/discussion in Singapore, the local contact must be a Singapore registered business entity . The person acting on behalf of the business entity must be a Singapore Citizen/Singapore Permanent Resident who is at least 21 years old . If you are not able to furnish a LOI from a local contact, you may approach your Embassy to issue a LOI to support your visa application.

(b) For Social Visit (visiting families, friends, relatives and for tourism)

1) Completed Form 14A (original)

2) One recent passport-sized colour photograph (to be pasted on the top right-hand corner of (Form 14A) which meets the following requirements:

- Image must be taken within the last 3 months .

- Photograph should be in colour, must be taken against a white background with a matt or semi-matt finish.

- Image must show the full face and without headgear (headgear worn in accordance with religious or racial customs is acceptable but must not hide the facial features).

3) Photocopy of the applicant's passport biodata page. Please ensure that the passport is valid for at least 6 months from the date of entry.

4) Completed Form V39A (Letter of Introduction for Visa Application)[2].

5) Local contact's Singapore Identity Card (original and photocopy).

[2] Letter of Introduction (LOI) may be issued by a local contact in Singapore. Any Singapore Citizen or Singapore Permanent Resident who is at least 21 years old can act as a local contact. If you are not able to furnish a LOI from a local contact, you may approach your Embassy to issue a LOI to support your visa application.

Other requirements

The applicant and the local contact may be required to furnish additional documents and information whenever necessary. Official translations of the documents are required if they are not in the English language.

Processing fee

A processing fee of S$30 per visa application will be collected at the time of submission. The fee collected is non-refundable regardless of the outcome of the application or if you withdraw the application after submission.

Security deposit

Where applicable, a security deposit may be required from the local contact or the visa applicant upon approval of the application. ICA will advise whether the security deposit should be in the form of a Banker's Guarantee, Cashier's Order or NETS. Insurance guarantees are not accepted. The amount of security deposit is S$1 000.

Refund of security deposit

The security deposit will be refunded to the local contact or the visa applicant if the applicant has not breached any of the conditions stated in the security bond executed by the local contact (or the visa applicant) and his/her departure from Singapore is confirmed by Immigration & Checkpoints Authority (ICA). A completed Direct Credit Authorisation Form is required for refunding purpose.

The processing time for refund is about **4 weeks**. To avoid any delay, visa applicant is advised to surrender the visa card to the Immigration Officer at the checkpoint upon his/her final departure. Any unused visa(s) should also be returned to ICA as soon as possible to facilitate the refund.

Processing time

The processing time is 1 working day (excluding the date of submission, Saturdays, Sundays and Public Holidays) to process. However, some applications may take a longer time to process.

Collection of visa

If the application is approved, the local contact/strategic partner/authorised visa agent can print a copy of the e-Visa for the visa applicant via Submission of Application for Visa Electronically (SAVE).

Important Notes

Each application for a visa will be considered on its own merits.

Possession of a valid visa alone does not guarantee entry into Singapore. Visitors must also meet entry requirements such as holding a valid passport with at least 6 months validity, sufficient funds for the period of stay in Singapore and confirmed onward/return air ticket.

ICA may share your personal information with other Government agencies to process any applications you have made or to render you a service, so as to serve you in a most efficient and effective way, unless such sharing is prohibited by legislation.

Last updated on 26 October 2014

Source: Singapore Immigration & Checkpoint Authority

http://www.ica.gov.sg/

Malaysia Visa Requirements

Types of Visa

The Malaysian Government issues Three (3) types of visas to foreign nationals:

1. **Single Entry Visa**
   This is issued to foreign nationals who require a visa to enter Malaysia mainly for a social visit. It is normally valid for a single entry and for a period of three (3) months from the date of issue.

2. **Multiple Entry Visa**
   This is issued to foreign nationals who require a visa to enter Malaysia mainly for business or government-to-government matters. It is normally valid for a period within three (3) months to twelve (12) months from the date of issue. Citizens of India and the People's Republic of China who wish to enter Malaysia for the purpose of a Social Visit are eligible to apply for the Multiple Entry Visa. The validity of the Multiple Entry Visa is one (1) year. Each entry is for 30 days only and the extension of stay is not allowed.
   Conditions for the Multiple Entry Visa are:

   i.   The applicant must show proof of sufficient funds for staying in Malaysia.

   ii. The applicant must possess a valid and confirmed return ticket.

   iii. Tour groups are not eligible to apply for Multiple Entry Visa.

   iv. The Multiple Entry Visa costs RM100.00 for Indian Citizens and RM30.00 for citizens of the People's Republic of China.

3. **Transit Visa**

   This is issued to foreign nationals who require a visa to enter Malaysia on transit to other countries. Foreign nationals on transit without leaving the airport premises and who continue their journey to the next destination with the same flight do not require a transit visa.

How to apply for a Visa

Visa applications must be made at any nearest Malaysian Representative Office Abroad.

Applications can also be made online through I-Visa System (Applicable for tourist from India and China only).

1. Application for a Visa without Reference

Documents required for the application of a visa without reference (approval of visa is given by High Commission of Malaysia) are:

a. Original passport

b. Two (2) photocopies of the applicant's passport

c. Two (2) photocopies of the visa application form (Form IMM.47)

d. Two (2) passport size photographs of the applicant

e. Original and two (2) photocopies of the ticket (confirmed and returned ticket)

f. Bank statement/travellers cheque

g. Invitation letter (if any)

h. Payment of visa fee

Note: Visa Without Reference is required for the purpose of a social visit.

2. Application for a Visa with Reference

Documents which are required for the application of a visa with reference (visa will issued after the application is being referred and approved by the Department of Immigration Malaysia/Other Agencies of Authority):

a. Original approval letter from the Immigration Department of Malaysia/other authority agencies

b. Original passport

c. Two (2) photocopies of the applicant's passport

d. Two (2) photocopies of visa application form (Form IMM.47)

e.   Two (2) passport size photograph of applicant

f.   Original and two (2) photocopies of an air ticket

g.   Payment of visa fee

Note: Visa With Reference is required for students, those seeking employment, dependants and professionals on a visit pass.

Visa Requirements by Country

1.   Commonwealth countries that require visa

- Bangladesh
- Cameroon*
- Ghana*
- Pakistan
- Nigeria*
- Mozambique*

2. Visa Requirements for other countries

Afghanistan (Visa with reference)	Equatorial Guinea*	Myanmar
Angola*	Eritrea*	Nepal
Bhutan	Ethiopia*	Niger*
Burkina Faso*	Guinea-Bissau*	Rwanda*
Burundi*	Hong Kong (C.I/D.I)	Serbia Montenegro
Central African Republic*	India	Sri Lanka
China	Israel**	United Nation (Laissez Passer)
Colombia*	Ivory Coast (Côte D'Ivoire)*	Western Sahara*
Congo Democratic Republic*	Liberia*	Yugoslavia
Djibouti*	Mali*	

Note:

The countries marked as (*) are allowed to enter Malaysia by air only.

Israel citizens** who wish to enter are required Visa and approval from Ministry of Home Affairs, Malaysia.

Visa is not required for a stay of less than one (1) month for ASEAN nationals except Myanmar. Visas are required for duration of stay exceeds (1) month except for Brunei and Singapore nationals.

Yellow Fever certificate is required to be produced upon landing in Malaysia for countries as listed below:

Angola	Ethiopia	Senegal
Benin	Gabon	Sierra Leone
Bolivia	Gambia	South Africa
Brazil	Ghana	Sri Lanka
Burkina Faso	Guinea-Bissau	St Kitts & Nevis
Burundi	Kenya	Suriname
Cameroon	Mali	Tanzania
Central African Republic	Niger	Togo
Chad	Nigeria	Uganda
Djibouti	Panama	Venezuela
Ecuador	Peru	Zaire
Guinea	Rwanda	Zambia
Eritrea	Sao Tome & Principe	

Last Updated on Thursday, 04 April 2013 00:39

Visa Fee According to the Country

Countries	Single/Multiple Entry Visa (RM)	Transit Visa (RM)
Argentina	20.15	4.10
Bangladesh	20.00	20.00
Bhutan	20.00	20.00
Bolivia	11.00	11.00
Burma	19.50	6.60
Brazil	17.00	17.00
Bulgaria	21.90	11.00
Chile	24.50	24.50
Republic of China	30.00	30.00
Costa Rica	9.00	20.00
Czech & Slovak	19.30	8.20
Denmark	6.00	–
Dominican Republic	12.90	9.65
Ecuador	7.00	0.50
Finland	7.00	–
France	12.90	–
Haiti	16.00	6.00
Hungary	21.45	10.30
India	50.00	50.00
Indonesia	15.00	3.50
Israel	9.70	1.10

Countries	Single/Multiple Entry Visa (RM)	Transit Visa (RM)
Italy	9.50	–
South Korea	30.00	15.00
Liberia	13.00	13.00
Mexico	17.50	17.50
Myanmar	20.00	20.00
Nepal	20.00	20.00
Panama	14.50	14.50
Pakistan	20.00	20.00
Peru	20.00	20.00
Poland	26.20	8.00
Portugal	6.50	6.50
Saudi Arabia	17.20	8.60
Sri Lanka	15.00	15.00
Sudan	12.90	4.30
United States of America	6.00	20.00
Uruguay	13.50	13.50
Venezuela	18.00	18.00
Vietnam	13.00	1.50
Countries which are not listed are to pay RM 20.00		

Last Updated on Thursday, 09 May 2013 00:54

Source: Philippine Immigration Department of Malaysia

http://www.imi.gov.my/index.php/en/

Thailand Visa Requirements

List of countries and territories entitled for Visa Exemption and Visa on Arrival

Period of stay 15 days

Bhutan	China	Cyprus	Czech Republic	Ethiopia	Hungary
India	Kazakhstan	Latvia	Liechtenstein	Lithuania	Maldives
Mauritius	Oman	Poland	Principality of Andorra	Russia	Republic of Bulgaria
Republic of Malta	Romania	Republic of San Marino	Saudi-Arabia	Slovak	Slovenia
Taiwan	Ukraine	Uzbekistan			

TOURIST VISA EXEMPTION

Period of stay 30 days

Australia	Austria	Bahrain	Belgium	Brazil	Brunei Darussalam
Canada	Czech Republic	Denmark	Estonia	Finland	France
Germany	Greece	Hong Kong	Hungary	Iceland	Indonesia
Ireland	Israel	Italy	Japan	South Korea	Kuwait
Luxembourg	Liechtenstein	Malaysia	Monaco	Netherlands	New Zealand
Norway	Oman	Peru	Philippines	Portugal	Poland
Qatar	Singapore	Slovak	Slovenia	Spain	South Africa
Sweden	Switzerland	Turkey	United Arab Emirates	United Kingdom	United States of America
Vietnam					

Remark

- Via airport, period of stay 30 days
- Via land border, period of stay 15 days

except Malaysian nationals who cross the borderline from Malaysia whose granted period of stay will not exceed 30 days each time.

Notice: For a holder of this type of visa may apply for a 7 day extension of stay.

Period of stay 90 days (*country member (ABTC))

Australia*	Brunei*	Canada	Chile*	China*	Hong Kong*
Indonesia*	Japan*	South Korea*	Malaysia*	Mexico*	New Zealand*
Papua New Guinea*	Peru*	Philippines*	Russia	Singapore*	Taiwan*
Vietnam*	United States of America*				

List of countries which have concluded bilateral agreements on visa fee exemption with Thailand

Period of stay 14 days

Cambodia

Period of stay 30 days

Hong Kong	Macau	Mongolia	Vietnam	Laos	Russia

Period of stay 90 days

Brazil*	Chile	South Korea*	Peru*	Argentina
* Diplomatic/Official Passport holder				

List of Countries which have concluded agreements on the exemption of visa requirements for holders of diplomatic or official or service/special passports with Thailand

Period of stay 30 days

Cambodia	China	Laos	Mongolia	Myanmar	Oman	Vietnam

List of countries which are declared Yellow Fever infected Areas

Angola	Argentina	Benin	Bolivia	Brazil
Burknan Faso	Burundi	Cameron	Central Africa	Chad
Columbia	Congo	Cote d'Ivoire	Ecuador	Equatorial Guin
Ethiopia	French-Guiana	Gabon	Gambia	Ghana
Guinea	Guyana	Guinea Bissau	Kenya	Liberia
Mali	Mauritania	Niger	Nigeria	Panama
Peru	Paraguay	Rwanda	Senegal	Sao Tome & Principe
Sierra Leone	Somalia	Sudan	Suriname	Tanzania
Togo	Trinidad & Tobago	Uganda	Venezuela	Zaire

Fees (adjusted):

Residence certificate (TM. 15)

Arrival prior to immigration act: 19 000.- Baht per piece

Residence certificate (TM. 16)

- For shared investment or special investment: 191 400.- Baht
- For employment or expert: 191 400.- Baht
- For foreigner married to Thai national: 95 700.- Baht
- For foreign head of family taking care of children of Thai nationality: 95 700.- Baht
- For spouse of foreign resident in the Kingdom: 95 700.- Baht
- For children of foreign resident in the Kingdom or of Thai nationals:
  - Underage: 95 700.- Baht
  - Adult: 191 400.- Baht
- For non-quota immigrants (original resident): 95 700.- Baht

Residence certificate (TM. 17)

In case of damage or loss or insufficient space in passport: 1 900.- Baht per piece

Re-entry permit endorsement

1 900.- Baht per piece

Non-quota immigrant visa outside the annual quota for immigrants admitted to the Kingdom:

- Single entry: 1 900.- Baht
- Multiple entries within 1 year: 3 800.- Baht

Visa

- Transit visa: 800.- Baht
- Tourist visa: 1 000.- Baht
- Non-immigrant visa:
  - single entry: 2 000.- Baht
  - multiple entries within 1 year: 5 000.- Baht
  - multiple entries within 3 years for holders of passports or other travel documents from the Asia-Pacific cooperation group who travel in and out of the Kingdom for business:
- Immigrant visa: 1 900.- Baht
- Non-quota immigrant visa:
  - single entry: 1 900.- Baht
  - multiple entries within 1 year: 3 800.- Baht

Appeal in Reference to Section 22

(persona non grata) each person 1 900 baht

Application for extension of temporary stay

1 900 baht per time

Appeal in Reference to Section 36

(revoked visa) 1 900.- Baht per person

Application for re-entry permit

- Single entry: 1 000.- Baht
- Multiple entries within remaining period of admission: 3 800.- Baht

Application for permanent residence in the Kingdom

7 600.- Baht per person

Request for verification of nationality

800 baht per person

Note

The ministerial order 27 (2003) was issued according to the 1979 immigration act and announced in the Royal Gazette, Decrees vol. 120, part 59a, on June 27, 2003 and has been enforced since August 26, 2003.

Applying for a resident's visa in Thailand

1. **Criterion and conditions of foreign nationals' residential permit consideration**

2. **Detailed information and required documents needed of Residence Permit applications**

   - Detailed information needed of Residence Permit applications
     - TM. 9
     - Personal information sheet
     - Health certificate from a government hospital
     - Map of residence and place of work
     - Example for the employment certification letter
     - Example for the letter of employment history to Department of Labour

3. **Required documents**

   - Investment
     - Working/Business
     - Supporting Thai citizen or being supported by Thai citizen
     - Supporting alien who already had residence permit or being supported by alien who already had residence permit
     - Experts

General Information

1. Generally, a foreign citizen who wishes to enter the Kingdom of Thailand is required to obtain a visa from a Royal Thai Embassy or a Royal Thai Consulate-General. However, nationals of certain countries do not require a visa if they meet visa exemption requirements as follows: (1) they are nationals of countries which are exempted from visa requirements when entering Thailand for tourism purposes. Such nationals will be permitted to stay in the Kingdom for a period of not exceeding 30 days. For more information, please see Tourist Visa Exemption; (2) they are nationals of countries which hold bilateral agreements with Thailand on the exemption of visa requirements. For more information, please see List of Countries which has Concluded Agreements with Thailand on the Exemption of Visa Requirements.

2. Nationals of certain countries may apply for visa upon arrival in Thailand. Travellers with this type of visa are permitted to enter and stay in Thailand for a period of not exceeding 15 days. For more information, please see Visa on Arrival.

3. Travellers travelling from/through countries which have been declared Yellow Fever Infected Areas must acquire an International Health Certificate verifying the receiving of a Yellow Fever vaccination. For more information, please see List of Countries which is Declared Yellow Fever Infected Areas.

4. Nationals of certain countries are required to apply for a visa only at the Royal Thai Embassy or the Royal Thai Consulate-General in the applicant's country of residence, or at the Royal Thai Embassy which has jurisdiction over his or her country of residence. Travellers are advised to enquire about authorised office for visa issuance at any Royal Thai Embassy or Royal Thai Consulate-General before departure. Contact details and locations of Royal Thai Embassies and Royal Thai Consulates-General are available at www.mfa.go.th/web/10.php.

5. To apply for a visa, a foreigner must possess a valid passport or travel document that is recognised by the Royal Thai Government and comply with the conditions set forth in the Immigration Act of Thailand B.E.2522 (1979) and its relevant regulations. In addition, the visa applicant must be outside of Thailand at the time of application. The applicant will be issued with a type of visa in accordance to his or her purpose of visit. For more information on types of visas and general requirements for each type of visa, please see Types of Visa and Issuance of Visa.

6. In general, applicants are required to apply for a visa in person. However, Royal Thai Embassies and Royal Thai Consulates-General in some countries and in some cases may also accept applications sent through representatives, authorised travel agencies or by post. Please enquire at the Royal Thai Embassy or Royal Thai Consulate-General where you intend to submit your application of acceptable ways of application.

7. Please note that the period of visa validity is different from the period of stay. Visa validity is the period during which a visa can be used to enter Thailand. In general, the validity of a visa is 3 months, but in some cases, visas may be issued to be valid for 6 months, 1 year, or 3 years. The validity of a visa is granted with discretion by the Royal Thai Embassy or Royal Thai Consulate-General and is displayed on the visa sticker.

8. On the other hand, the period of stay is granted by an immigration officer upon arrival at the port of entry and in accordance with the type of visa. For example, the period of stay for a transit visa is not exceeding 30 days, for a tourist visa is not exceeding 60 days, and for a non-immigrant visa is not exceeding 90 days from the arrival date. The period of stay granted by the immigration officer is displayed on the arrival stamp. Travellers who wish to stay longer than such period may apply for extension of stay at offices of the Immigration Division 1 in Bangkok, located at Government Centre B, Chaengwattana Soi 7, Laksi, Bangkok 10210, Tel 0-2141-9889 or at an Immigration office located in the provinces. For information on application for extension of stay, see the Immigration Bureau website at www.immigration.go.th

9. Foreigners entering Thailand are not permitted to work, regardless of their types of visa, unless they are granted a work permit. Those who intend to work in Thailand must hold the correct type of visa to be eligible to apply for a work permit. Information on Work Permit applications could be obtained from the website of the Office of Foreign Workers Administration, Department of Employment, and Ministry of Labour

10. Royal Thai Embassies and Royal Thai Consulates-General have the authority to issue visas to foreigners for travel to Thailand. The authority to permit entry and stay in Thailand, however, is with the immigration officers. In some cases, the immigration officer may not permit foreigner holding a valid visa entry into Thailand should the immigration officer find reason to believe that he or she falls into the category of aliens prohibited from entering Thailand under the Immigration Act B.E. 2522 (1979).

11. According to the Immigration Act of Thailand B.E. 2522 (1979), foreigners who fall into any of the following categories are prohibited to enter Thailand:

    i.   Having no genuine valid passport or document used in lieu of passport; or having a genuine valid passport or document used in lieu of passport without valid visa issuance by the Royal Thai Embassies, the Royal Thai Consulates-General or the Ministry of Foreign Affairs, with exception of those who meet visa exemption requirements. The terms and conditions of visa issuance and visa exemption are prescribed by the Ministerial Regulations.

    ii.   Having no appropriate means of living following entry into the Kingdom.

    iii. Having entered the Kingdom to be employed as an unskilled or untrained labourer, or to work in violation of the Alien Work Permit Law.

    iv.   Being mentally unstable or having any of the diseases stated in the Ministerial Regulations.

    v.   (5) Having not yet been vaccinated against smallpox; or inoculated, or undergone any other medical treatment for protection against disease; and having refused to have such vaccinations administered by the Immigration Doctor.

    vi.   Having been imprisoned by judgment of the Thai Court; or by lawful injunction or judgment of the Court of a foreign country, except for when the penalty is for a petty offence, or negligence, or is provided for as an exception by the Ministerial Regulations.

    vii. Having behaviour which could cause possible danger to the public; or having the likelihood of being a nuisance or constituting any violence to the peace, safety and security of the public or to the security of the nation; or being under warrant of arrest by competent officials of foreign governments.

    viii. Reason to believe that entry into Kingdom is for the purpose of being involved in prostitution, the trafficking of women or children, drug smuggling, or other types of smuggling which are against public morality.

    ix.   Having no money or bond as prescribed by the Minister under Section 14 of the Immigration Act B.E. 2522 (1979).

    x.   Being a person prohibited by the Minister under Section 16 of the Immigration Act B.E. 2522 (1979).

> xi. Being deported by either the Government of Thailand or that of other foreign countries; or having been revoked the right of stay in the Kingdom or in foreign countries; or having been expelled from the Kingdom by competent officials at the expense of the Government of Thailand unless exemption is provided by the Minister on an individual basis.

Source: Immigration Bureau (Thailand)
http://www.immigration.go.th/nov2004/en/base.php?page=voa

Germany Visa Requirements

EU nationals

EU nationals do not require a visa to enter the Federal Republic of Germany.

Non-EU nationals

Generally speaking, all other foreigners require a visa for stays in Germany. A visa is not required for visits of up to 90 days in an 180-day period for nationals of those countries for which the European Community has abolished the visa requirement.

You will find an overview on visa requirements here:

Table of countries whose citizens require/do not require visas to enter Germany

http://www.auswaertiges-amt.de/EN/EinreiseUndAufenthalt/
StaatenlisteVisumpflicht_node.html

Bodies responsible for issuing visas

Under German law (section 71 (2) of the Residence Act), responsibility for issuing visas lies with the missions of the Federal Republic of Germany, i.e. its embassies and consulates-general. In principle, the Federal Foreign Office is not involved in decisions on individual visa applications, nor does it have any knowledge of the status of individual applications being processed by the missions.

Ratione loci competence (local responsibility) for issuing the visa lies with the mission responsible for the area in which the applicant has his/her ordinary residence or domicile.

Ratione materiae competence (subject-matter responsibility) lies with the mission of the Schengen state in whose territory the sole or main destination is situated.

Visa fees

Since 14 May 2008, the fee for all types of visas has been EUR 60.
Exemptions may be possible. Please refer to our fees page for information:

http://www.auswaertiges-amt.de/cae/servlet/contentblob/480896/
publicationFile/186903/Gebuehrenmerkblatt.pdf

Time required to process a visa application

As a rule, missions require between two and ten working days to decide on an application for a short stay visa. Applications for visas entitling the holder to a longer stay or to take up gainful employment may take several months to process.

During the peak travel season there may be a waiting period for making an application to a German mission. Persons requiring a visa to enter Germany should therefore submit their applications in good time.

Application procedure

As a rule, applicants must submit visa applications, together with all necessary documents, in person at the German mission responsible for their place of residence. In order to avoid time-consuming requests for additional information or documentation, applicants should consult the website of the respective mission well in advance of their departure date to find out about the visa procedure and about the documentation which has to be submitted.

Visa application forms can be obtained from the mission free of charge (in the local language). Applicants may also download the forms here (see right). The forms submitted must be original versions in the appropriate language of the mission in question. Application forms may also be downloaded free of charge from the website of the competent mission.

Requirements for the issue of short stay (Schengen) visas

Since 5 April 2010, Regulation (EC) No. 810/2009 of the European Parliament and of the Council of 13 July 2009 establishing a Community Code on Visas (Visa Code) forms the statutory basis under European law in all Schengen states for the issuing of visas for transit through the Schengen area or for short-term stays in the Schengen area not exceeding 90 days in any 180-day period.

The Visa Code standardises the visa requirements which must be examined by the mission in the course of the visa procedure. The respective mission makes a decision on the visa application at its own discretion, taking into account all the circumstances in any given individual case.

There is no automatic entitlement to a Schengen visa.

The mission must ensure that the following requirements have been met in each individual case:

1. The purpose of the trip to Germany must be plausible and comprehensible.

2. The applicant must be in a position to finance his/her living and travel costs from his/her own funds or income.

3. The visa holder must be prepared to leave the Schengen area before the visa expires.

4. Documentary evidence must be provided of travel health insurance with a minimum coverage of 30 000 euros valid for the entire Schengen area.

Should an applicant be unable to prove that he/she can finance the journey and stay from his/her own funds, a third person may undertake to cover all costs associated with the trip in accordance with sections 66 and 68 of the Residence Act. This undertaking is normally to be made to the foreigners authority in the place of residence of the person making the undertaking.

Persons whose entry into the Schengen area would jeopardise security or public order in the Schengen states or who do not fulfil one or more of the above-mentioned requirements, cannot be granted a visa.

Should a visa application be rejected, the applicant will be informed of the main reasons for the rejection. Every applicant is entitled to take legal recourse against the mission's decision.

Requirements for the issue of visas for longer stays and/or stays entitling the holder to take up gainful employment

As a rule, all foreigners require visas for stays of more than three months or stays leading to gainful employment. Exemptions apply to EU and EEA (European Economic Area) citizens and Swiss nationals.

Furthermore, citizens of Australia, Canada, Israel, Japan, New Zealand, the Republic of Korea and the United States of America may obtain any residence permit that may be required after entering Germany. Citizens of all other countries planning a longer stay in Germany must apply for visas at the competent mission before arriving in the country. Such visa applications must be approved by the relevant foreigners authority in Germany, i.e. the foreigners authority in the place where the applicant intends to take up residence. If the approval of the foreigners authority is necessary before a visa can be issued, the procedure can take up to three months, in some cases longer, since the foreigners authority will often consult other authorities (e.g. the Federal Employment Agency). Missions may only issue visas once they have obtained the approval of the foreigners authority.

Visas entitling holders to take up gainful employment often do not require the approval of the foreigners authority, which speeds up the application process.

Visa application forms for a long-term stay (longer than three months) can be obtained from the relevant mission free of charge. They can also be downloaded here (German, English, French, Italian). The forms submitted must be original versions (at least two sets) in the appropriate language of the mission in question. Please contact the mission beforehand to find out exactly which forms are required.

The foreigners authorities are also responsible for measures and decisions pertaining to residence law for foreigners already residing in Germany. Foreigners authorities are not subordinate agencies of the Federal Foreign Office, and the Federal Foreign Office cannot influence their decisions. They are in fact accountable to and operate under the supervision of the respective interior ministries and senators of the Länder (federal states).

As a result of Regulation 265/2010 it is now possible for anyone in possession of a national visa (D visa) and a valid travel document to move freely in the Schengen area up to three months in any six-month period.

Simplifying the procedure for applying for Schengen visas

The possibility of downloading and filling in visa application forms online, and then taking the completed and printed out form to the interview at the visa section where they can be scanned in electronically via a barcode has done much to reduce the time required to process the application at the visa counter. In addition, many German missions have introduced an electronic appointments system to help manage the number of visitors to the mission and thus shorten waiting times.

The increasing number of visas issued which entitle holders to multiple short stays in the Schengen area over a long period of time means it is no longer necessary to submit visa applications repeatedly. This option is of particular benefit to persons who have to travel frequently for professional or private reasons and have proven their reliability by using previous visa legally.

In future all missions will electronically scan in applicants' fingerprints when accepting visa applications. This biometric procedure will be introduced gradually region by region, probably by the end of 2014. Once a person's fingerprints have been scanned in, an interview at the mission will only be necessary in exceptional cases when submitting a visa application. A renewed biometric procedure is envisaged after five years.

Source: Federal Foreign Office (Germany)
http://www.auswaertiges-amt.de/EN/EinreiseUndAufenthalt/Visabestimmungen_node.html

Internet references or resource guide for information on visa requirements for various countries

North America	Canada	http://www.cic.gc.ca/english/index.asp
	The United States of America	http://www.usembassy.gov/index.html
South America	Brazil	http://www.brasil.gov.br/
Western Europe	Denmark	https://www.nyidanmark.dk/en-us/
	France	http://www.diplomatie.gouv.fr/en/coming-to-france/getting-a-visa/
	The United Kingdom	https://www.gov.uk/browse/visas-immigration
Eastern Europe	Russia	http://www.russianvisa.org/ http://www.russianembassy.org/page/general-visa-information
Asia Pacific	Australia	http://www.immi.gov.au/Pages/Welcome.aspx
	India	http://boi.gov.in/
	Indonesia	http://www.imigrasi.go.id/index.php/en/
	Japan	http://www.mofa.go.jp/j_info/visit/visa/
	New Zealand	http://www.immigration.govt.nz/
	People's Republic of China	http://www.visaforchina.org/
	Philippines	http://www.immigration.gov.ph/
	Taiwan	http://www.immigration.gov.tw/mp.asp?mp=2

Africa	South Africa	http://www.dha.gov.za/index.php/immigration-services
Middle East	Dubai	http://www.dubai.ae/en/pages/default.aspx
	Kingdom of Saudi Arabia	http://www.mofa.gov.sa/sites/mofaen/Pages/Default.aspx
	Qatar	http://portal.www.gov.qa/wps/portal/homepage

APPENDIX 3
EXPATRIATE POLICY EXAMPLE
Barbara Parry

Expatriate management is complex, and as such it is important to ensure that all criteria relating to the management, conditions of assignment and benefits are stipulated in the Expatriate Policy.

The policy must reflect the Expatriate Strategy, and enable the company strategy by comprehensively stating all criteria that govern the assignments of all classes of assignees. Many companies are classifying the assignments in order to provide relevant policies for assignments that may be short term, commuter, virtual or long term.

The business requirement must drive the need for Expatriates, as they are very expensive employees on the payroll, and costs need to be contained. While this a major focus in Expatriate management, it is very important to understand that the individuals and their families being sent on assignment need to be prepared properly before departing, and supported during and after the assignment. This is critical to avoiding failed assignments.

There is a fine line between attracting the right people and skills as well as keeping the costs within budgets. Many people have assumed that Expatriates earn extremely high salaries, but in reality, their salaries and benefits are designed to maintain their quality of life experienced in their home country, and not to make them unduly wealthy.

The decisions on methodology applied in structuring the salaries as well as the benefits provided will have to be made prior to formulating the policy.

Once these decisions are made, it is important to structure the policy to include all of the criteria, and to state the conditions and limitations of benefits. If these are not stated in the policy, you may find that Expatriates will find the gaps and attempt to manipulate the policy for personal gain.

The Expatriate families do meet socially in the host country, and they certainly do discuss and compare salaries and benefits, as well as the level of support the company provides. Thus it is vital to know and understand the diverse methods applied globally in structuring Expatriate benefits and support.

The Expatriate Policy that follows is purely an example, and should not be copied and applied. It is an illustration of the criteria that need to be included in the policy, and the manner in which the provisions should be stated.

There is no one-size-fits-all way to select, reward or manage Expatriates, and each company needs a policy that adheres to their objectives in using Expatriates to conduct business and achieve business goals.

Expatriate management must include the consideration of the incumbent's career, and should be closely integrated with talent management within the organisation, in order to assure the Expatriate that the assignment is a fundamental part of their career progression.

The life-cycle of the Expatriate starts with selection and ends with repatriation, but there are a multitude of processes that need to be executed in order to have sound financial management and successful assignments.

Any dissatisfied Expatriate within a company can create disillusionment for potential assignees which will impact on the ability to attract those families, which could, in turn, drive costs up unnecessarily.

Always remember that you are not dealing with only the employee, but the entire family, whether they accompany the Expatriate on assignment or not.

DEFINITIONS

Name	Definition

REMUNERATION

SALARY

- The remuneration for the duration of the assignment is calculated according to salary bands and adjusted by the specific hardship and cost-of-living factors for each country.

    – The hardship factor is based on a diverse set of criteria based on the difference between living in the home and the host country.

- – The cost of living is based on a basket of goods to evaluate the difference in the costs of goods between the host and the home country.

- – These factors are researched by specialist survey companies each year or twice per annum in volatile economies.

- These factors vary per host and home country.

- This salary includes these factors which are paid for the duration of an assignment in a specific host country.

- Should the Expatriate be re-assigned to another host country, the factors will be adjusted accordingly.

- The gross salary will be fixed and declared in [currency] in the Expatriate contract of employment or secondment agreement.

- A review may be appropriate if inflation in the host country is running in excess of 10 percent per annum.

INCREASES

- Annual increases are at the discretion of the [company] remuneration committee. If increases are awarded, they will be based on the performance of the company and the individual. Increases are processed in [month] each year. Increases are not considered on anniversary of employment start date. Increases will be based on the normal performance outcomes, as well as the CPIX and the inflation versus the [currency applied].

- Annual performance Reviews are conducted [month, and must be completed between the Expatriate and his Line Manager in order to qualify for an increase.

- Extensions of contracts do not necessarily result in salary increases or re-negotiation of salary. In the event of the job description changing or a promotion will the salary be reviewed

PERFORMANCE BONUSES

- The Board of Directors may in its discretion pay a performance bonus, which will be determined by the Expatriate's performance as well as the performance of the Company. Balanced Score Card targets and requirements are defined and recorded and agreed to between the Expatriate and his manager. Performance Evaluations will be conducted by management in order to establish personal performance scores for the performance bonus.

- All bonuses will be calculated on the base salary not including the hardship and cost-of-living factors.

- The bonus determined would be payable pro rata to the Expatriate's period of service with the Operation.

- A *pro rata* bonus shall be paid in the Expatriate's' home country for any period worked in the company prior to the secondment to the operation.

  - The payment of a bonus and the amount of the bonus is entirely within the discretion of the [operation] board of Directors, which may withhold the payment of a bonus in its discretion.

  - Expatriates will be entitled to a bonus only if they are working in the operation on the date of the bonus. If the assignment has expired, and all commitments to the operation have been – ed, Expatriates will be eligible for a pro rata bonus for the time worked in the operation.

  - If any Expatriate has been dismissed for any reason whatsoever, they will not qualify for any bonus payment.

MEDICAL INSURANCE

- Medical insurances will be paid for by the operation for the Expatriate and all accompanying legal dependants.

- Medical insurance for South African and Third Country Nationals employed by an operation will be paid into the [name of the fund] Medical fund or any fund of their choice (provided that the fund covers expenses in the foreign territories).

PENSION, PROVIDENT, LIFE AND DISABILITY INSURANCES ("INSURANCE")

Insurance and retirement investments will be made by [company] into the [fund name] fund.

TAX

- As all salaries are paid gross of tax, the employee will be accountable for any and all taxes on benefits offered by the company.

HOST COUNTRY

- Tax will be determined by the tax legislation of the host country and be withheld and paid to the tax authorities by the operation.

- The Composition of the net salary will be negotiated with the Expatriate or Secondee according to the tax legislation in the host country at the time.

TAX RETURN PREPARATION AND PROVISIONAL TAX PAYMENTS

South African Nationals

- South African Expatriates sent on assignment outside South Africa are required to file South African tax returns for the duration of their assignments, and to report all worldwide income earned. As a result, the operation will cover the cost of assistance with tax return preparation.

- The Expatriate is required to provide to the income tax service-provider, all information and documentation required in preparing the tax return filings and payments in South Africa. This must be done timeously in order to avoid the incurral of penalties or interest for late filing or payment of taxes due. Where this is not adhered to, the employee will be responsible for the payment of any penalties or interest levied by SARS.

- For the chosen service-provider see " Addendum 1"

- The South African Revenue Services (SARS) renders the Assignee's Expatriate income tax exempt if he remains outside of South Africa for a minimum of 183 days per annum of which 60 days must be continuous in any tax year.

- In order to comply with this requirement, The Expatriate is accountable to ensure that all his home trips are scheduled accordingly. Failure to do so will result in taxes being raised by SARS, plus penalties and interest for which the Expatriate will be solely liable. The same applies to all penalties and interest raised due to late submission of data to the tax consultants in order to meet the tax deadlines.

Third Country Nationals

- The operation pays gross remuneration and tax will be deducted in the host country by the operation and paid to the authorities in the host country.

- The [company name] appointed tax consultants will provide assistance and tax return preparation for the home country tax submissions required in the home country.

- Any taxes due in the home country on the income earned either in the host country or the home country will be the individual's responsibility.

- In order for a Third Country National to comply with his home country tax exemption requirements it is important that he establish these requirements through the tax consultants. His failure to plan his leave trips accordingly will result in his being solely liable for any taxes plus any interest or penalties raised. The same applies if any interest or penalties are raised due to his late submission of data to the tax consultants.

RECRUITMENT

All Expatriate recruitment is carried out by the [designation]. The following processes form part of the recruitment process, and are compulsory for all short-listed applicants:

MEDICAL TESTS

- Pre-Medical tests for all Expatriates and their accompanying family members are compulsory to ensure that the Expatriate and his family members are physically able to cope in the host country for the duration of the Expatriate's assignment. These medical tests will also identify any pre-existing conditions which the medical evacuation insurance may not cover, to facilitate decisions being made with full knowledge of the financial impact that these pre-existing medical conditions may have on the Expatriate.

- All medical test and inoculation costs are paid for by the Operation. Regular medical check-ups which the Expatriate is required to attend, must be scheduled with the company selected Tropical Diseases Specialist appointed at the time.

PSYCHOMETRIC ASSESSMENTS

- Psychometric assessments with the company appointed Industrial Psychologist for the Expatriate and their spouse or significant other are compulsory. These assessments are to ensure that they are able to cope emotionally in the host country for the duration of the assignment.

- The costs of these assessments are paid for by the Operation, as well as any counselling that may be required throughout the assignment.

EXPATRIATION PREPARATION TRAINING

- Expatriate preparation training. This is 2 (two) full days' cultural training for the whole family consisting of adult training for the parents as well as children's educationalists and psychologists to train the children in geography, history, culture, language and integration into the host country.

- The costs of this training are paid for by the Operation.

LOOK, SEE, DECIDE (LSD) TRIPS

- A familiarisation trip will only be granted to Long-term Expatriates and Expatriates.

- Familiarisation trips may not be traded or banked.

- The Long-term Expatriate and their family will be sent to the host country on a Look, See, Decide (LSD) trip, and the Operation will pay for:

  - travel by air or road

  - accommodation in a hotel or B&B establishment for 3 nights (or more depending on the flights in and out of the country)

  - If the trip falls over a public holiday or weekend, [home company] will not credit prospective Expatriates with leave. If the trip falls over normal working days (Monday to Friday) the days absent from work for [home company] employees will not be deducted from annual leave in the home country.

VISAS, WORK PERMITS AND RESIDENCE PERMITS

- The Operation in the host country will apply for and pay for all permits required to enable the Expatriate and his accompanying family members to travel to, work and reside in the host country.

- No permits may be obtained illegally or in any manner that may result in the [company] Group coming into disrepute in the host country.

- Certified copies of all qualifications, ID books and passports are to be handed to the [designation] for work permit applications.

RELOCATION LEAVE

- Once all the recruitment processes are completed and the offer has been accepted by the Expatriate, an official period time of 5 (five) working days will be provided. This period is to be used to arrange offshore bank accounts; update wills; notify bank managers of offshore payments coming through; pack up home; farewells to family and friends.

- This leave will be permitted to pack up home and prepare for relocation.

STORAGE OF GOODS

- The Operation pays for reasonable storage and insurance costs of household goods and 1 (one) vehicle in the home country for the duration of the assignment if accompanied by the family.

- The [designation] will notify you of the storage company appointed by [company] at that time.

SHIPPING OF PERSONAL EFFECTS

- The Operation will pay for the shipping and insurance of Long-term Assignment Expatriate's personal goods to the host country. The allowance is 6 cubic metres per adult and an additional 6 cubic metres for children. The maximum is 18 cubic metres per family.

- The [designation] will notify the Expatriate of the shipping company to contact to arrange for packing and shipping of these goods

RELOCATION ALLOWANCE

- A relocation allowance of [value and currency] will only be granted to Long-term Expatriates.

- The allowance will be paid prior to departure from the home country and prior to departure from the host country.

EXCESS BAGGAGE REIMBURSEMENT

Excess baggage will be paid for by the Company (over and above the airline allowance) as follows:

- the same as the airline allowance

- If vouchers are not provided documentation must be submitted to the operation in the host country on arrival for reimbursement.

ACCOMMODATION IN THE HOST COUNTRY

- The Operation will provide a monthly housing allowance.

- The Operation will pay deposits and sign leases with the landlords.

- The standard of accommodation will depend on the availability and standard of housing available in the host country.

- The type of accommodation will depend on a number of factors including, but not limited to, the length of assignment; the cost of shipping furniture and personal goods; the size of the Expatriate's family.

- Accommodation will include:

    - DSTV if there is reception in remote areas

    - Sufficient electrical power supply (back-up generator or gas if necessary)

    - The Expatriate must verify the inventory list on moving in, as well as moving out of the premises.

- Should the Expatriate be able to select the house or apartment, the lease will be signed by the Operation on approval of the lease agreements.

- When renewing rental agreements or entering into new rental agreements the reasonable personal preferences of the Expatriate for whom the house is intended, as to location and standard will be taken into account. The final decision rests with the Operation.

SCHOOLING OF CHILDREN IN THE HOST COUNTRY

- The Operation will pay for school fees of children attending schools in the host country.

- The following conditions apply to schooling:

- The child must be a legal child of the Expatriate.

  - In the case of children that are not legal dependants, the Expatriate must prove to the Operation that the school fees have been fully paid for by the Expatriate in the home country for at least 12 months prior to the assignment.

  - The child must have reached compulsory school-going age in the host country.

  - The Operation will not pay for any expenses other than tuition such as school uniforms; books; extra-curricular activities; extra lessons.

UTILITIES IN THE HOST COUNTRY

- The Operation will pay electricity consumption, water consumption and local council service charges. Should gas be required in specific countries, then the Operation will provide this.

- This includes telephone installation costs (fixed line) and Internet.

SECURITY

The Operation will pay for one security guard at the home, should it be necessary to do so for the level of the Expatriate and dependant on the norm for Expatriates in each country.

PERSONAL COSTS NOT PAID FOR BY THE OPERATION

- The Operation will not pay for the services and/or the employment of domestic staff in the host country

- Insurance of Personal Goods

- It is the Expatriate's responsibility to insure personal household goods and personal effects in the host country.

RECREATIONAL/CLUB EXPENSES

- The Operation will not pay club fees.

- Should reasonable recreational expenses result from entertaining business clients, these may be reimbursed on submission of documentation to the relevant Manager.

TRANSPORT

- The Operation will provide the Expatriate with transport.

- The Operation will provide a driver if required in the host country.

LEAVE AND PUBLIC HOLIDAYS WHILE EXPATRIATED

- The leave entitlement is [number of days] per annum, which includes travelling time.

- Any accumulated leave due in the home country to Long-term Expatriates will be paid out by the home country company.

- The Expatriate is not entitled to home country public holiday leave whilst in the host country, but host country public holidays will be considered as paid leave

- Any accumulated leave in the host country may be taken at the end of the contract period.

- No more than 5 days may be accumulated in any 6-month period.

- Leave not taken will be paid out at the end of the assignment, although regular leave is encouraged whilst on assignment

SICK LEAVE

- Sick leave will be afforded where necessary, a maximum of 30 working days in a 36 (thirty six) month period. Should your absence extend for more than 2 (two) consecutive working days, you will be required to produce a valid medical certificate from a registered medical practitioner. Such medical certificate must contain information relating to the nature of sickness; the date upon which you became ill; the dates of your appointments with the medical practitioner; the date on which you will be fit to return to work and the name, telephone number and address of the medical practitioner who attended to you.

- You are required to take all reasonable precautions to safeguard your health and agree to undergo such medical treatment(s) or test(s) including inoculations and other preventative measures as [company appointed Dr] may prescribe from time to time.

MEDICAL MANAGEMENT WHILE EXPATRIATED

- [Company] has identified a Tropical Diseases Medical Specialist who will be on 24 hour call to assist Expatriates and their families in the host country. The Doctor has been to the host country to evaluate the facilities, meet with the medical practitioners there and has advised [company] on the most suitable facilities and medical practitioners in the country. There is a Medical Incident Report (MIR) form which Expatriates are to take to the host country Doctor when going for treatment. The Doctor must complete this form and it is to be faxed to the [company] Doctor in South Africa, so that he is able to monitor the diagnosis made, the treatment given and the patient's progress. He can also advise the host country Doctor on the patient's pre-existing conditions and allergies (from the medical tests prior to the assignment) and advice on medication.

- If a medical evacuation is required, our Doctor will liaise with the [Operation] safety and security staff, the host country HR manager and the treating Doctor in the host country. Our Doctor will visit the patient in hospital in South Africa and notify [designation] of the evacuee's progress and anticipated return to the host country.

MEDICAL EVACUATION INSURANCE

- The Operation pays for full medical evacuation insurance for the Expatriate and accompanying dependants for the full duration of assignment.

- [Company] has a blanket policy for all Expatriates and their accompanying dependants. Policy details will be included in your Expatriate Pack, which you will be given on acceptance of expatriation.

COMPASSIONATE LEAVE AND OTHER EVENTUALITIES

Serious illness or death of a close relative:

- In the event of death of a close relative in the home country, the Operation will pay for return tickets to the home country for the Expatriate and his accompanying dependants for the purpose of attending the funeral. The duration of compassionate leave will be at the discretion of the CEO of the Operation.

- In the event of serious illness of a close relative in the home country, provision of air tickets will be at the discretion of the Operation, provided that such benefit will be limited to one visit in respect of the same relative and the same incident.

DEATH IN THE HOST COUNTRY

- In the event of a death of an Expatriate or any accompanying dependant in the host country, the Operation will pay the costs of transporting the human remains to the home country. The Expatriate Manager, CEO of the Operation and the appointed Doctor will advise and assist with the logistics in such a case.

- In such an instance, the authorities are to be notified and the work permit and residential permits will be cancelled, requiring the accompanying family to return to their home country within a specified time period according to that country's legislation.

NOTICE PERIOD

- Contracts may be terminated on 3 (three) months written notice one to the other, subject to the provisions in the Expatriate's contractual probation period.

- Termination at any time prior to the expiry of a period of 1 (one) year from inception of assignment may result in the Operation claiming the costs associated with relocation to and from the host country.

RESIGNATION FROM ANY ASSIGNMENT

In the event of any resignation at any time prior to the expiry of the Expatriate's contract, the Expatriate contemporaneously resigns from [name] Group.

REPATRIATION ON EXPIRY OF EXPATRIATION

- Quotations to be obtained in the host Country for the packing and shipping of goods back to the Home Country, and given to the Senior Manager or his nominee.

- Approval to be given on one quotation, and the order given to the selected supplier.

- Exit interviews to be conducted by the Senior Manager in the host country and records to be sent to the Expatriate Manager.

- Accommodation to be checked and inventory lists to be reconciled with the Landlord of the building by the Expatriate and the Senior Manager or his nominee.

- The Senior Manager or his nominee in the host country to arrange flights home for the family and assist with any logistics involved with the move.

- All Company equipment to be handed back to the Senior Manager or his nominee on departure from the Host Country.

- Excess baggage to be paid for by the company as was paid in original relocation costs.

- [Designation] will assist and advise all Repatriates.

- Long-term expatriate employed by [company] in South Africa prior to secondment:

  - [Company] will use its best endeavours to enable the Long-term Expatriate to take up a position, similar to that held prior to assignment, within the [Company] Group.

- Short-term secondee employed in any [name] company prior to secondment:

  - Is guaranteed a position in the specific [Name] Group company he was employed by prior to secondment.

  - In the event that the [Name] Group cannot, for whatever reason, place him in the position he occupied prior to his secondment, he will be placed in a similar position with no loss of benefits.

- Third country and South African national not previously employed in [name] group:

  - Is not guaranteed any position on expiry of his assignment.

REPATRIATION TRAINING DAY

- Once the families have returned to South Africa, the Expatriate and spouse or significant other will be required to attend a full day of training/counselling on reintegration into the country and if applicable, into [Company] This is a full day session with the [Company] appointed Industrial Psychologist who will assist with the process of reintegration back into the society/family/corporate world back home.

- For Third Country Nationals this service is not available, as we are not able to identify or contract with professionals in all of the diverse home countries.

REPATRIATION LEAVE

Long-term Expatriates returning to [Company] will be granted one week (5 working days) settling in leave, which time should be used to arrange for moving into home, receiving goods shipped from the Host Country, delivery of goods in storage, schooling for children, and all other personal issues back in the home country.

OTHER EVENTUALITIES

- As Expatriate Management is a complex and subjective area of Human Resources, we understand that not all eventualities may have been covered in this policy.

- Should Expatriates have any queries not dealt with in this document, please contact the Expatriate Manager for assistance and advice.

APPENDIX 4
INTERNATIONAL SOS

When one wants quick evacuation from one's current location to a different location, then one needs to consider a specialist service provider. International SOS is one such provider and set out below is an excerpt from their service offering and how it works.

Travellers' and Expatriates' Frequently Asked Questions

Introduction

Your company has partnered with International SOS to provide you with medical and security advice and assistance before, during and after assignments overseas.

Prior to travel, it is highly recommended that you view the country information online. If you need more in-depth information or have questions specific to your personal health and safety, call the International SOS assistance centre before you travel.

While away from home, the services are for your everyday assistance needs as well as any emergency assistance needs. These include, but are not limited to:

- Medical advice on vaccinations and travel safety tips before travelling overseas.

- If you become unwell with a cold or experience a minor cut; you are injured in a car accident; or have concerns for your safety (these are examples only).

Speak to your company's programme manager today to find out more about what is available to you in terms of the membership. There are many ways to access International SOS services.

Watch a presentation ▶

Browse our portal 🌐

Download our mobile app 📱

Call our experts 💬

FAQs

- **Q. Who or what is International SOS?**

  International SOS is the world's leading medical and security services company operating from over 700 sites in 70 countries with 10 000 employees, led by 1 200 physicians and 200 security specialists. Our global services include medical and risk planning, preventative programmes, in-country expertise and emergency response for travellers, expatriates and their dependents of over 70 percent of the Fortune 500 companies.

  At the core of our service is a comprehensive, members-only website (internationalsos.com) and more than 27 assistance centres around the world, staffed by multilingual professionals. With 34 International SOS clinics and a fleet of air ambulances, members are assured of the very best routine or emergency medical and security assistance.

- **Q. When should I call International SOS?**

  You can call International SOS with a simple medical question or in an emergency. As an International SOS member you get 24-hour expert advice and assistance – whether you want to arrange vaccinations before travelling; get medical advice when you're abroad; or receive immediate care in a medical emergency. International SOS assistance services are designed to help you with any medical, personal, travel or legal problems when you are outside your home country.

- **Q. What is an assistance centre?**

  International SOS assistance centres are 24/7/365 call centres staffed by doctors and nurses, security experts, multi-lingual coordinators, and logistics support personnel. We can respond rapidly to any type of emergency or call for assistance.

- **Q. Is International SOS an insurance company?**

  International SOS is not an insurance company. We are a 24-hour medical assistance company. Simplified, insurance takes care of financial aspect and we help keep your employees safe, healthy and secure around the world, through expert advice, referral, medical monitoring, activating ambulances, alerting the emergency staff is required, arranging hotel/home visits, arranging bedside nursing, all done by our in-house doctors, nurses and security specials.

  Our medical staff credentials a worldwide network of our providers prior to any referral. Also we have signed agreements with many of these providers and are able to provide guarantee of payments on your behalf and in most cases, preferred pricing with these providers.

- **Q. Do I have to pay to use International SOS services?**

If you are a member, all of our advisory services are complimentary to you. Your organisation subscribes to a membership programme to access these services.

- **Q. Will International SOS pay my medical bills?**

Many countries around the world have medical systems that require upfront payment before treatment, even in an emergency. After approval from your company, International SOS will guarantee and pay upfront costs associated with your medical care to ensure that you receive immediate treatment. We can arrange a guarantee of payment from your company's insurance provider for medical fees and expenses.

Your company, through a medical insurance company or any other source, typically covers fees for outpatient and in-patient care at our own or other hospitals or clinics, including medication. You should review your company's medical insurance policy for medical care coverage.

- **Q. Do I need to activate my membership?**

No, your membership is already active. Simply download the assistance app on your mobile phone and carry the International SOS card in your wallet at all times when travelling. Whenever you need assistance, the mobile will direct you to the nearest assistance centre.

- **Q. Do I have to carry my membership card with me at all times?**

No. However it is a good idea always to carry your membership card with you since it includes the telephone numbers of our assistance centres and your company's membership number. Our website (www.internationalsos.com) includes all our contact information, but members will receive service more promptly if they have their membership number handy. (Some organisations include membership information on their intranets.)

- **Q. What information should I have available before calling International SOS?**

To ensure a prompt response when calling, you should be prepared to provide the following:

1. Your company's membership number (this can be found on the membership card or on the mobile app) – it's all right if you don't have this; International SOS will assist you.

2. Basic contact information so that International SOS can call you back if you are cut off.

3. A brief description of your issue or concern so that you can be put through to the appropriate medical or security assistance.

4. Answers to personal questions. The information you provide is bound by privacy laws, so please be frank with your consultant so that you can receive the best possible care and advice.

- **Q. Does International SOS have any pre-travel information available?**

In addition to calling the assistance centre for any pre-trip questions you may have, you will be able to access the Country Guides by logging in with your membership number at www.internationalsos.com.

Members can access this comprehensive and up-to-date site providing essential information, which includes the following:

- Vaccination requirements
- Passport and visa requirements
- Quality of healthcare
- Advice on prevalent diseases
- Personal and driving safety information
- Hygiene: quality of food and water
- Culture and customs
- Currency
- Weather and what clothes to take
- Compatibility of electrical items
- Personal safety advice.

- **Q. How do I sign up for travel email alerts for my destinations?**

As a traveller you should sign up for email alerts at least 7 (seven) days prior to travel. If you are a programme manager, for non-critical monitoring, you may prefer to sign up for a daily digest on all countries of operations or destinations. If it is a high-risk destination, the recommendation is to receive real-time email alerts in order to monitor activity.

Go to www.internationalsos.com and insert your company membership number in the top right corner.

On the left-hand menu, click on email alerts and follow the on-screen instructions. When you return, if you are not travelling to the same destination in the near future, don't forget to log back in to unsubscribe from email alerts.

- **Q. What if I need medical advice or a referral to a doctor or dentist?**

  If you have any medical concerns, minor or serious, your first contact should be International SOS. Our multilingual medical staff will listen to your concerns, offer advice, and, if necessary, direct you to the appropriate local healthcare provider for treatment. Also, we can help you to arrange an appointment at the nearest approved medical centre.

  In some countries you can attend International SOS clinics which have expatriate staff and offer general practice and accident and emergency facilities. Many of our International SOS clinics also have facilities such as a laboratory and X-ray and pharmacy departments, and hold events for members, including family medicine and first aid training. Some additional fees may apply for the use of these services.

- **Q. What if I am hospitalised?**

Call International SOS as soon as possible or have someone do so on your behalf. We will immediately take steps to evaluate the care you are receiving and determine what actions must be taken to ensure your safe and speedy recovery.

- **Q. What if I need medicine or equipment?**

If you've lost or run out of medication, first aid equipment or other supplies, we can help you replace it (in accordance with local and international regulations). In some cases we can send fresh supplies, get you a prescription from your doctor at home, or, if required, a prescription from a local physician.

- **Q. What if local medical facilities are not adequate?**

If you are hospitalised in an area where adequate medical facilities are not available, International SOS will obtain approval from your company to move you to a medical facility capable of providing the required care. A physician supervises these movements, and when necessary, a medical specialist or nurse will accompany you during the transportation. A commercial flight or air ambulance will be used as required.

- **Q. What happens if I am discharged from hospital and still need help?**

When your condition is stabilised and International SOS has determined that it is medically advisable to bring you home or to a facility near your permanent residence, International SOS will again obtain approval from your company and arrange the repatriation under medical supervision.

- **Q. What other travel assistance services do you help members with?**

International SOS assists you with replacing important travel documents (such as your passport, or credit cards). If you have a change in plans, we can advise you on how to extend your visa or get further vaccinations.

International SOS can refer you to a lawyer or interpreter, help to replace lost tickets, and if your company authorises, we can also provide emergency cash advances. However, for routine travel arrangements, please use your company's travel management provider.

Some important notes to remember

- The questions and answers above relate to all International SOS Membership types. For specific details regarding your membership programme, contact your company's programme manager, or your International SOS Client Service Manager or closest assistance manager.

- International SOS provides a wide range of medical, security, and travel services to assist people in almost every situation, whether it is an emergency or routine advice.

- The International SOS assistance app and card is the best resource a traveller can have. They provide critical contact numbers for assistance, as well as being a source of up-to-date medical and security information provided by International SOS experts who monitor global situations 24/7.

- International SOS provides pre-travel information to help you prepare for the trip.

- Members can access this information by logging in to the members' section of our website (www.internationalsos.com.) or calling any of our assistance centres.

- International SOS is not just for trips with a return ticket. International SOS can help expatriates manage their health and safety while abroad. You can contact our assistance centres for information about ongoing health issues, medical referrals, and safety concerns that can make your life abroad as worry free as possible.

For more information about International SOS, please visit www.internationalsos. com.

INDEX

www.ingramcontent.com/pod-product-compliance
Lightning Source LLC
Chambersburg PA
CBHW082131210326
41599CB00031B/5940